Cooking Light

good mood food

Cook Up Some Feel-Good Vibes!

Oxmoor House®

contents

get happy

This book started with a conversation about food that makes us happy. Nutritionists urge us to see food as fuel—and with good reason, given the little-changed national weight stats. But eating isn't just about nutrients, calories, and checking off your five-or-more leafy greens and dark yellows every day.

As we explored what good mood food is, people shared stories about foods that have meaning to them. For one person, a road trip just isn't a road trip without Cajun peanuts bought at Louisiana gas stations. An empty-nester mom welcomes her adult children home with homemade chicken fried rice—the same dish she made for them on Friday nights as they were growing up. For a young gardener, the first salad of the

season made entirely of vegetables she grew isn't just enviably fresh—it's a celebration of her accomplishment. And one woman shared that her uncle's very simple Saturday morning pancakes still make her as giddy as a six-year-old. In sharing our stories, we learned just how much food—humble or grand, quirky or common—can become more than the sum of ingredients and cooking.

We present this collection of recipes meant to inspire happiness and good moods—dishes to share with family and friends as you celebrate life. For 25 years, *Cooking Light* has shown Americans how to make food healthy, and all along, we've believed in enjoying the foods we love, prepared in light, fresh ways. *Cooking Light*'s motto is "life lived deliciously"—it's a motto we embrace, and we hope you will, too.

the editors of *Cooking Light*

COOK UP SOME FEEL-GOOD VIBES!

We asked our staff and members of the *Cooking Light* Bloggers Connection about the dishes they love and the moods they associate with those foods, and here is our list of the most mentioned. Create the perfect mood with one of these recipes. (Read more about the foods that bloggers love in Kitchen Memory stories you'll find throughout the book.)

stir up some nostalgia

Dishes like pound cake or tomato soup with a grilled cheese hold a special place in our imaginations: They're delicious, surely, but we also associate them with holidays, people we love, comfort, and precious times.

13 Canola Oil
Pound Cake

relax and bliss out

Looking for just the thing to add to your prescription for a moment of calm? Cheesy, creamy, and bready foods topped our list of foods to help us unwind.

149 French
Onion Soup

get happy

Bright colors, fruity flavors, take-out favorites, and foods that remind us of being children were themes among the dishes that make us happy.

47 Strawberry-Lemon Shortcakes

take a flavor adventure

Shake things up and try something new or different! Spicy foods, trendy ingredients, and dishes inspired by cuisines from around the world wake up your taste buds.

191 Korean-Style Beef Tacos

start a little romance

Light some candles, put on a crooner's tunes, and serve a meal for two: These recipes are sure to win the heart of someone special.

017 Chocolate Pots de Creme

SWEET

rapture:

EAT DESSERT

first!

BLACKBERRY CURD TART

Made with a technique similar to making lemon curd, the blackberry curd features a fruit switch that takes advantage of fresh summer berries.

Hands-on time: 51 min. ★ **Total time: 3 hr. 40 min.**

4.5 ounces all-purpose flour (about 1 cup)
⅓ cup powdered sugar
¼ cup almonds, toasted and finely ground
⅜ teaspoon salt, divided
8 tablespoons chilled butter, divided
Baking spray with flour
3 cups fresh blackberries
1¾ cups granulated sugar, divided
¼ cup fresh lemon juice
2 tablespoons cornstarch
2 large egg yolks
¼ teaspoon cream of tartar
3 large egg whites
⅓ cup water

1. Preheat oven to 350°.

2. Weigh or lightly spoon flour into a dry measuring cup; level with a knife. Place flour, powdered sugar, almonds, and ⅛ teaspoon salt in a food processor; pulse to combine. Cut 7 tablespoons butter into small pieces. Add to flour mixture; pulse just until mixture resembles coarse meal. Press in bottom and up sides of a 9-inch round removable-bottom tart pan coated with baking spray. Bake at 350° for 30 minutes or until golden. Cool on a wire rack.

3. Combine berries, ¾ cup granulated sugar, and juice in a sauce-pan over medium-high heat; bring to a boil. Reduce heat, and simmer 6 minutes. Place mixture in a blender; let stand 5 minutes. Blend until smooth. Strain mixture through a cheese-cloth-lined sieve into a medium bowl, pressing on solids. Discard solids. Wipe pan clean; return mixture to pan. Combine corn-starch and egg yolks, stirring until smooth. Stir yolk mixture into berry mixture; bring to a boil over medium-low heat. Cook 1 minute, stirring constantly. Remove from heat; stir in ⅛ teaspoon salt and 1 tablespoon butter. Scrape mixture into a bowl; cover surface directly with plastic wrap. Chill at least 2 hours.

4. Combine ⅛ teaspoon salt, cream of tartar, and egg whites in a large bowl; beat with a mixer at high speed until soft peaks form. Combine 1 cup granulated sugar and ⅓ cup water in a saucepan; bring to a boil. Cook, without stirring, until a candy thermometer registers 250°. Gradually pour hot sugar syrup in a thin stream over egg whites, beating at medium speed, and then at high speed until stiff peaks form.

5. Preheat broiler.

6. Spoon curd over crust; top with meringue. Broil 2 minutes or until golden.

Serves 12 (serving size: 1 slice)

CALORIES 285; FAT 10.2g (sat 5.3g, mono 3.3g, poly 0.9g); PROTEIN 3.7g; CARB 46.6g; FIBER 2.5g; CHOL 55mg; IRON 0.9mg; SODIUM 90mg; CALC 27mg

BOURBON-GLAZED PEACHES WITH YOGURT

Peaches and yogurt might sound like a very simple dessert, but with perfectly ripe fruit, bourbon, and vanilla bean–infused yogurt, it's absolutely decadent.

Hands-on time: 10 min. ★ **Total time: 1 hr. 30 min.**

1 (2-inch) piece vanilla bean, split lengthwise
1 cup plain 2% reduced-fat Greek yogurt
5 ½ tablespoons dark brown sugar, divided
⅛ teaspoon fine sea salt, divided
3 tablespoons bourbon
½ teaspoon vanilla extract
4 firm, ripe peaches, halved and pitted

1. Scrape seeds from vanilla bean into a medium bowl. Combine seeds, bean, yogurt, 1½ tablespoons sugar, and a dash of salt. Let stand 1 hour; discard bean.

2. Preheat oven to 350°.

3. Combine ¼ cup sugar, dash of salt, bourbon, and vanilla in a large bowl, stirring with a whisk. Add peaches; toss gently. Arrange peaches, cut sides down, on a parchment paper–lined baking sheet. Reserve sugar mixture. Bake peaches at 350° for 10 minutes. Turn peach halves over; drizzle cavities with reserved sugar mixture. Bake an additional 10 minutes or just until tender. Serve with yogurt mixture and juices.

Serves 4 (serving size: 2 peach halves and about ¼ cup yogurt mixture)

CALORIES 201; **FAT** 1.8g (sat 1g, mono 0g, poly 0g); **PROTEIN** 6.7g; **CARB** 36.4g; **FIBER** 2g; **CHOL** 3mg; **IRON** 0.5mg; **SODIUM** 87mg; **CALC** 76mg

BLUEBERRY CRISP

Celebrate summer's bounty with a dessert that will remind you of an old-time indulgence— or of picking berries as a child. Serve warm with a scoop of low-fat ice cream.

Hands-on time: 20 min. ★ Total time: 50 min.

Cooking spray
4   teaspoons cornstarch, divided
2   tablespoons brown sugar
½   teaspoon vanilla extract
1   pound fresh or frozen blueberries
2.25 ounces all-purpose flour (about ½ cup)
½   cup packed brown sugar
¼   cup old-fashioned rolled oats
3   tablespoons chopped walnuts
2   tablespoons cornmeal
½   teaspoon salt
¼   teaspoon ground cinnamon
¼   cup chilled butter, cut into small pieces

1. Preheat oven to 375°.

2. Coat an 8-inch square glass or ceramic baking dish with cooking spray. Sprinkle 2 teaspoons cornstarch evenly in dish.

3. Combine 2 teaspoons cornstarch, 2 tablespoons brown sugar, vanilla, and blueberries in a large bowl; toss. Place in prepared baking dish.

4. Weigh or lightly spoon flour into a dry measuring cup; level with a knife. Place flour and next 6 ingredients (through cinnamon) in a food processor; pulse twice to combine. Add butter; pulse 5 times or until mixture resembles coarse meal. Spoon topping evenly over blueberries, packing down lightly. Bake at 375° for 30 minutes or until filling is bubbly and topping is golden.

Serves 8 (serving size: about ½ cup)

CALORIES 217; FAT 8.1g (sat 3.9g, mono 1.8g, poly 1.7g); PROTEIN 2.2g; CARB 35.9g; FIBER 2.4g; CHOL 15mg; IRON 0.9mg; SODIUM 195mg; CALC 25mg

CANOLA OIL POUND CAKE
with browned butter glaze

Many well-loved home cooks create memories with a tender, buttery pound cake with a perfect crust. Here's an equally memorable lighter version featuring heart-healthy canola oil. Soaking the vanilla bean in the oil boosts its flavor.

Hands-on time: 25 min. ★ **Total time: 1 hr. 50 min.**

Cake:
- **6** tablespoons canola oil
- **1** vanilla bean, split lengthwise
- **1 ³/₄** cups sugar
- **¹/₂** cup unsalted butter, softened
- **2** large eggs
- **12** ounces cake flour (about 3 cups)
- **2** teaspoons baking powder
- **¹/₂** teaspoon salt
- **1** cup nonfat buttermilk
- **Cooking spray with flour**

Glaze:
- **1** tablespoon unsalted butter
- **¹/₄** cup sugar
- **2** tablespoons 2% reduced-fat milk
- **¹/₂** teaspoon vanilla extract

1. Preheat oven to 350°.

2. To prepare cake, combine oil and vanilla bean in a small skillet over medium-high heat, and bring to a simmer. Remove from heat. Let stand 10 minutes or until mixture cools to room temperature. Scrape seeds from bean, and stir into oil; discard bean.

3. Combine oil mixture, 1¾ cups sugar, and ½ cup butter in a large bowl; beat with a mixer at medium speed until well blended (about 5 minutes). Add eggs, 1 at a time, beating well after each addition. Weigh or lightly spoon flour into dry measuring cups; level with a knife. Combine flour, baking powder, and salt, stirring well with a whisk. Add flour mixture and buttermilk alternately to sugar mixture, beginning and ending with flour mixture.

4. Spoon batter into a 10-inch tube pan coated with cooking spray; spread evenly. Bake at 350° for 1 hour or until a wooden pick inserted in center comes out clean. Cool in pan 10 minutes on a wire rack; remove from pan.

5. To prepare glaze, melt 1 tablespoon butter in a small skillet over medium heat; cook 2 minutes or until lightly browned. Remove from heat. Add next 3 ingredients (through vanilla), stirring until smooth. Drizzle glaze over warm cake.

Serves 16 (serving size: 1 slice)

CALORIES 294; **FAT** 12.6g (sat 4.7g, mono 5.3g, poly 1.9g); **PROTEIN** 3.2g; **CARB** 42.8g; **FIBER** 0.4g; **CHOL** 44mg; **IRON** 1.7mg; **SODIUM** 149mg; **CALC** 60mg

CARROT CAKE

Warm spices and brown sugar enhance the rich, caramelized flavors of carrot cake. Buttermilk and less butter help lighten the still tender cake, creating room for real cream cheese frosting.

Hands-on time: 35 min. ★ **Total time: 1 hr. 53 min.**

Cake:
- **10.1** ounces all-purpose flour (about 2¼ cups)
- **2** teaspoons baking powder
- **1½** teaspoons ground cinnamon
- **¼** teaspoon salt
- **2** cups grated carrot
- **1** cup granulated sugar
- **½** cup packed brown sugar
- **6** tablespoons butter, softened
- **3** large eggs
- **1** teaspoon vanilla extract
- **½** cup low-fat buttermilk
- Cooking spray

Frosting:
- **7** ounces cream cheese, softened
- **2** tablespoons butter, softened
- **½** teaspoon vanilla extract
- **⅛** teaspoon salt
- **3** cups powdered sugar
- **¼** cup chopped pecans, toasted

1. Preheat oven to 350°.

2. To prepare cake, weigh or lightly spoon flour into dry measuring cups; level with a knife. Combine flour, 2 teaspoons baking powder, ground cinnamon, and ¼ teaspoon salt in a medium bowl, stirring with a whisk. Add 2 cups grated carrot, tossing to combine.

3. Place granulated sugar, brown sugar, and 6 tablespoons butter in a large bowl. Beat with a mixer at medium speed until combined. Add eggs, 1 at a time, beating well after each addition. Stir in 1 teaspoon vanilla. Add flour mixture and buttermilk alternately to sugar mixture, beginning and ending with flour mixture. Spread batter into a 13 × 9-inch metal baking pan coated with cooking spray. Bake at 350° for 28 minutes or until a wooden pick inserted in center comes out clean. Cool cake completely in pan on a wire rack.

4. To prepare frosting, place softened cream cheese and next 4 ingredients (through ⅛ teaspoon salt) in a medium bowl. Beat with a mixer at medium speed until fluffy. Gradually add powdered sugar, beating at medium speed until combined (don't overbeat). Spread frosting evenly over top of cooled cake. Sprinkle evenly with toasted pecans. Yield: 20 servings (serving size: 1 piece)

CALORIES 285; **FAT** 9.9g (sat 5.2g, mono 2.9g, poly 0.8g); **PROTEIN** 3.5g; **CARB** 46g; **FIBER** 0.9g; **CHOL** 51mg; **IRON** 0.9mg; **SODIUM** 184mg; **CALC** 59mg

CHOCOLATE POTS DE CRÈME

Pots de crème are decadent, creamy custards served in tiny cups—and they're a perfect ending to a cozy dinner. Make this dessert the night before, and chill until you're ready to serve.

Hands-on time: 14 min. ★ **Total time: 9 hr. 29 min.**

2   large eggs
2 1/2 cups fat-free milk
3/4   cup granulated sugar
1/4   cup unsweetened cocoa
1/8   teaspoon salt
1   teaspoon vanilla extract
4   ounces semisweet or
       bittersweet chocolate,
       chopped
Powdered sugar (optional)

1. Preheat oven to 350°.

2. Place eggs in a medium bowl; stir with a whisk until eggs are lightly beaten.

3. Combine milk, sugar, cocoa, and salt in a medium saucepan over medium heat. Cook until sugar dissolves, stirring occasionally (about 3 minutes). Add vanilla and chocolate; stir until chocolate melts.

4. Gradually add 1/4 cup hot milk mixture to eggs, stirring constantly with a whisk. Add egg mixture to milk mixture in pan, stirring with a whisk to combine. Pour into 8 (4-ounce) ramekins. Place ramekins in a 13 x 9–inch metal baking pan; add hot water to pan to a depth of 1 inch. Bake at 350° for 35 minutes or until a knife inserted in center comes out clean. Remove ramekins from pan; cool completely on a wire rack. Chill 8 hours or overnight. Sift powdered sugar over custards, if desired.

Serves 8 (serving size: 1 custard)

CALORIES 196; **FAT** 7.8g (sat 3.7g, mono 2.7g, poly 0.4g); **PROTEIN** 5.7g; **CARB** 31.3g; **FIBER** 1.9g; **CHOL** 54mg; **IRON** 1mg; **SODIUM** 87mg; **CALC** 106mg

CHOCOLATE SANDWICH COOKIES
with marshmallow cream filling

Hands-on time: 24 min. ★ **Total time: 39 min.**

Cookies:

1	**cup sugar**
5	**tablespoons butter, softened**
1	**teaspoon vanilla extract**
2	**large eggs**
9	**ounces all-purpose flour (about 2 cups)**
5	**tablespoons unsweetened cocoa**
1	**teaspoon salt**
1	**teaspoon baking powder**
1	**teaspoon baking soda**
1	**cup nonfat buttermilk**

Cooking spray

Filling:

1	**envelope unflavored gelatin (about 2 ½ teaspoons)**
¾	**cup cold water, divided**
½	**cup sugar**
¼	**cup light-colored corn syrup**
⅛	**teaspoon salt**
½	**teaspoon vanilla extract**

1. Preheat oven to 375°.

2. To prepare cookies, combine 1 cup sugar and butter in a large bowl. Beat with a mixer at medium speed until well blended (about 2 minutes). Add 1 teaspoon vanilla and eggs; beat until combined. Lightly spoon flour into dry measuring cups; level with a knife. Combine flour, cocoa, 1 teaspoon salt, baking powder, and baking soda; stir well with a whisk. Add flour mixture and buttermilk alternately to sugar mixture, beginning and ending with flour mixture.

3. Drop dough by rounded tablespoonfuls 2 inches apart onto baking sheets coated with cooking spray. Bake at 375° for 10 minutes or until set. Cool on pans 5 minutes. Remove from pans; cool completely on wire racks.

4. To prepare filling, sprinkle gelatin over ½ cup cold water in a large bowl; set aside. Combine ¼ cup water, ½ cup sugar, syrup, and ⅛ teaspoon salt in a medium saucepan over medium-high heat. Cook, without stirring, until a candy thermometer registers 244°. Remove from heat. Gradually pour hot sugar syrup into softened gelatin mixture, beating with a mixer at low speed, and then at high speed until thick (about 6 minutes), scraping sides of bowl occasionally. Add ½ teaspoon vanilla; beat until well blended.

5. Quickly spread about 2 tablespoons filling over bottom side of 1 cookie; top with another cookie. Repeat procedure with remaining filling and cookies.

Serves 16 (serving size: 1 cookie)

CALORIES 197; FAT 4.6g (sat 2.6g, mono 1.3g, poly 0.3g); PROTEIN 3.7g; CARB 36.6g; FIBER 1g; CHOL 36mg; IRON 1.1mg; SODIUM 329mg; CALC 46mg

make it ahead
Have the cookies ready before you make the marshmallow filling—the filling firms up quickly as it cools. You can make the sandwiches ahead and freeze them tightly wrapped in plastic wrap; they will last up to a month.

make it foolproof

If you prefer a slightly chewier cookie, reduce baking time to 10 minutes.

CINNAMON-SUGAR COOKIES

Hands-on time: 21 min. ★ Total time: 1 hr. 33 min.

1 **cup granulated sugar**
6 **tablespoons butter, softened**
1 **tablespoon light corn syrup**
1 **teaspoon vanilla extract**
1 **large egg**
4 **ounces cake flour (about 1 cup)**
3.3 **ounces all-purpose flour (about ¾ cup)**
1 **teaspoon baking powder**
1 **teaspoon baking soda**
¼ **teaspoon salt**
¾ **teaspoon ground cinnamon, divided**
¼ **cup turbinado sugar**

1. Place granulated sugar and butter in a bowl; beat with a mixer at medium speed until well blended (about 3 minutes). Add corn syrup, vanilla, and egg; beat 3 minutes or until well blended.

2. Lightly spoon cake flour and all-purpose flour into dry measuring cups; level with a knife. Combine flours, baking powder, baking soda, salt, and ¼ teaspoon cinnamon. Add flour mixture to butter mixture; stir until just combined. Wrap in plastic wrap; chill 1 hour.

3. Preheat oven to 375°.

4. Combine turbinado sugar and ½ teaspoon cinnamon in a small bowl. Shape dough into 48 balls, about 1 teaspoon each. Roll balls in cinnamon-sugar mixture. Place 2 inches apart on ungreased baking sheets. Bake at 375° for 12 minutes or until golden on bottom. Cool on wire racks.

Serves 48 (serving size: 1 cookie)

CALORIES 105; **FAT** 3.1g (sat 1.9g, mono 0.8g, poly 0.2g); **PROTEIN** 1.2g; **CARB** 18.2g; **FIBER** 0.3g; **CHOL** 16mg; **IRON** 0.5mg; **SODIUM** 122mg; **CALC** 15mg

CREAM PUFFS
with ice cream and caramel

Hands-on time: 19 min. ★ **Total time: 1 hr. 49 min.**

**4.75 ounces bread flour
(about 1 cup)**
1 cup water
3 tablespoons butter
¼ teaspoon salt
3 large egg whites
2 large eggs
2 cups vanilla low-fat ice cream
**½ cup fat-free caramel sundae
syrup**

1. Preheat oven to 425°. Cover a heavy baking sheet with parchment paper; set aside. Lightly spoon flour into a dry measuring cup; level with a knife. Set aside.

2. Combine 1 cup water, butter, and salt in a large heavy saucepan over medium-high heat; bring to a boil, stirring occasionally. Add flour, stirring well until mixture is smooth and pulls away from sides of pan. Cook 30 seconds, stirring constantly. Remove from heat. Place dough in bowl of a stand mixer. Add egg whites and eggs, 1 at a time, beating at medium speed with a paddle attachment until well combined. Beat 2 minutes at medium speed.

3. Scoop dough by ¼ cupfuls into 8 mounds 2 inches apart on prepared pan. Bake at 425° for 20 minutes. Reduce oven temperature to 350° (do not remove pan from oven); bake an additional 30 minutes. Turn oven off. Pierce top of each cream puff with a knife; return pan to oven. Cool cream puffs in closed oven 20 minutes. Remove from oven; cool completely on a wire rack.

4. Split cream puffs in half horizontally. Fill each puff with ¼ cup ice cream; top each with cream puff tops. Drizzle 1 tablespoon syrup over the top.

Serves 8 (serving size: 1 filled cream puff)

CALORIES 229; **FAT** 6.8g (sat 3.6g, mono 1.6g, poly 0.5g); **PROTEIN** 7g; **CARB** 34.6g; **FIBER** 0.9g; **CHOL** 67mg; **IRON** 1mg; **SODIUM** 213mg; **CALC** 61mg

CREMA CATALANA

A Spanish version of crème brûlée, this luscious custard is just the thing to make for your sweetheart—or to enjoy as a calm, meditative treat. If you don't have a kitchen blowtorch, caramelize the sugar under the broiler for a minute.

Hands-on time: 27 min. ★ Total time: 4 hr. 57 min.

2   cups whole milk
3   (3 x 1-inch) strips fresh lemon rind
1   (2-inch) cinnamon stick
7   tablespoons sugar, divided
2   tablespoons cornstarch
⅛   teaspoon salt
3   large egg yolks

1. Heat milk over medium-high heat in a small heavy saucepan to 180° or until tiny bubbles form around edge (do not boil). Remove from heat. Add rind and cinnamon; cover and let stand 30 minutes. Discard rind and cinnamon.

2. Combine ¼ cup sugar, cornstarch, and salt in a small bowl, stirring well with a whisk. Add ¼ cup milk to sugar mixture, stirring until smooth. Return milk mixture to pan; cook over medium-low heat 7 minutes or until almost thick, stirring constantly with a whisk. Place egg yolks in a small bowl. Gradually pour one-third of hot milk mixture into yolks, stirring constantly with a whisk. Carefully return yolk mixture to pan. Cook over low heat 4 minutes or until a thermometer registers 180°, stirring constantly with a whisk. Divide custard evenly among 6 (4-ounce) custard cups; press plastic wrap against surface of custard. Chill at least 4 hours or until ready to serve.

3. Remove plastic; discard. Sprinkle 3 tablespoons sugar evenly over custards. Holding a kitchen blowtorch about 2 inches from top of each custard, heat sugar, moving torch back and forth, until sugar is completely melted and caramelized (about 1 minute). Serve immediately or within 1 hour.

Serves 6 (serving size: 1 custard)

CALORIES 142; **FAT** 4.9g (sat 2.3g, mono 1.6g, poly 0.5g); **PROTEIN** 3.9g; **CARB** 21g; **FIBER** 0g; **CHOL** 111mg; **IRON** 0.3mg; **SODIUM** 86mg; **CALC** 103mg

make it ahead
Custards are a great make-ahead dessert. You can make these through step 2 up to three days in advance. Wait until right before serving time to caramelize the tops.

LEMON SQUARES

Sunny lemon evokes happiness, and paired with a tender, short cookie crust and a dusting of powdered sugar, it works a special smile-inducing magic.

Hands-on time: 15 min. ★ **Total time: 3 hr.**

3.4 ounces all-purpose flour (about ³/₄ cup)
¹/₄ cup powdered sugar
3 tablespoons pine nuts, toasted and coarsely chopped
¹/₈ teaspoon salt
2 tablespoons chilled unsalted butter, cut into small pieces
2 tablespoons canola oil
Cooking spray
³/₄ cup granulated sugar
1 teaspoon grated lemon rind
¹/₂ cup fresh lemon juice
2 tablespoons all-purpose flour
2 large eggs
1 large egg white
2 tablespoons powdered sugar

1. Preheat oven to 350°.

2. Weigh or lightly spoon flour into dry measuring cups; level with a knife. Place flour, ¼ cup powdered sugar, pine nuts, and salt in a food processor; pulse 2 times to combine. Add butter and canola oil. Pulse 3 to 5 times or until mixture resembles coarse meal. Place mixture in bottom of an 8-inch square glass or ceramic baking dish coated with cooking spray; press into bottom of pan. Bake at 350° for 20 minutes or until lightly browned. Reduce oven temperature to 325°.

3. Combine granulated sugar and next 5 ingredients (through egg white) in a medium bowl, stirring with a whisk until smooth. Pour mixture over crust. Bake at 325° for 20 minutes or until set. Remove from oven, and cool completely in pan on a wire rack. Cover and chill at least 2 hours. Cut into 16 squares. Sift 2 tablespoons powdered sugar evenly over squares.

Serves 16 (serving size: 1 square)

CALORIES 124; FAT 5g (sat 1.3g, mono 2g, poly 1.2g); PROTEIN 2g; CARB 18.5g; FIBER 0.3g; CHOL 30mg; IRON 0.5mg; SODIUM 31mg; CALC 6mg

mom's little helper

I feel very fortunate to have grown up with a mother who loved to cook. She made nearly everything from scratch, and I loved learning from her. As far back as I remember, I was always in the kitchen helping Mom. I have a favorite photo of myself at age 5, standing on a stool to reach the kitchen counter, wearing my pajamas and a huge smile, stirring a big bowl of pie filling—rich maple pecan pie filling. A holiday does not go by without the memory of me making that pie. Every holiday still includes a pecan pie.

-Kristina Sloggett,
Braverton, Oregon

MAPLE-BOURBON PECAN PIE

Maple syrup and bourbon lend the pie an old-time sweetness. For a decadent treat, top warm pie with vanilla low-fat ice cream.

Hands-on time: 12 min. ★ **Total time: 1 hr. 23 min.**

½ (14.1-ounce) package refrigerated pie dough	2 tablespoons butter, melted
Cooking spray	2 tablespoons bourbon
¾ cup pecan halves	1 teaspoon vanilla extract
½ cup maple syrup	¼ teaspoon kosher salt
½ cup dark corn syrup	2 large eggs, lightly beaten
¼ cup finely chopped pecans	2 large egg whites, lightly beaten
3 tablespoons brown sugar	

1. Preheat oven to 350°.

2. Roll dough into a 12-inch circle. Fit dough into a 9-inch pie plate coated with cooking spray, draping excess dough over edges. Fold edges under, and flute. Chill in freezer 15 minutes.

3. Combine pecans and next 10 ingredients (through egg whites) in a bowl, stirring well to combine. Pour filling into prepared crust. Bake at 350° for 38 minutes or until center of pie is almost set (shield edges of piecrust with foil to prevent overbrowning). Cool on a wire rack.

Serves 10 (serving size: 1 wedge)

CALORIES 308; **FAT** 16.2g (sat 4.4g, mono 7g, poly 3.8g); **PROTEIN** 3.3g; **CARB** 37.6g; **FIBER** 1g; **CHOL** 51mg; **IRON** 0.7mg; **SODIUM** 203mg; **CALC** 29mg

make it special

Serve New York Cheesecake with seasonal fruit: Berries, cherries, and sliced stone fruit are all good options. For a stunning presentation, find some fresh mint leaves, and top the whole cake with a mound of fruit and whole mint.

NEW YORK CHEESECAKE

For a denser, creamier texture, cool the cake in the oven one hour with the oven door ajar instead of closed. Make a day ahead since the cooled cake needs to chill overnight.

Hands-on time: 38 min. ★ **Total time: 11 hr. 43 min.**

Crust:

- 1 cup graham cracker crumbs (about 7 cookie sheets)
- 3 tablespoons sugar
- 1 large egg white

Cooking spray

Filling:

- 1 ounce all-purpose flour (about 1/4 cup)
- 1/2 cup 1% low-fat cottage cheese
- 3 (8-ounce) blocks fat-free cream cheese, softened, divided
- 2 (8-ounce) blocks 1/3-less-fat cream cheese, softened
- 1 3/4 cups sugar
- 1 1/2 teaspoons finely grated lemon rind
- 2 tablespoons fresh lemon juice
- 1/2 teaspoon vanilla extract
- 3 large eggs
- 3 large egg whites

1. Preheat oven to 350°.

2. To prepare crust, combine crumbs, 3 tablespoons sugar, and 1 egg white in a bowl; toss with a fork until well blended. Lightly coat hands with cooking spray. Press crumb mixture into bottom of a 9-inch springform pan coated with cooking spray. Bake at 350° for 8 minutes; cool on a wire rack. Reduce oven temperature to 325°.

3. To prepare filling, weigh or lightly spoon flour into a dry measuring cup; level with a knife. Place cottage cheese and 8 ounces fat-free cream cheese in a food processor, and process until smooth. Add 16 ounces fat-free cream cheese, 1/3-less-fat cream cheese, flour, and next 4 ingredients (through vanilla); process until smooth. Add eggs and 3 egg whites; process until blended. Pour cheese mixture into prepared pan. Bake at 325° for 65 minutes or until almost set (center will not be firm but will set as it chills). Turn oven off; cool cheesecake in closed oven 1 hour. Remove from oven; cool on wire rack. Cover and chill 8 hours.

Serves 16 (serving size: 1 wedge)

CALORIES 259; FAT 8g (sat 4.8g, mono 2.5g, poly 0.4g); PROTEIN 12.7g; CARB 33.9g; FIBER 0.2g; CHOL 58mg; IRON 0.6mg; SODIUM 446mg; CALC 111mg

PEACH "FRIED" PIES

Dried peaches make this dessert a year-round option.
Keeping dough ingredients chilled ensures a crisp, tender
crust, which is baked rather than fried.

Hands-on time: 40 min. ★ **Total time: 3 hr.**

Crust:
- **12.4 ounces all-purpose flour (about 2 ³/₄ cups), divided**
- **1 teaspoon salt**
- **2 tablespoons sugar**
- **9 tablespoons frozen unsalted butter, cut into small pieces**
- **¹/₄ cup vodka, chilled**
- **¹/₄ cup cold water**

Filling:
- **8 ounces dried peaches**
- **1 cup water**
- **¹/₂ cup orange juice**
- **³/₄ cup sugar**
- **1 teaspoon ground cinnamon**
- **1 tablespoon fat-free milk**
- **1 large egg, lightly beaten**
- **Cooking spray**

1. To prepare crust, weigh or lightly spoon flour into dry measuring cups; level with a knife. Place 12.4 ounces (about 2½ cups) flour, salt, and 2 tablespoons sugar in a food processor; pulse 10 times. Add frozen butter, and process until mixture resembles coarse meal. Place food processor bowl and flour mixture in freezer 15 minutes.

2. Return bowl to processor. Combine vodka and ¼ cup cold water. Add vodka mixture slowly through food chute, pulsing just until combined.

3. Divide dough into 12 equal portions. Shape each dough portion into a ball; flatten each ball into a 3-inch circle on a lightly floured surface. Roll each dough portion into a 5-inch circle, adding ¼ cup flour as needed to prevent dough from sticking. Stack dough circles between single layers of wax paper or plastic wrap to prevent sticking. Cover stack with plastic wrap; refrigerate at least 2 hours or overnight.

4. To prepare filling, combine peaches, 1 cup water, orange juice, ¾ cup sugar, and cinnamon in a medium saucepan. Bring to a simmer; cover and cook 1 hour, stirring occasionally. Remove from heat, and mash with a potato masher; cool.

5. Preheat oven to 425°. Place a large foil-lined baking sheet in oven.

6. Remove dough from refrigerator. Working with 1 circle at a time, spoon 2 level tablespoons peach mixture into center of each circle. Fold dough over filling; press edges together with a fork.

7. Combine milk and egg in a small bowl, stirring with a whisk. Brush pies evenly with egg mixture. Cut 3 diagonal slits across top of each pie. Remove hot baking sheet from oven, and coat with cooking spray. Place pies, cut sides up, on baking sheet, and place on middle oven rack. Bake at 425° for 18 minutes or until lightly browned. Cool slightly on a wire rack.

Serves 12 (serving size: 1 pie)

CALORIES 312; **FAT** 9.4g (sat 5.7g, mono 2.4g, poly 0.5g); **PROTEIN** 4.6g; **CARB** 49.7g; **FIBER** 2.3g; **CHOL** 41mg; **IRON** 2mg; **SODIUM** 203mg; **CALC** 15mg

PEACH AND BASIL SHORTCAKE

Try a different twist on a summer shortcake: Basil, part of the mint family, adds a refreshing herbal flavor. Here is where you can show off the season's sweetest, juiciest peaches.

Hands-on time: 29 min. ★ **Total time: 3 hr.**

Topping:

4	cups sliced peeled peaches (about 3 pounds)
1/3	cup sugar
1/3	cup small basil leaves
1 1/2	tablespoons fresh lemon juice

Shortcake:

9	ounces cake flour (about 2 1/4 cups)
1/2	cup sugar, divided
1	tablespoon baking powder
1/2	teaspoon baking soda
1/4	teaspoon salt
6	tablespoons chilled butter, cut into small pieces
1	cup low-fat buttermilk

Cooking spray

1 1/2	teaspoons fat-free milk
1/4	cup slivered almonds
3/4	cup plain fat-free Greek yogurt

1. To prepare topping, combine peaches, 1/3 cup sugar, basil, and juice in a bowl; let stand 1 hour.

2. Preheat oven to 400°.

3. To prepare shortcake, weigh or lightly spoon flour into dry measuring cups; level with a knife. Combine flour, 7 tablespoons sugar, baking powder, baking soda, and salt in a bowl; stir with a whisk. Cut in butter with a pastry blender or 2 knives until mixture resembles coarse meal. Stir in buttermilk with a fork just until combined (do not overmix). Spoon dough into a 9-inch round cake pan coated with cooking spray. Gently brush dough with milk. Sprinkle with 1 tablespoon sugar and almonds.

4. Bake at 400° for 23 minutes or until a wooden pick inserted in center comes out clean. Cool 5 minutes in pan on a wire rack. Remove shortcake from pan; cool completely on wire rack.

5. Cut shortcake into 12 wedges. Top each wedge with 1/3 cup peach mixture and 1 tablespoon yogurt.

Serves 12 (serving size: 1 wedge)

CALORIES 261; **FAT** 7.8g (sat 4g, mono 2.4g, poly 0.7g); **PROTEIN** 5.5g; **CARB** 44g; **FIBER** 2.3g; **CHOL** 17mg; **IRON** 2mg; **SODIUM** 266mg; **CALC** 119mg

PEAR TARTE TATIN

Tarte tatin is an impressive dessert: an upside-down tart with a flaky crust and a delicious syrup made in the pan from fruit juices and caramelized sugar.

Hands-on time: 16 min. ★ Total time: 57 min.

2 tablespoons butter, divided
½ cup sugar, divided
4 peeled ripe Anjou pears, cored and halved lengthwise
1 tablespoon canola oil
5 (14 x 9-inch) sheets frozen phyllo dough, thawed
3 tablespoons crème fraîche

1. Preheat oven to 400°.

2. Coat a 10-inch cast-iron skillet with 1½ tablespoons butter. Sprinkle 6 tablespoons sugar into pan. Arrange 7 pear halves, cut sides up, in a circle in pan; place remaining pear half in center. Cover skillet, and place over medium-low heat. Cook, without stirring, 15 minutes or until sugar mixture is bubbly and caramelized. Place pan in oven. Bake at 400° for 5 minutes.

3. Place 1½ teaspoons butter and oil in a microwave-safe bowl. Microwave at HIGH 30 seconds or until butter melts. Place 1 phyllo sheet horizontally on a flat work surface (cover remaining dough to keep from drying); brush lightly with butter mixture. Sprinkle 2 teaspoons sugar evenly over phyllo. Place 1 phyllo sheet vertically on top of first. Repeat procedure twice with remaining butter mixture, sugar, and phyllo, ending with phyllo. Fold edges to form a 9-inch circle.

4. Place phyllo circle in pan over pears, pressing gently. Bake at 400° for 16 minutes or until filling is bubbly and crust is browned. Remove from oven, and let stand 5 minutes. Place a plate upside down on top of pan; invert tart onto plate. Cut tart into 6 wedges. Top each wedge with 1½ teaspoons crème fraîche.

Serves 6 (serving size: 1 wedge)

CALORIES 258; **FAT** 10.3g (sat 4.4g, mono 2.9g, poly 1g); **PROTEIN** 2g; **CARB** 41.7g; **FIBER** 3g; **CHOL** 17mg; **IRON** 0.5mg; **SODIUM** 79mg; **CALC** 70mg

make it special

Serve Pear Tarte Tatin with a dessert wine, such as a muscat. Ideally, you want a wine that is less sweet than the tart, with a little acidity to balance the caramel flavors of the dessert.

PLUM KUCHEN

Almost any slightly firm plum will work in this lovely cake. In fact, a mix of black, red, and yellow fruit gives contrasting flavor and color.

Hands-on time: 35 min. ★ **Total time: 2 hr. 10 min.**

6.75 ounces all-purpose
   flour (about 1 1/2 cups)
2/3 cup plus 2 tablespoons
   granulated sugar, divided
2 tablespoons brown sugar
1 teaspoon baking powder
3/8 teaspoon salt, divided
1/8 teaspoon ground
   cardamom
7 tablespoons chilled
   butter, cut into pieces
   and divided
1/2 cup fat-free milk
1/2 teaspoon vanilla extract
1 large egg
Cooking spray
1 1/2 pounds plums, quartered
   and pitted
1 teaspoon grated lemon
   rind
1/4 teaspoon ground allspice

1. Preheat oven to 425°.

2. Weigh or lightly spoon flour into dry measuring cups; level with a knife. Combine flour, 2 tablespoons granulated sugar, brown sugar, baking powder, 1/4 teaspoon salt, and cardamom in a medium bowl, stirring well with a whisk. Cut in 4 tablespoons butter with a pastry blender or 2 knives until mixture resembles coarse meal.

3. Combine milk, vanilla, and egg in a bowl, stirring with a whisk. Add milk mixture to flour mixture; stir until just combined.

4. Spoon batter into a 9-inch round cake pan or springform pan coated with cooking spray. Arrange plums in a circular pattern over batter.

5. Combine 2/3 cup granulated sugar, 1/8 teaspoon salt, lemon rind, and allspice in a small bowl, stirring well. Place 3 tablespoons butter in a microwave-safe bowl. Microwave at HIGH 30 seconds or until butter melts. Stir into sugar mixture. Sprinkle plums evenly with sugar mixture. Bake at 425° for 35 minutes or until browned and bubbly. Cool in pan 1 hour on a wire rack. Cut into 10 wedges.

Serves 10 (serving size: 1 wedge)

CALORIES 256; FAT 8.7g (sat 5.3g, mono 2.3g, poly 0.5g); PROTEIN 3.6g; CARB 42.5g; FIBER 1.5g; CHOL 40mg; IRON 1.2mg; SODIUM 144mg; CALC 48mg

RASPBERRY LINZER COOKIES

Hands-on time: 54 min. ★ **Total time: 2 hr. 39 min.**

7.5 ounces all-purpose flour
    (about 1¹/₂ cups plus 2
    tablespoons), divided
1   cup whole blanched
    almonds
¹/₂ teaspoon baking powder
¹/₂ teaspoon ground
    cinnamon
¹/₄ teaspoon salt
²/₃ cup granulated sugar
¹/₂ cup unsalted butter,
    softened
¹/₂ teaspoon grated lemon
    rind
4   large egg yolks
6   tablespoons raspberry
    preserves with seeds
2   teaspoons powdered
    sugar

1. Weigh or lightly spoon 2.25 ounces (about ½ cup) flour into a dry measuring cup; level with a knife. Place 2.25 ounces flour and almonds in a food processor; process until finely ground. Weigh or lightly spoon remaining 5.25 ounces (about 1 cup plus 2 tablespoons) flour into a dry measuring cup; level with a knife. Combine almond mixture, remaining 5.25 ounces flour, baking powder, cinnamon, and salt, stirring well with a whisk.

2. Place granulated sugar, butter, and rind in a large bowl; beat with a mixer at medium speed until light and fluffy (about 3 minutes). Add egg yolks; beat until well blended. Beating at low speed, gradually add flour mixture; beat just until a soft dough forms. Turn dough out onto a sheet of plastic wrap; knead lightly 3 times or until smooth. Divide dough into 2 equal portions; wrap each portion in plastic wrap. Chill 1 hour.

3. Preheat oven to 350°. Roll each dough portion to a ⅛-inch thickness on a floured surface; cut with a 2-inch rectangular cookie cutter with fluted edges to form 36 cookies. Repeat procedure with remaining dough portion; use a 1-inch rectangular fluted cutter to remove centers of 36 rectangles. Arrange 1 inch apart on baking sheets lined with parchment paper. Bake, 1 batch at a time, at 350° for 10 minutes or until edges are lightly browned. Cool on pans 5 minutes. Remove from pans; cool on wire racks.

4. Spread center of each whole cookie with about ½ teaspoon preserves. Sprinkle cutout cookies with powdered sugar. Place 1 cutout cookie on top of each whole cookie.

Serves 36 (serving size: 1 cookie)

CALORIES 96; FAT 5.1g (sat 1.9g, mono 2.2g, poly 0.7g); PROTEIN 1.8g; CARB 11.4g; FIBER 0.6g; CHOL 29mg; IRON 0.5mg; SODIUM 25mg; CALC 18mg

RHUBARB-APPLE PIE

Get rhubarb at its peak between April and June, and look for bright red stalks—they will have the most flavor.

Hands-on time: 28 min. ★ **Total time: 1 hr. 28 min.**

½ (14.1-ounce) package refrigerated pie dough
Cooking spray
1 cup granulated sugar
3½ cups sliced fresh rhubarb (about 1¼ pounds)
1 tablespoon fresh lemon juice
2 Granny Smith apples, peeled, cored, and sliced
½ teaspoon ground cinnamon
³⁄₈ teaspoon salt, divided
4.22 ounces all-purpose flour (about 1 cup), divided
½ cup packed brown sugar
6 tablespoons chilled butter, cut into small pieces
⅓ cup chopped walnut halves

1. Preheat oven to 425°.

2. Place pie dough on a lightly floured work surface; roll into a 12-inch circle. Fit dough into a 9-inch pie plate coated with cooking spray. Turn edges under; flute. Combine granulated sugar, rhubarb, juice, and apples; toss. Sprinkle rhubarb mixture with cinnamon, ¼ teaspoon salt, and 3 tablespoons flour; toss. Spoon rhubarb mixture into prepared crust.

3. Weigh or lightly spoon remaining 3.38 ounces flour (about ¾ cup) into dry measuring cups; level with a knife. Combine 3.38 ounces flour, ⅛ teaspoon salt, and brown sugar in a medium bowl; cut butter into flour mixture with a pastry blender or 2 knives until mixture resembles coarse meal. Stir in walnuts. Sprinkle butter mixture evenly over rhubarb mixture. Bake at 425° for 15 minutes.

4. Reduce oven temperature to 375° (do not remove pie). Bake at 375° for 30 minutes or until golden and bubbly (shield edges of crust with foil to prevent overbrowning). Let pie stand on a cooling rack 15 minutes before slicing.

Serves 12 (serving size: 1 wedge)

CALORIES 296; FAT 12.4g (sat 5.4g, mono 1.8g, poly 1.8g); PROTEIN 2.6g; CARB 46.2g; FIBER 1.5g; CHOL 15mg; IRON 0.8mg; SODIUM 192mg; CALC 47mg

STONE FRUIT COBBLER

Tender and buttery, this cobbler's crust is a nice foil for the flavor-packed filling. You can bake this dessert in any 2-quart glass or ceramic baking dish, from round to rectangular. Just be sure to roll the dough to fit your dish.

Hands-on time: 45 min. ★ **Total time: 5 hr. 55 min.**

Crust:

9 ounces all-purpose flour (about 2 cups)
1 tablespoon sugar
½ teaspoon salt
6 tablespoons cold butter cut into small pieces
2 teaspoons fresh lemon juice
4 to 5 tablespoons ice water

Filling:

1¼ cups sugar
6 tablespoons all-purpose flour
½ teaspoon salt
½ teaspoon ground nutmeg
¼ teaspoon ground allspice
2½ pounds red plums, pitted and cut into ½-inch-thick slices
2 peaches (about 1 pound), pitted and cut into ½-inch-thick slices
1 tablespoon butter, melted
½ teaspoon vanilla extract

Remaining ingredients:

Cooking spray
2 teaspoons fat-free milk
1 tablespoon sugar

1. Weigh or lightly spoon 9 ounces (about 2 cups) flour into dry measuring cups; level with a knife. Combine flour, 1 tablespoon sugar, and ½ teaspoon salt in a bowl; cut in 6 tablespoons butter with a pastry blender or 2 knives until mixture resembles coarse meal. Sprinkle surface with juice and ice water, 1 tablespoon at a time; toss with a fork until moist and crumbly (do not form a ball). Gently press two-thirds of dough into a 4-inch circle on plastic wrap, and cover. Press remaining dough into a 4-inch circle on plastic wrap, and cover. Chill 3 hours or overnight.

2. Preheat oven to 425°. Place a foil-lined baking sheet on middle rack.

3. To prepare filling, combine 1¼ cups sugar and next 4 ingredients (through allspice) in a small bowl, stirring with a whisk. Combine plums and peaches in a large bowl; sprinkle flour mixture over plum mixture. Drizzle with melted butter and vanilla; toss gently.

4. Working with large portion, roll dough out on a lightly floured surface into a 13 x 9–inch rectangle. Fit into a 2-quart glass or ceramic baking dish coated with cooking spray. Spoon plum mixture into crust. Roll remaining portion of dough into an 11 x 7–inch rectangle. Cut dough lengthwise into ½-inch-thick strips; arrange strips in a lattice design over plum mixture. Seal dough strips around edges of crust. Lightly brush strips with milk; sprinkle evenly with 1 tablespoon sugar. Place baking dish on preheated pan; bake at 425° for 20 minutes.

5. Reduce oven temperature to 375° (do not remove cobbler from oven). Bake an additional 50 minutes or until crust is golden and filling is bubbly. Cool at least 1 hour.

Serves 12 (serving size: about ¾ cup)

CALORIES 301; FAT 7.1g (sat 4.3g, mono 1.8g, poly 0.4g); PROTEIN 3.7g; CARB 58g; FIBER 2.5g; CHOL 18mg; IRON 1.5mg; SODIUM 199mg; CALC 10mg

STRAWBERRIES, PEACHES, AND BASIL
with orange vinaigrette

Vinaigrette isn't just for salad: This dessert vinaigrette is an adaptation of a recipe by Dan Barber, chef of Blue Hill at Stone Barns in Pocantico Hills, New York. Serve within 20 minutes of preparing for maximum flavor and optimal temperature.

Hands-on time: 18 min. ★ **Total time: 18 min.**

1   cup fresh orange juice
1½ tablespoons sugar
1½ tablespoons champagne
    vinegar or white wine
    vinegar
1   tablespoon extra-virgin
    olive oil
Dash of salt
1½ cups fresh blueberries
1   pound fresh strawberries,
    halved
1   large ripe peach or
    nectarine, cut into 16
    wedges
¼   cup small basil
    leaves

1. Combine first 3 ingredients in a small saucepan; bring to a boil. Cook until reduced to ½ cup (about 15 minutes). Add oil and salt to pan, stirring with a whisk. Let stand 2 minutes.

2. Combine berries and peach in a large bowl. Add juice mixture, stirring gently. Sprinkle with basil.

Serves 4 (serving size: 1¼ cups)

CALORIES 163; FAT 4.2g (sat 0.5g, mono 2.6g, poly 0.7g); PROTEIN 2.1g; CARB 32.5g; FIBER 4.4g; CHOL 0mg; IRON 1mg; SODIUM 39mg; CALC 36mg

STRAWBERRY-LEMON SHORTCAKES

Tender biscuits get a little lift from sweet, floral lemon rind. For slightly taller shortcakes with soft sides, pack biscuits into a round cake pan; for separate shortcakes with crisp edges, arrange on a baking sheet with space between.

Hands-on time: 35 min. ★ **Total time: 1 hr. 30 min.**

9   **ounces all-purpose flour (about 2 cups)**
¼   **cup granulated sugar**
1   **tablespoon baking powder**
½   **teaspoon baking soda**
¼   **teaspoon salt**
6   **tablespoons chilled butter, cut into small pieces**
1¼ **cups low-fat buttermilk**
1   **tablespoon grated lemon rind**
Cooking spray
½   **cup all-purpose flour**
1   **tablespoon butter, melted**
1   **tablespoon turbinado sugar**
4   **cups sliced strawberries**
¼   **cup granulated sugar**
1   **tablespoon fresh lemon juice**
1¼ **cups frozen fat-free whipped topping, thawed**

1. Preheat oven to 425°.

2. Weigh or lightly spoon 9 ounces (about 2 cups) flour into dry measuring cups; level with a knife. Combine 9 ounces flour, ¼ cup granulated sugar, baking powder, baking soda, and ¼ teaspoon salt in a large bowl. Cut in chilled butter with a pastry blender or 2 knives until mixture resembles coarse meal. Combine buttermilk and grated lemon rind. Add buttermilk mixture to flour mixture, and toss gently with a fork to combine (dough should be wet and about the texture of cottage cheese).

3. Coat a 9-inch round cake pan or baking sheet with cooking spray. Place ½ cup flour in a shallow dish. Scoop 10 equal dough portions into dish. Gently shape each portion into a round by tossing in flour to help shape the dough. Arrange in pan. Discard excess flour. Brush dough with melted butter, and sprinkle evenly with 1 tablespoon turbinado sugar. Bake at 425° for 22 minutes or until shortcakes are lightly browned. Cool in pan on a wire rack 10 minutes. Remove shortcakes from pan. Cool on wire rack.

4. Combine berries, ¼ cup granulated sugar, and lemon juice; toss to coat. Let stand 15 minutes. Split each shortcake in half; spoon about ⅓ cup berry mixture and 2 tablespoons whipped topping onto bottom half of shortcake. Place top half over whipped topping.

Serves 10 (serving size: 1 filled shortcake)

CALORIES 267; **FAT** 8.8g (sat 5.3g, mono 2.2g, poly 0.5g); **PROTEIN** 4.5g; **CARB** 46.2g; **FIBER** 2.2g; **CHOL** 23mg; **IRON** 1.6mg; **SODIUM** 338mg; **CALC** 126mg

STRAWBERRY-BUTTERMILK SHERBET

This five-ingredient recipe uses raspberry-flavored liqueur to enhance the fruit flavor; it also helps create a nice texture. Taste the strawberries; if they're super-sweet, you can use lemon juice to boost the tartness of the sherbet.

Hands-on time: 10 min. ★ **Total time: 1 hr. 40 min.**

2	cups chopped strawberries
⅓	cup agave nectar
1½	cups whole buttermilk
3	tablespoons Chambord (raspberry-flavored liqueur)
1	tablespoon fresh lemon juice (optional)

1. Place berries and nectar in a blender; process until smooth (about 1 minute). Add buttermilk; process until well blended. Add liqueur; pulse to mix. Add juice, if desired. Chill mixture 1 hour. Pour into freezer can of an ice-cream freezer; freeze according to manufacturer's instructions.

Serves 6 (serving size: about ¾ cup)

CALORIES 135; FAT 2.2g (sat 1.3g, mono 0.6g, poly 0.2g); PROTEIN 2.4g; CARB 24.4g; FIBER 1.1g; CHOL 9mg; IRON 0.2mg; SODIUM 73mg; CALC 9mg

SWEET AND SALTY PEANUT CHOCOLATE CHUNK COOKIES

Hands-on time: 18 min. ★ **Total time: 1 hr. 22 min.**

⅓	**cup coarsely chopped unsalted, dry-roasted peanuts**
4.5	**ounces all-purpose flour (about 1 cup)**
½	**teaspoon baking powder**
¼	**teaspoon baking soda**
½	**cup granulated sugar**
½	**cup packed brown sugar**
¼	**cup unsalted butter, softened**
1	**teaspoon vanilla extract**
1	**large egg**
⅓	**cup semisweet chocolate chips**
½	**teaspoon coarse sea salt**

Cooking spray

1. Preheat oven to 350°.

2. Place nuts in a small metal baking pan. Bake at 350° for 8 minutes or until lightly toasted; cool.

3. Lightly spoon flour into a dry measuring cup; level with a knife. Combine flour, baking powder, and baking soda, stirring well with a whisk.

4. Place sugars and butter in a large bowl; beat with a mixer at medium speed until well blended (about 2 minutes). Add vanilla and egg; beat until combined. Add flour mixture to sugar mixture; beat at low speed until well blended. Stir in peanuts, chocolate chips, and salt.

5. Drop dough by teaspoonfuls 2 inches apart onto baking sheets coated with cooking spray. Bake at 350° for 10 minutes or until edges are lightly browned. Cool on pans 5 minutes. Remove cookies from pans; cool on wire racks.

Serves 38 (serving size: 1 cookie)

CALORIES 61; **FAT** 2.4g (sat 1.2g, mono 0.8g, poly 0.3g); **PROTEIN** 0.9g; **CARB** 9.2g; **FIBER** 0.3g; **CHOL** 9mg; **IRON** 0.3mg; **SODIUM** 48mg; **CALC** 9mg

WARM COCONUT RICE PUDDING

Flecks of coconut, aromatic cardamom and cinnamon, and a crunchy pistachio topping make this chai–inspired rice pudding comforting and transcendent.

Hands-on time: 20 min. ★ **Total time: 20 min.**

1	cup water	¼	cup flaked sweetened coconut
1	cup uncooked instant rice		
½	cup sugar	1	teaspoon vanilla extract
3	tablespoons cornstarch	¼	teaspoon ground cinnamon
¼	teaspoon salt		
1½	cups 2% reduced-fat milk, divided	¼	teaspoon ground cardamom
2	large egg yolks	1	tablespoon chopped pistachios
1	cup light coconut milk		

1. Bring 1 cup water to a boil in a saucepan. Stir in rice; cover and reduce heat to medium-low. Simmer 5 minutes. Remove from heat; uncover. Set aside.

2. Combine sugar, cornstarch, and salt in a small bowl.

3. Combine ¼ cup milk and yolks in a bowl, stirring with a whisk. Add sugar mixture to milk mixture, stirring with a whisk until blended.

4. Bring 1¼ cups milk and coconut milk to a boil in a small saucepan. Gradually add hot milk mixture to yolk mixture, stirring with a whisk. Return milk mixture to pan. Bring to a boil, and cook 1 minute, stirring constantly. Remove from heat; stir in cooked rice, coconut, and next 3 ingredients (through cardamom). Top with pistachios.

Serves 6 (serving size: ½ cup pudding and ½ teaspoon pistachios)

CALORIES 228; **FAT** 5.4g (sat 3g, mono 1.4g, poly 0.5g); **PROTEIN** 4.6g; **CARB** 40g; **FIBER** 0.8g; **CHOL** 75mg; **IRON** 1.3mg; **SODIUM** 141mg; **CALC** 87mg

learning to love dessert

"Mom, why do we always have rice pudding (kheer) at every special occasion in our home?" I asked my mother when I was 7 years old, secretly wishing for chocolate cake. My mother would respond, "It is the king of desserts! Slow-boiled reduced milk and rice with nuts, saffron, and raisins brings out the incredible taste, flavor, and texture." Throughout my childhood, we had kheer for all celebrations and feasts. And I grew to love it. Today, I continue to make kheer in my home for all important life experiences. When my kids started solids, their lips were dabbed with kheer in their *Annaprashan*, or "first rice-eating" ceremony, and when they started kindergarten, I made kheer for their breakfasts in the mornings.

-Rashmi Nigam, Studio City, California

NIBBLE

&

SIP:

STARTERS & SNACKS

CREOLE DEVILED EGGS

Start a party with some wow and update deviled eggs with this New Orleans–inspired twist: The filling is a tangy, spicy, creamy, and crunchy mix; hot pickled okra adds a unique garnish and a kick.

Hands-on time: 22 min. ★ Total time: 37 min.

8 large eggs
1 tablespoon cider vinegar
1 ounce (2 tablespoons) 1/3-less-fat cream cheese
1/4 cup plain 2% reduced-fat Greek yogurt
1 tablespoon finely chopped green bell pepper
1 tablespoon finely chopped celery
1 tablespoon Creole mustard
2 teaspoons minced fresh chives
1/4 teaspoon freshly ground black pepper
1/4 teaspoon hot pepper sauce
1/8 teaspoon salt
Dash of ground red pepper
2 pieces hot pickled okra, each cut into 8 slices (optional)

1. Place eggs in a large saucepan. Cover with water to 1 inch above eggs; stir in vinegar. Bring just to a rolling boil. Remove from heat; cover and let stand 15 minutes. Drain and rinse with cold running water until cool.

2. Peel eggs; cut in half lengthwise. Place yolks in a medium bowl; add cream cheese, and mash with a fork until smooth. Add yogurt and next 8 ingredients (through ground red pepper). Spoon mixture into egg white halves (about 1 tablespoon in each half). Garnish each egg half with 1 okra slice, if desired.

Serves 8 (serving size: 2 egg halves)

CALORIES 90; FAT 4.9g (sat 1.8g, mono 1.9g, poly 0.8g); PROTEIN 7.2g; CARB 2.5g; FIBER 0.1g; CHOL 183mg; IRON 1mg; SODIUM 163mg; CALC 36mg

make it ahead

Deviled eggs are a great party food in part because they're easy to make ahead. You can boil the eggs and mix the filling a day in advance. Store the filling in a zip-top plastic bag, and when you're ready to assemble, snip off a corner of the bag and pipe the filling into the egg white halves.

MARINATED PEPPERS AND MOZZARELLA

Serve this stunning dish solo as a pre-dinner nosh, or spoon over mixed lettuces for a fresh spin on salad. Reserve excess oil, and toss it with steamed brown rice or noodles.

Hands-on time: 13 min. ★ **Total time: 8 hr. 43 min.**

4	cups baby sweet peppers
½	cup extra-virgin olive oil
1	teaspoon grated lemon rind
½	teaspoon crushed red pepper
½	teaspoon salt
3	ounces fresh baby mozzarella balls
3	garlic cloves, crushed
¼	cup small basil leaves
1	teaspoon fresh lemon juice

1. Preheat broiler.

2. Arrange sweet peppers in a single layer on a foil-lined jelly-roll pan; broil peppers 4 minutes on each side or until blackened and tender. Cool. Combine peppers, olive oil, lemon rind, crushed red pepper, salt, baby mozzarella balls, and garlic; toss. Cover and refrigerate overnight, tossing occasionally. Let stand at room temperature 30 minutes. Stir in basil leaves and lemon juice before serving. Serve with a slotted spoon.

Serves 6 (serving size: about ¼ cup)

CALORIES 83; **FAT** 7.7g (sat 1.8g, mono 4.3g, poly 0.7g); **PROTEIN** 1.5g; **CARB** 2.1g; **FIBER** 0.6g; **CHOL** 6mg; **IRON** 0.2mg; **SODIUM** 104mg; **CALC** 5mg

go ahead, break a holiday rule

Traditional holiday recipes are funny fare. Why are some dishes served only once a year? In my family, it seems almost sacrilegious, even impossible, to serve those special foods at non-holiday times of the year. If I actually had the nerve to prepare my family's Baked Crab Meat Casserole, served in crab shells, any day other than Christmas Eve, I wouldn't dare tell Mom or my sisters, and I'd be a little worried that Grandma would admonish me from heaven. So, when I found this recipe for Cajun Hot Crab Dip, I was overjoyed that I could still have the comfort food flavors my heart craved without breaking any family rules.

- Serena Ball,
Worden, Illinois

CAJUN HOT CRAB DIP

Spoon this dip into a baking dish up to a day ahead, but top with panko and chives just before baking. If it's chilled, leave the dish out at room temperature while the oven preheats. Serve with toasted baguette slices.

Hands-on time: 30 min. ★ **Total time: 65 min.**

Cooking spray
2 tablespoons minced shallots
1 teaspoon minced garlic
1 pound lump crabmeat, shell pieces removed, divided
¼ cup water
1 tablespoon hot pepper sauce
2 teaspoons salt-free Cajun seasoning
½ cup canola mayonnaise
⅓ cup ⅓-less-fat cream cheese, softened
¼ cup minced red bell pepper
2 tablespoons lemon juice
¼ teaspoon salt
¼ teaspoon freshly ground black pepper
3 tablespoons panko (Japanese bread crumbs)
3 tablespoons minced fresh chives

1. Preheat oven to 450°.

2. Heat a small saucepan over medium heat. Coat pan with cooking spray. Add shallots and garlic to pan; cook 2 minutes, stirring frequently. Place 1 cup crab in a food processor. Add shallot mixture, ¼ cup water, pepper sauce, and Cajun seasoning to crab; process until smooth. Spoon mixture into a large bowl, and stir in remaining crab, mayonnaise, and next 5 ingredients (through black pepper).

3. Transfer mixture to a 1-quart glass or ceramic baking dish lightly coated with cooking spray. Combine panko and chives in a small bowl; sprinkle over crab mixture. Coat panko mixture with cooking spray. Bake at 450° for 30 minutes or until browned and bubbly. Let stand 5 minutes.

Serves 12 (serving size: ¼ cup)

CALORIES 95; **FAT** 5.3g (sat 1.1g, mono 1.8g, poly 1.3g); **PROTEIN** 8.4g; **CARB** 2g; **FIBER** 0.1g; **CHOL** 43mg; **IRON** 0.4mg; **SODIUM** 253mg; **CALC** 46mg

PAN-FRIED EGG ROLLS

Rather than the usual filling mishmash, these egg rolls keep the ingredients more distinct, similar to spring or summer rolls. Pan-fry these to get a crisp wrap without the fuss and mess of deep-frying.

Hands-on time: 54 min. ★ Total time: 54 min.

¼   cup sweet chili sauce, divided
12   ounces fresh bean sprouts, chopped
12   (8-inch) egg roll wrappers
12   cooked jumbo shrimp, peeled, deveined, and split in half lengthwise (about 13 ounces)
6   tablespoons chopped fresh cilantro
¼   cup peanut oil
1   tablespoon rice vinegar
2   teaspoons lower-sodium soy sauce
¼   teaspoon grated peeled fresh ginger
⅛   teaspoon freshly ground black pepper

1. Combine 3 tablespoons chili sauce and bean sprouts, tossing well to coat.

2. Working with 1 egg roll wrapper at a time (cover remaining wrappers to prevent drying), place wrapper onto work surface with 1 corner pointing toward you (wrapper should look like a diamond). Spoon about 2 heaping tablespoons bean sprout mixture into center of wrapper; top with 2 shrimp halves and 1½ teaspoons cilantro. Fold lower corner of wrapper over filling; fold in side corners. Moisten top corner of wrapper with water; roll up jelly-roll fashion. Place egg roll, seam side down, on a baking sheet. Repeat procedure with remaining wrappers, bean sprout mixture, shrimp, and cilantro.

3. Heat 2 tablespoons oil in a large nonstick skillet over medium-high heat. Add 6 egg rolls, seam sides down; cook 7 minutes or until golden, turning occasionally. Place on a wire rack. Repeat procedure with 2 tablespoons oil and 6 egg rolls.

4. Combine 1 tablespoon chili sauce, vinegar, and next 3 ingredients (through pepper). Serve sauce with egg rolls.

Serves 12 (serving size: 1 egg roll and 1½ teaspoons sauce)

CALORIES 103; **FAT** 4g (sat 0.7g, mono 1.7g, poly 1.3g); **PROTEIN** 7.9g; **CARB** 8.7g; **FIBER** 0.7g; **CHOL** 48mg; **IRON** 1.3mg; **SODIUM** 207mg; **CALC** 23mg

ROASTED OYSTERS
with pancetta and breadcrumbs

Oysters crusted with nuts and pancetta elevate any gathering. You can prepare the crumb mix a few hours ahead; just make sure your oysters are freshly shucked right before you broil and serve them.

Hands-on time: 19 min. ★ **Total time: 24 min.**

2 tablespoons pine nuts, toasted
2 (1-ounce) slices white bread
Cooking spray
1 ounce finely chopped pancetta or cured bacon
2 tablespoons chopped fresh flat-leaf parsley
¼ teaspoon freshly ground black pepper
18 shucked oysters on the half shell
6 lemon wedges

1. Preheat oven to 450°.

2. Place nuts and bread in a mini food processor; process until coarsely ground. Heat a medium skillet over medium-high heat, and lightly coat pan with cooking spray. Add pancetta; sauté 2 minutes or until crisp, stirring frequently. Remove from heat. Stir in pine nut mixture, parsley, and black pepper. Carefully arrange oysters in a single layer on a broiler pan, and spoon 1 tablespoon bread mixture onto each oyster. Bake at 450° for 5 minutes or until oysters are opaque. Serve immediately with lemon wedges.

Serves 6 (serving size: 3 oysters)

CALORIES 92; FAT 4.9g (sat 1.1g, mono 0.7g, poly 1.4g); PROTEIN 4.7g; CARB 7.7g; FIBER 0.7g; CHOL 26mg; IRON 3.3mg; SODIUM 212mg; CALC 38mg

make it foolproof

If you're using bamboo skewers, be sure to soak them in water for 30 minutes to keep them from burning on the grill.

CHICKEN SATAY

Make your own peanut-based marinade for this popular party appetizer.

Hands-on time: 24 min. ★ **Total time: 1 hr. 24 min.**

⅓ cup unsalted, dry-roasted peanuts

1 tablespoon toasted cumin seeds

2 tablespoons fresh lime juice

1 tablespoon dark sesame oil

1 teaspoon toasted coriander seeds

2 garlic cloves

1 shallot, peeled

⅓ cup light coconut milk

3 tablespoons brown sugar

1 tablespoon grated peeled fresh ginger

¼ teaspoon ground turmeric

1 serrano chile, stem removed

6 skinless, boneless chicken thighs, cut into 36 pieces

¼ teaspoon salt

1. Place first 7 ingredients in a food processor, and process until smooth. Add coconut milk and next 4 ingredients (through serrano chile); process until smooth. Spoon peanut mixture into a large zip-top plastic bag. Add chicken to bag, and seal. Marinate in refrigerator 1 hour, turning after 30 minutes.

2. Preheat grill to medium-high heat.

3. Remove chicken from bag, and discard marinade. Thread chicken evenly onto 12 (6-inch) skewers; sprinkle evenly with salt. Grill 6 minutes on each side or until chicken is done.

Serves 12 (serving size: 1 skewer)

CALORIES 153; FAT 7.2g (sat 1.4g, mono 2.9g, poly 2.2g); PROTEIN 15.2g; CARB 7.3g; FIBER 0.7g; CHOL 57mg; IRON 2mg; SODIUM 161mg; CALC 23mg

BAKED FETA
with romesco and olive tapenade

Romesco comes from Spanish cuisine; nuts thicken the base, made of roasted red bell peppers. (For the best flavor, roast your own fresh peppers.) Serve this warm, cheesy dip with crostini or other thin slices of lightly toasted bread.

Hands-on time: 45 min. ★ **Total time: 1 hr. 12 min.**

Romesco:
1   red bell pepper
Cooking spray
2   cups chopped peeled plum tomato
5   garlic cloves, minced
1/2 cup fat-free, lower-sodium chicken broth
2   tablespoons chopped hazelnuts, toasted
1   (1-ounce) slice white bread, chopped
1/4 teaspoon freshly ground black pepper

Tapenade:
1/2 cup pitted kalamata olives
1/2 cup pitted picholine or other fruity olives
1/4 cup chopped fresh flat-leaf parsley
2   tablespoons sherry vinegar
1   tablespoon olive oil
1/4 teaspoon freshly ground black pepper

Remaining ingredients:
1 1/4 cups (5 ounces) crumbled feta cheese
2   tablespoons chopped fresh flat-leaf parsley, optional

1. Preheat broiler.

2. To prepare romesco, cut red bell pepper in half lengthwise, and discard seeds and membranes. Place pepper halves, skin sides up, on a foil-lined baking sheet; flatten with hand. Broil 8 minutes or until blackened. Place in a paper bag; fold to close tightly. Let stand 10 minutes. Peel and chop.

3. Reduce oven temperature to 425°.

4. Heat a large skillet over medium heat. Coat pan with cooking spray. Add tomato and garlic; cook 4 minutes or until garlic lightly browns, stirring frequently. Add red bell pepper and broth; cover and cook 10 minutes, stirring occasionally. Stir in nuts and bread; cook 1 minute. Transfer mixture to a food processor or blender; add 1/4 teaspoon black pepper. Process until smooth; transfer to a bowl.

5. To prepare tapenade, place olives, 1/4 cup parsley, and next 3 ingredients (through 1/4 teaspoon black pepper) in a food processor. Process until finely chopped. Transfer to a bowl.

6. Coat a 1 1/2-quart broiler-safe glass or ceramic baking dish with cooking spray. Spoon half of romesco sauce into prepared dish, and top with 3/4 cup cheese. Dollop tapenade over cheese. Spoon remaining romesco sauce over tapenade, and top with 1/2 cup crumbled feta cheese. Bake at 425° for 20 minutes or until thoroughly heated. Remove dish from oven.

7. Preheat broiler.

8. Broil 3 minutes or until top browns. Sprinkle with 2 tablespoons parsley, if desired.

Serves 12 (serving size: 1/4 cup)

CALORIES 88; FAT 6.1g (sat 2g, mono 2.4g, poly 0.6g); PROTEIN 3.6g; CARB 4.9g; FIBER 0.7g; CHOL 8mg; IRON 0.4mg; SODIUM 240mg; CALC 47mg

make it ahead
Make the romesco sauce
and tapenade up to three days
ahead, and keep them
chilled separately.

BAKED BLACK BEANS
with chorizo

Add a little zip to your next party and serve this dip warm or at room temperature with chips, or as a tasty side to tacos.

Hands-on time: 35 min. ★ **Total time: 65 min.**

1	tablespoon olive oil
½	cup diced Spanish chorizo

Cooking spray

1½	cups chopped onion
1	jalapeño pepper, sliced
½	teaspoon salt
½	teaspoon ground cumin
¼	teaspoon ground red pepper
5	garlic cloves, minced
¾	cup fat-free, lower-sodium chicken broth
2	(15-ounce) cans no-salt-added black beans, rinsed and drained
1	cup chopped seeded tomato
½	cup (2 ounces) shredded Monterey Jack cheese
¼	cup thinly sliced green onions

1. Preheat oven to 425°.

2. Heat a large nonstick skillet over medium-high heat. Add oil to pan; swirl to coat. Add chorizo; sauté 2 minutes. Remove chorizo from pan. Coat pan with cooking spray. Add onion and jalapeño; sauté 4 minutes, stirring occasionally. Add salt, cumin, red pepper, and garlic; sauté 1 minute, stirring constantly. Stir in broth and beans; bring to a boil. Cook 5 minutes. Mash to desired consistency. Spoon bean mixture into an 8-inch square glass or ceramic baking dish coated with cooking spray.

3. Top with chorizo, tomato, and cheese. Bake at 425° for 30 minutes or until lightly browned. Top with green onions.

Serves 6 (serving size: about ½ cup)

CALORIES 189; FAT 8.4g (sat 3g, mono 3.6g, poly 0.7g); PROTEIN 10.2g; CARB 19.4g; FIBER 6.2g; CHOL 8mg; IRON 1.7mg; SODIUM 307mg; CALC 142mg

make it foolproof

Take the casing off the Spanish chorizo (made of smoked pork) before starting the recipe. Spanish chorizo doesn't need to be cooked, but warming it in a skillet releases its flavors for other ingredients.

ONION, GRUYÈRE, AND BACON SPREAD

Serve this, and watch the cheese lovers gather around and swoon. Offer crackers or bread slices on the side. If you can't find Gruyère, substitute raclette, fontina, or Swiss cheese.

Hands-on time: 35 min. ★ **Total time: 1 hr. 15 min.**

Cooking spray
3 ½ cups chopped onion
¼ cup (2 ounces) shredded Gruyère cheese, divided
2 tablespoons chopped fresh chives, divided
⅓ cup canola mayonnaise
⅓ cup fat-free sour cream
¼ teaspoon salt
¼ teaspoon freshly ground black pepper
3 bacon slices, cooked and crumbled

1. Preheat oven to 425°.

2. Heat a large cast-iron skillet over medium-high heat. Coat pan lightly with cooking spray. Add onion to pan; sauté 5 minutes, stirring frequently. Reduce heat to low; cook 20 minutes or until golden brown, stirring occasionally. Cool slightly.

3. Reserve 2 tablespoons cheese. Combine remaining cheese, caramelized onion, 1 tablespoon chives, and next 5 ingredients (through bacon) in a medium bowl. Transfer mixture to a 1-quart glass or ceramic baking dish lightly coated with cooking spray. Sprinkle with reserved 2 tablespoons cheese. Bake at 425° for 20 minutes or until browned and bubbly. Sprinkle with 1 tablespoon chives.

Serves 8 (serving size: 3 tablespoons)

CALORIES 101; **FAT** 6.8g (sat 1.9g, mono 2.9g, poly 1.3g); **PROTEIN** 4.2g; **CARB** 5.3g; **FIBER** 0.7g; **CHOL** 12mg; **IRON** 0.2mg; **SODIUM** 236mg; **CALC** 97mg

PROSCIUTTO-WRAPPED STUFFED DATES

You've seen a version of these popular party noshes: Dates wrapped in or stuffed with salty, cheesy, or nutty ingredients that play off their intense sweetness. Here's a lighter, faster version that uses goat cheese and prosciutto.

Hands-on time: 9 min. ★ **Total time: 17 min.**

¾ **cup (6 ounces) goat cheese**
1 **tablespoon minced shallots**
1 **tablespoon chopped fresh thyme**
¼ **teaspoon freshly ground black pepper**
24 **whole pitted dates**
6 **thin slices prosciutto**

1. Preheat oven to 350°.

2. Combine first 4 ingredients in a small bowl, stirring with a fork. Slice dates lengthwise, cutting to, but not through, other side. Open dates; place 1 rounded teaspoon cheese mixture into each date. Cut 1 prosciutto slice in half lengthwise and then crosswise to make 4 equal pieces. Repeat procedure with remaining prosciutto to form 24 pieces. Wrap each date with 1 prosciutto piece; place dates on a baking sheet lined with parchment paper. Bake at 350° for 8 minutes or until filling is thoroughly heated. Serve immediately.

Serves 12 (serving size: 2 stuffed dates)

CALORIES 91; **FAT** 3.7g (sat 2.3g, mono 1g, poly 0.2g); **PROTEIN** 4.6g; **CARB** 10.8g; **FIBER** 1.2g; **CHOL** 11mg; **IRON** 0.5mg; **SODIUM** 159mg; **CALC** 27mg

BOURBON-MAPLE SOUR

The perfect mix of sweet maple, tart lemon, and the warmth of bourbon makes this cocktail a keeper. For an extra hit of maple, dip wet glass rims in maple sugar.

Hands-on time: 4 min. ★ **Total time: 4 min.**

6   **tablespoons bourbon**
2   **tablespoons maple syrup**
2   **tablespoons fresh lemon juice**
½   **cup ice cubes**
Additional ice (optional)

1. Combine bourbon, maple syrup, and fresh lemon juice, stirring well. Pour mixture into a cocktail shaker filled with ½ cup ice. Cover and shake. Strain mixture; divide evenly between 2 glasses. Serve over ice, if desired.

Serves 2 (serving size: about ⅓ cup)

CALORIES 152; **FAT** 0g (sat 0g, mono 0g, poly 0g); **PROTEIN** 0.1g; **CARB** 14.7g; **FIBER** 0.1g; **CHOL** 0mg; **IRON** 0.3mg; **SODIUM** 2mg; **CALC** 14mg

CAMPARI AND ORANGE SPARKLING COCKTAIL

Campari, an Italian aperitif, gives this cocktail a bitter edge and beautiful rosy color.

Hands-on time: 6 min. ★ Total time: 6 min.

1⅓ **cups sparkling rosé wine,
      chilled**
6   **tablespoons fresh orange juice,
      chilled**
6   **tablespoons Campari, chilled**
Orange rind curls (optional)

1. Combine first 3 ingredients. Garnish with rind curls, if desired.

Serves 4 (serving size: ½ cup)

CALORIES 127; **FAT** 0g (sat 0g, mono 0g, poly 0g); **PROTEIN** 0.2g; **CARB** 10g; **FIBER** 0.1g; **CHOL** 0mg; **IRON** 0.1mg; **SODIUM** 0mg; **CALC** 3mg

CILANTRO-JALAPEÑO LIMEADE

Hands-on time: 12 min. ★ **Total time: 3 hr. 42 min.**

4 ½ cups water
¾ cup sugar
½ cup agave nectar
1 cup coarsely chopped cilantro
2 large jalapeño peppers, seeded and chopped (about ½ cup)
2 tablespoons sugar
¼ teaspoon salt
9 lime wedges, divided
1 ½ cups fresh lime juice (about 10 limes)
4 cups ice cubes

1. Combine first 3 ingredients in a medium saucepan over medium-high heat; bring to a boil. Remove from heat; stir in cilantro and jalapeño. Let stand 30 minutes. Pour jalapeño mixture into a large bowl; cover and chill at least 3 hours.

2. Combine 2 tablespoons sugar and salt in a shallow dish. Rub rims of 8 glasses with 1 lime wedge. Dip rims of glasses in sugar mixture.

3. Strain cilantro mixture through a fine sieve over a bowl, discarding solids. Stir in lime juice. Fill each prepared glass with ½ cup ice. Add ¾ cup limeade to each glass. Garnish with remaining 8 lime wedges.

Serves 8

CALORIES 162; **FAT** 0g (sat 0g, mono 0g, poly 0g); **PROTEIN** 0.2g; **CARB** 44g; **FIBER** 0.7g; **CHOL** 0mg; **IRON** 0mg; **SODIUM** 74mg; **CALC** 7mg

FIZZY PLUM BELLINI

Treat someone to this twist on a brunch cocktail. (Breakfast in bed, perhaps?)
Plums stand in for peaches; pluots, which are sweeter, can also be used.

Hands-on time: 26 min. ★ **Total time: 1 hr. 41 min.**

½ cup water
3 tablespoons sugar
2 ripe red-skinned plums, pitted and quartered
1 teaspoon eau-de-vie or brandy
2 cups prosecco

1. Combine ½ cup water, sugar, and plums in a medium saucepan over medium-high heat; bring to a boil. Cook 5 minutes, stirring occasionally. Remove from heat; cool completely. Strain syrup through a sieve over a bowl; reserve plums. Stir eau-de-vie or brandy into syrup; chill. Discard plum skins; puree flesh until smooth. Chill puree. Spoon 2 teaspoons puree into each of 6 flutes; discard remaining puree. Divide syrup evenly among glasses. Top each serving with ⅓ cup prosecco; stir.

Serves 6

CALORIES 93; **FAT** 0.1g (sat 0g, mono 0g, poly 0g); **PROTEIN** 0.2g; **CARB** 10.1g; **FIBER** 0.3g; **CHOL** 0mg; **IRON** 0mg; **SODIUM** 0mg; **CALC** 1mg

FRESH RASPBERRY LEMONADE

Sweet raspberries and fresh lemon make this lemonade sunshine in a glass. You can make the sugar syrup up to a week ahead, but wait to blend until no more than an hour or two before you serve. Adults might want to stir in a favorite clear liquor, or Chambord.

Hands-on time: 26 min. ★ **Total time: 1 hr. 26 min.**

2 cups water, divided
³/₄ cup sugar
2 cups fresh raspberries
1³/₄ cups fresh lemon juice (about 13 medium lemons)
¹/₂ cup fresh orange juice (about 1 orange)
16 ounces sparkling water, chilled

1. Combine ¾ cup water and sugar in a small saucepan; bring to a boil. Cook 2 minutes, stirring until sugar dissolves. Cool to room temperature.

2. Place remaining 1¼ cups water and raspberries in a blender; pulse 10 times or until well blended. Strain mixture through a fine sieve into a large pitcher; discard solids. Add lemon juice, orange juice, sparkling water, and cooled syrup to pitcher; stir to combine. Serve immediately over ice.

Serves 8 (serving size: about 1 cup)

CALORIES 108; FAT 0.4g (sat 0g, mono 0g, poly 0.1g); PROTEIN 0.7g; CARB 28g; FIBER 2.2g; CHOL 0mg; IRON 0.3mg; SODIUM 12mg; CALC 13mg

BLUEBERRY THRILL

For a fizzy cocktail, pour gin, cardamom syrup, and lemon juice over ice with chilled club soda.

Hands-on time: 11 min. ★ **Total time: 1 hr. 11 min.**

2   **cups blueberries**
1½ **cups dry gin**
¾   **cup water**
½   **cup sugar**
3   **cardamom pods**
Crushed ice
½   **cup fresh lemon juice**
Additional blueberries (optional)
Lemon slices (optional)

1. Place 2 cups blueberries in a large heavy stainless-steel saucepan; mash with a fork or potato masher. Place over medium-high heat, and cook 3 minutes or until berries begin to release juice. Remove from heat; add gin. Cover and let stand at least 1 hour or overnight. Strain mixture through a fine sieve into a bowl, pressing berries with the back of a spoon to remove as much juice as possible; discard solids.

2. Combine ¾ cup water, sugar, and cardamom pods in a small saucepan; bring to a boil. Cook 2 minutes or until sugar dissolves. Cool completely; discard cardamom pods.

3. To serve, add crushed ice to a cocktail shaker to come halfway up sides of container. Add ¼ cup blueberry gin, 1½ tablespoons cardamom syrup, and 1 tablespoon lemon juice; shake until chilled. Strain cocktail into a chilled martini glass. Garnish with additional blueberries and lemon slices, if desired. Serve immediately. Repeat procedure with remaining ingredients.

Serves 8

CALORIES 159; **FAT** 0g (sat 0g, mono 0g, poly 0g); **PROTEIN** 0.1g; **CARB** 14.5g; **FIBER** 0.2g; **CHOL** 0mg; **IRON** 0mg; **SODIUM** 1mg; **CALC** 1mg

MINTED LEMON-LIME WATERMELON AGUA FRESCA

Garnish this family-friendly drink with mint, lime wedges, or small watermelon wedges.

Hands-on time: 20 min. ★ Total time: 40 min.

1¼ cups water
½ cup sugar
⅓ cup coarsely chopped fresh mint
1 tablespoon grated lime rind
1 tablespoon grated lemon rind
12 cups cubed seeded watermelon
¼ cup fresh lime juice
3 tablespoons fresh lemon juice

1. Combine 1¼ cups water and sugar in a small saucepan; bring to a boil over medium-high heat. Cook 30 seconds or until sugar dissolves, stirring frequently.

2. Remove from heat; stir in mint, lime rind, and lemon rind. Let stand 20 minutes. Strain mixture through a fine sieve over a bowl; discard solids.

3. Place one-third each of sugar syrup and watermelon in a blender; process until smooth. Pour puree into a large pitcher. Repeat procedure twice with remaining sugar syrup and watermelon. Stir in lime juice and lemon juice. Serve over ice, or refrigerate until ready to serve. Stir before serving.

Serves 9 (serving size: 1 cup)

CALORIES 108; FAT 0.3g (sat 0g, mono 0.1g, poly 0.1g); PROTEIN 1.3g; CARB 27.7g; FIBER 1g; CHOL 0mg; IRON 0.6mg; SODIUM 3mg; CALC 19mg

SALTY CHIHUAHUA

Red grapefruit juice and Cointreau combine for this riff on a Salty Dog. As the name implies, a dash of salt is put in the cocktail or on the rim. Squeeze your own juice to get the grapefruit's sweetest flavor. Make the juice mixture up to one day ahead, and chill.

Hands-on time: 15 min. ★ **Total time: 15 min.**

8 cups fresh red grapefruit juice (about 12 grapefruits)

1½ cups silver tequila

¾ cup Cointreau (orange-flavored liqueur)

1½ teaspoons kosher salt

Ice cubes

Lime slices (optional)

1. Combine juice, tequila, and liqueur; stir well. Coat rim of each of 12 glasses with ⅛ teaspoon salt. Fill each glass with ice; pour 1 cup juice mixture into each glass. Garnish each glass with a lime slice, if desired.

Serves 12 (serving size: 1 cup)

CALORIES 187; FAT 0.2g (sat 0g, mono 0.1g, poly 0.1g); PROTEIN 0.8g; CARB 20g; FIBER 0g; CHOL 0mg; IRON 0.3mg; SODIUM 242mg; CALC 15mg

SWEET & SOUR PLUM QUENCHER

Cachaça is a distilled alcohol from Brazil, made from sugar cane juice. It'll carry the herbal, spicy flavors of the mint and ginger, making this quencher beautiful to look at and drink.

Hands-on time: 8 min. ★ **Total time: 8 min.**

1   **lime**
2   **ounces cachaça**
6   **thin ginger slices**
6   **mint leaves**
6   **ounces Japanese plum sake**
Ice cubes
2   **ounces sparkling rosé wine**
1   **plum, thinly sliced**

1. Thinly slice lime; place in a cocktail shaker. Add cachaça, ginger slices, and mint leaves; muddle. Add sake and ice to shaker. Cover and shake 30 seconds. Strain and divide mixture evenly between 2 glasses. Float 1 ounce sparkling rosé wine atop each serving. Garnish with a thin plum slice.

Serves 3 (serving size: about ⅓ cup)

CALORIES 151; **FAT** 0g (sat 0g, mono 0g, poly 0g); **PROTEIN** 0.5g; **CARB** 8g; **FIBER** 0.9g; **CHOL** 0mg; **IRON** 0.1mg; **SODIUM** 2mg; **CALC** 4mg

THE MICHELADA

This tangy, spicy beer-based Mexican refresher is a good way to kick off taco night. Prepare the base ahead, chill, and stir in the beer just before serving.

Hands-on time: 4 min. ★ **Total time:** 4 min.

6	tablespoons spicy Bloody Mary mix
¼	cup fresh lime juice
1	tablespoon lower-sodium soy sauce
1	teaspoon hot pepper sauce
2	(12-ounce) bottles light beer
	Lime wedges (optional)

1. Combine spicy Bloody Mary mix, fresh lime juice, soy sauce, hot pepper sauce, and beer. Serve over ice. Garnish with lime wedges, if desired.

Serves 4 (serving size: about 1 cup)

CALORIES 64; **FAT** 0g (sat 0g, mono 0g, poly 0g); **PROTEIN** 0.9g; **CARB** 5.8g; **FIBER** 0.1g; **CHOL** 0mg; **IRON** 0.1mg; **SODIUM** 199mg; **CALC** 14mg

THE WHOOPSY DAISY

To make simple syrup, combine equal amounts of sugar and water in a small saucepan; bring to a boil. Cook 1 minute or until sugar dissolves. Store up to 2 weeks in an airtight container in the fridge.

Hands-on time: 6 min. ★ Total time: 6 min.

½ cup tequila blanco
¼ cup mescal
6 tablespoons fresh lime juice
6 tablespoons simple syrup
2 teaspoons pomegranate
   molasses

1. Combine all ingredients; stir with a whisk. Strain through a cheesecloth-lined colander into a bowl.

2. Ladle ⅓ cup tequila mixture into a cocktail shaker; add ice. Cover and shake 30 seconds. Strain and pour into a martini glass. Repeat 3 times to make a total of 4 drinks.

Serves 4 (serving size: about ⅓ cup)

CALORIES 158; **FAT** 0g (sat 0g, mono 0g, poly 0g); **PROTEIN** 0.1g; **CARB** 15.8g; **FIBER** 0.1g; **CHOL** 0mg; **IRON** 0.4mg; **SODIUM** 1mg; **CALC** 13mg

make it ahead
Steep juice mixture up to a week ahead; cool to room temperature, and refrigerate. Warm over medium-low heat, and add rum and lime juice shortly before serving.

WARM SPICED CRAN-POM TODDIES

For a nonalcoholic version, simply omit the rum; to make it sweeter, replace the rum with apple juice.

Hands-on time: 5 min. ★ Total time: 38 min.

2   (3-inch) cinnamon sticks
1   (64-ounce) bottle cranberry-
     pomegranate juice drink
1   (1-inch) piece fresh ginger,
     peeled and cut into thin slices
1³⁄₄ cups gold rum
3   tablespoons fresh lime juice
Cinnamon sticks (optional)

1. Combine cinnamon sticks, juice drink, and ginger slices in a large Dutch oven, and bring to a simmer. Cover and cook over low heat 30 minutes. Discard cinnamon sticks and ginger slices. Stir in rum and lime juice; serve warm. Garnish with cinnamon sticks, if desired.

Serves 10 (serving size: about 1 cup)

CALORIES 175; FAT 0g (sat 0g, mono 0g, poly 0g); PROTEIN 0.1g; CARB 20.7g; FIBER 0.8g; CHOL 0mg; IRON 3mg; SODIUM 30mg; CALC 32mg

WHISKEY SOUR PUNCH

Take a nostalgic cocktail and turn it into a punch: You'll set the pace for a lively party.

Hands-on time: 5 min. ★ Total time: 25 min.

⅓   **cup sugar**
⅓   **cup water**
2½ **cups refrigerated fresh
    orange juice**
2   **cups bourbon**
½   **cup fresh lemon juice
    (about 3 large lemons)**
3   **cups chilled club soda**
Ice (optional)
Fresh orange slices (optional)

1. Combine sugar and ⅓ cup water in a 1-cup glass measure. Microwave at HIGH 2 minutes; stir until sugar dissolves. Cool to room temperature.

2. Combine sugar mixture, orange juice, bourbon, and lemon juice in a large pitcher; stir well. Stir in club soda just before serving. Serve over ice, if desired, and garnish with orange slices, if desired.

Serves 10 (serving size: about ¾ cup)

CALORIES 160; FAT 0.1g (sat 0g, mono 0g, poly 0g); PROTEIN 0.5g; CARB 14.2g; FIBER 0.2g; CHOL 0mg; IRON 0.2mg; SODIUM 16mg; CALC 11mg

GARDEN

fresh

GOODNESS:

SALADS

CABBAGE SLAW

with tangy mustard seed dressing

What's a family picnic without slaw? Update a get-together favorite with mustard seed, cilantro, and cumin to give this coleslaw an exciting Indian spin.

Hands-on time: 20 min. ★ **Total time: 37 min.**

8 cups presliced green cabbage (about 1½ pounds)
1 cup thinly vertically sliced red onion
½ cup grated carrot
½ cup chopped fresh cilantro
2 tablespoons canola oil
2 tablespoons brown mustard seeds
1 tablespoon cumin seeds
1 large garlic clove, minced
½ jalapeño pepper, finely chopped
¼ cup white wine vinegar
1½ teaspoons sugar
¾ teaspoon salt
¾ teaspoon freshly ground black pepper

1. Combine first 4 ingredients in a large bowl.

2. Heat a small saucepan over medium heat. Add oil to pan; swirl to coat. Add mustard and cumin seeds; cook 90 seconds or until mustard seeds begin to pop. Remove from heat. Stir in garlic and jalapeño; let stand 2 minutes. Add vinegar, sugar, salt, and pepper, stirring with a whisk. Pour vinegar mixture over cabbage mixture; toss to coat. Let stand 15 minutes.

Serves 10 (serving size: about 1 cup)

CALORIES 67; FAT 3.5g (sat 0.3g, mono 2.3g, poly 0.9g); PROTEIN 1.6g; CARB 7.5g; FIBER 2.4g; CHOL 0mg; IRON 1mg; SODIUM 199mg; CALC 54mg

make it foolproof

Cabbage will release a lot of water once it's been salted. For the best texture (and to avoid watering down a delicious dressing), wait to add salt or a salty dressing to a slaw until you're nearly ready to serve. Some cooks salt the cabbage and let it drain first before using it to make slaw; just remember that step will boost the sodium level in your final salad.

CANDIED WALNUT, PEAR, AND LEAFY GREEN SALAD

The sweet, crunchy nuts are great on their own—make a double batch, and give some as a gift.

Hands-on time: 18 min. ★ **Total time: 18 min.**

⅓ cup sugar

⅔ cup chopped walnuts, toasted

Cooking spray

½ teaspoon kosher salt, divided

2 tablespoons white balsamic vinegar

1½ teaspoons Dijon mustard

3 tablespoons extra-virgin olive oil

1 tablespoon capers, chopped

4 cups torn green leaf lettuce

4 cups chopped romaine lettuce

4 cups chopped radicchio

1 ripe red Anjou pear, thinly sliced

¼ teaspoon freshly ground black pepper

1. Place sugar in a small heavy saucepan over medium-high heat; cook until sugar dissolves, stirring gently as needed to dissolve sugar evenly (about 1 minute). Continue cooking 1 minute or until golden (do not stir). Remove from heat; carefully stir in nuts to coat evenly. Spread nuts on a baking sheet coated with cooking spray; separate nuts quickly. Sprinkle with ¼ teaspoon salt. Set aside until cool; break into small pieces.

2. Combine vinegar and mustard, stirring with a whisk. Gradually add oil, stirring constantly with a whisk. Stir in capers.

3. Combine lettuces and radicchio; top with pear and candied walnuts. Drizzle dressing evenly over salad; sprinkle with ¼ teaspoon salt and pepper. Toss gently to combine.

Serves 8 (serving size: about 1 cup)

CALORIES 171; FAT 11.6g (sat 1.3g, mono 4.6g, poly 5.2g); PROTEIN 2.7g; CARB 16.3g; FIBER 2.6g; CHOL 0mg; IRON 1mg; SODIUM 177mg; CALC 37mg

CHERRY TOMATO CAPRESE SALAD

*Caprese combos are so simple: tomato, basil, and fresh mozzarella.
Elevate it here with a colorful assortment of heirloom cherry or other
small tomatoes, and a splash of white wine vinegar.*

Hands-on time: 6 min. ★ **Total time: 6 min.**

1   **tablespoon white wine vinegar**
1   **tablespoon extra-virgin olive oil**
¼   **teaspoon kosher salt**
¼   **teaspoon freshly ground black
     pepper**
¼   **cup halved miniature
     mozzarella balls**
¼   **cup basil leaves**
1   **pint heirloom cherry tomatoes,
     halved**

1. Combine vinegar, olive oil, kosher salt, and freshly ground black pepper in a medium bowl, stirring well with a whisk. Add mozzarella balls, basil leaves, and cherry tomato halves. Toss to combine.

Serves 4 (serving size: about ½ cup)

CALORIES 86; FAT 7g (sat 2.5g, mono 3.6g, poly 0.5g); PROTEIN 3.1g; CARB 3.1g; FIBER 1g; CHOL 12mg; IRON 0.3mg; SODIUM 132mg; CALC 13mg

GOLDEN CORN SALAD
with fresh basil

Hands-on time: 32 min. ★ **Total time: 62 min.**

8	ounces small yellow Finnish potatoes or small red potatoes
3	cups fresh corn kernels (about 4 ears)
2	cups assorted tear-drop cherry tomatoes (pear-shaped), halved
1½	cups chopped red bell pepper
¼	cup minced shallots
3	tablespoons white balsamic vinegar
1	tablespoon Dijon mustard
½	teaspoon kosher salt
¼	teaspoon black pepper
3	tablespoons extra-virgin olive oil
6	cups baby arugula
½	cup torn basil leaves
2	ounces goat cheese, sliced

1. Place potatoes in a small saucepan; cover with water. Bring to a boil; cook 11 minutes or until tender. Drain and chill. Cut potatoes in half lengthwise. Combine potatoes, corn, tomatoes, and bell pepper in a large bowl.

2. Combine shallots and next 4 ingredients (through black pepper) in a small bowl, stirring with a whisk. Slowly pour oil into shallot mixture, stirring constantly with a whisk. Drizzle over corn mixture; toss well. Add arugula; toss. Sprinkle with basil; top evenly with goat cheese.

Serves 4 (serving size: 2¼ cups)

CALORIES 337; **FAT** 16.5g (sat 4.7g, mono 8.9g, poly 2.4g); **PROTEIN** 10g; **CARB** 43.2g; **FIBER** 6.8g; **CHOL** 11mg; **IRON** 2.2mg; **SODIUM** 376mg; **CALC** 131mg

make it ahead

Every component of the salad can be prepared and ready to serve well in advance. Prepare the dressing several hours or even a day ahead; just bring to room temperature before tossing with arugula. It takes time to peel and slice the oranges, so do that ahead, arranging the oranges on a plate and covering with plastic wrap.

ORANGE SALAD
with arugula and oil-cured olives

Make this salad in winter, when citrus fruits are at their peak. The lemony dressing and colorful orange slices perk up any heavy dish—and your spirits, too. If you can find fresh blood oranges, they make a stunning presentation.

Hands-on time: 15 min. ★ **Total time: 15 min.**

Dressing:
- ⅓ cup thinly sliced shallots
- ¼ cup fresh lemon juice
- 2 tablespoons finely chopped mint leaves
- 1 teaspoon sugar
- 2 teaspoons Dijon mustard
- ¼ teaspoon kosher salt
- ⅛ teaspoon freshly ground black pepper
- ¼ cup extra-virgin olive oil

Salad:
- 1 (5-ounce) package arugula
- 5 oranges, peeled and thinly sliced crosswise
- 30 oil-cured black olives
- Freshly ground black pepper (optional)

1. To prepare dressing, combine first 7 ingredients in a medium bowl, stirring with a whisk. Gradually add oil, stirring constantly with a whisk.

2. To prepare salad, combine arugula and three-fourths of dressing in a large bowl; toss gently to coat. Arrange about ½ cup arugula mixture on each of 10 salad plates; arrange orange slices evenly over salads. Drizzle remaining one-fourth of dressing evenly over salads; top each salad with 3 olives. Sprinkle evenly with black pepper, if desired. Serve immediately.

Serves 10

CALORIES 131; FAT 9g (sat 1.2g, mono 6.7g, poly 0.9g); PROTEIN 1.4g; CARB 13g; FIBER 3g; CHOL 0mg; IRON 1.4mg; SODIUM 298mg; CALC 82mg

RICE NOODLE SALAD

Wide rice noodles are great for stir-fries and cook better when broken into shorter lengths. Soften in hot water, and stir-fry as directed. If unavailable, substitute linguine or fettuccine.

Hands-on time: 35 min. ★ **Total time: 35 min.**

8	ounces uncooked wide rice sticks (banh pho)
2	tablespoons plus 1 teaspoon sesame oil, divided
½	cup organic vegetable broth
6	tablespoons ketchup
2	tablespoons lime juice
2	tablespoons lower-sodium soy sauce
1	teaspoon Sriracha (hot chile sauce)
8	ounces tempeh, cut into ½-inch cubes
6	garlic cloves, minced
2	shallots, thinly sliced
2	large eggs, lightly beaten
2	cups fresh bean sprouts
1½	cups thinly sliced English cucumber
1½	cups matchstick-cut carrots
½	cup basil leaves
½	cup mint leaves
½	cup chopped fresh cilantro
5	thinly sliced green onions
2	tablespoons finely chopped unsalted, dry-roasted peanuts
12	lime wedges

1. Cook noodles according to package directions. Drain and toss with 1 teaspoon sesame oil.

2. Combine broth and next 4 ingredients (through Sriracha), stirring with a whisk.

3. Heat a large nonstick skillet over medium-high heat. Add 2 tablespoons oil to pan; swirl to coat. Add tempeh, and stir-fry 3 minutes or until lightly browned. Add garlic and shallots; stir-fry 1 minute or until shallots begin to soften. Add eggs; stir-fry 30 seconds or until soft-scrambled, stirring constantly. Add soy sauce mixture, and bring to a boil. Add noodles and bean sprouts; toss gently to coat. Cook 1 minute or until sauce is thick.

4. Remove from heat, and top with cucumber and next 5 ingredients (through onions). Sprinkle each serving with 1 teaspoon dry-roasted peanuts and juice from 2 lime wedges.

Serves 6 (serving size: 1⅓ cups)

CALORIES 370; FAT 12.6g (sat 2.3g, mono 4.7g, poly 4.5g); PROTEIN 13g; CARB 55.3g; FIBER 3.9g; CHOL 60mg; IRON 3.4mg; SODIUM 420mg; CALC 112mg

TZATZIKI CHICKEN SALAD

A classic Greek sauce of creamy yogurt and cucumber makes the base of this tangy salad. Make this part of a salad plate combo—offer a mixed green salad and a fruit salad to go with it.

Hands-on time: 16 min. ★ Total time: 16 min.

⅔ cup plain 2% reduced-fat Greek yogurt
¼ cup finely chopped red onion
1 tablespoon fresh lemon juice
2 teaspoons chopped fresh dill
⅜ teaspoon kosher salt
¼ teaspoon freshly ground black pepper
1 cucumber, seeded and shredded
1 garlic clove, minced
2 cups shredded skinless, boneless rotisserie chicken breast
3 ounces multigrain pita chips

1. Combine first 8 ingredients in a medium bowl, stirring with a whisk. Add chicken; toss to coat. Serve with pita chips.

Serves 4 (serving size: about ⅔ cup salad and ½ cup chips)

CALORIES 230; **FAT** 7.5g (sat 1.5g, mono 1.4g, poly 2.1g); **PROTEIN** 23g; **CARB** 18.7g; **FIBER** 2.1g; **CHOL** 53mg; **IRON** 1mg; **SODIUM** 569mg; **CALC** 60mg

SWEET POTATO SALAD
with cranberry-chipotle dressing

Hands-on time: 25 min. ★ Total time: 60 min.

2½ pounds sweet potatoes, peeled and cut into 2-inch pieces
3 tablespoons olive oil, divided
¾ teaspoon kosher salt
½ teaspoon freshly ground black pepper
¾ cup fresh or frozen cranberries
¼ cup water
2 teaspoons honey
1 (7-ounce) can chipotle chiles in adobo sauce
½ cup pepitas (pumpkinseed kernels)
¾ cup sliced green onions
¼ cup cilantro leaves

1. Preheat oven to 450°. Place sweet potatoes on a jelly-roll pan. Drizzle with 2 tablespoons oil, and sprinkle with salt and pepper; toss to coat. Bake at 450° for 30 minutes or until tender, turning after 15 minutes.

2. Place 1 tablespoon oil, cranberries, ¼ cup water, and honey in a saucepan. Remove 1 or 2 chiles from can; finely chop to equal 1 tablespoon. Add chipotle and 1 teaspoon adobo sauce to pan. Place pan over medium-low heat; bring to a boil. Cover, reduce heat, and cook 10 minutes or until cranberries pop, stirring occasionally. Remove from heat. Mash with a fork until chunky.

3. Place pepitas in a medium skillet; cook over medium heat 4 minutes or until lightly browned, shaking pan frequently.

4. Combine potatoes, pepitas, onions, and cilantro in a bowl. Add cranberry mixture to bowl; toss gently to coat.

Serves 8 (serving size: ¾ cup)

CALORIES 189; FAT 8.4g (sat 1.3g, mono 5.5g, poly 0.9g); PROTEIN 3.7g; CARB 25.5g; FIBER 4.5g; CHOL 0mg; IRON 1.3mg; SODIUM 335mg; CALC 40mg

SOUR CREAM—DILL POTATO SALAD

Potato salad is a traditional must-have for outdoor gatherings. This version is ready in less than 20 minutes.

Hands-on time: 18 min. ★ **Total time: 18 min.**

¾ **pound fingerling potatoes**
½ **cup diced English cucumber**
2 **tablespoons reduced-fat sour cream**
1½ **tablespoons plain fat-free Greek yogurt**
1½ **teaspoons chopped fresh dill**
¼ **teaspoon kosher salt**
¼ **teaspoon freshly ground black pepper**

1. Place a saucepan filled two-thirds with water over high heat. Cut potatoes into 1-inch pieces. Add potatoes to pan; cover and bring to a boil. Reduce heat to medium-high; cook 5 minutes or until tender. Drain.

2. Combine cucumber, sour cream, yogurt, dill, salt, and pepper in a large bowl. Add drained potatoes to cucumber mixture, and toss gently to coat.

Serves 6 (serving size: ½ cup)

CALORIES 50; FAT 0.7g (sat 0.4g, mono 0.2g, poly 0.1g); PROTEIN 1.6g; CARB 9.7g; FIBER 1.1g; CHOL 2mg; IRON 1mg; SODIUM 87mg; CALC 15mg

PEACH AND TOMATO SALAD

You may be tempted to enjoy seconds of this salad, built on the novel pairing of peaches and tomatoes, two summer fruits that go very well together. Serve this with a nice piece of grilled fish, pork, or thinly sliced steak.

Hands-on time: 19 min. ★ **Total time: 19 min.**

¼ **cup thinly vertically sliced red onion**

½ **pound ripe peaches, pitted and cut into wedges**

¼ **pound heirloom beef steak tomatoes, cut into thick wedges**

¼ **pound heirloom cherry tomatoes, halved**

1 **tablespoon sherry vinegar**

1½ **teaspoons extra-virgin olive oil**

1 **teaspoon honey**

⅛ **teaspoon salt**

⅛ **teaspoon freshly ground black pepper**

¼ **cup (1 ounce) crumbled feta cheese**

2 **tablespoons small basil leaves or torn basil**

1. Combine first 4 ingredients in a large bowl.

2. Combine vinegar, olive oil, honey, salt, and pepper in a small bowl, stirring with a whisk. Drizzle vinegar mixture over peach mixture; toss well to coat. Sprinkle with cheese and basil.

Serves 4 (serving size: 1 cup)

CALORIES 75; **FAT** 3.5g (sat 1.3g, mono 1.6g, poly 0.3g); **PROTEIN** 2.1g; **CARB** 9.9g; **FIBER** 1.7g; **CHOL** 6mg; **IRON** 0.4mg; **SODIUM** 156mg; **CALC** 47mg

make it special

Peaches come in heirloom varieties, too. One to look for: the Indian Blood Peach, in season in August. Its flesh is white with red streaks—sure to make your salad a little more stunning.

TOMATO STACK SALAD
with corn and avocado

Here is the essence of summer in a standout side salad. This is the star of the meal; keep the entrée simple.

Hands-on time: 30 min. ★ **Total time: 30 min.**

2   bacon slices, halved
¼   cup low-fat buttermilk
1   tablespoon finely chopped fresh chives
1   tablespoon finely chopped fresh basil
2   tablespoons canola mayonnaise
2   teaspoons cider vinegar
1   garlic clove, minced
½   teaspoon freshly ground black pepper, divided
2   ears shucked corn
Cooking spray

2   large beefsteak tomatoes, cut into 8 (½-inch-thick) slices total
2   globe tomatoes, cut into 8 (½-inch-thick) slices total
⅛   teaspoon kosher salt
½   ripe peeled avocado, thinly sliced
4   teaspoons extra-virgin olive oil
Basil leaves

1. Preheat grill to high heat.

2. Heat a large nonstick skillet over medium heat. Add bacon to pan; cook 8 minutes or until crisp, tossing occasionally to curl. Drain bacon on paper towels.

3. Combine buttermilk and next 5 ingredients (through garlic), stirring with a whisk. Stir in ¼ teaspoon pepper.

4. Coat corn with cooking spray. Place corn on grill rack; grill 8 minutes or until well marked, turning occasionally. Remove from grill; cool slightly. Cut corn kernels from cobs.

5. Sprinkle tomato slices evenly with salt. Alternate layers of tomato and avocado on each of 4 plates. Scatter corn evenly onto plates. Drizzle each tomato stack with about 1½ tablespoons dressing and 1 teaspoon oil. Sprinkle ¼ teaspoon black pepper over salads; top each salad with 1 bacon piece and basil leaves.

Serves 4

CALORIES 191; **FAT** 13g (sat 1.9g, mono 8g, poly 2.2g); **PROTEIN** 5.1g; **CARB** 16.1g; **FIBER** 4.5g; **CHOL** 5mg; **IRON** 0.9mg; **SODIUM** 228mg; **CALC** 40mg

summer's best on one plate

My father grew up in rural Pennsylvania, so sweet corn was always a seasonal kitchen staple in our family. I have fond memories of eating ears of Silver Queen. And, from a young age, I was fortunate to experience the taste of beautiful, juicy homegrown tomatoes from both our suburban garden and my grandpop's backyard at the Jersey Shore. This stacked salad melds all those childhood delights together with a modern twist. I love the tang and freshness of the buttermilk herb dressing. Paired with bacon and avocado, this is summer vegetable heaven!

-Deanna Segrave-Daly, Havertown, Pennsylvania

GRILLED CAESAR SALAD

Flames are all you need to put an exciting spin on a salad invented nearly 100 years ago. Grilling lettuce gives it a hint of smokiness and lends the leaves crisp-tender contrast. Toasted garlic bread stands in for croutons.

Hands-on time: 25 min. ★ **Total time: 25 min.**

10 (½-ounce) slices diagonally cut French bread (about ¼ inch thick)
Cooking spray
3 garlic cloves, divided
7 canned anchovy fillets, rinsed, drained, and divided
¼ cup fresh lemon juice
1 teaspoon Dijon mustard
½ teaspoon freshly ground black pepper
¼ teaspoon salt
1 large pasteurized egg yolk
¼ cup extra-virgin olive oil
3 romaine lettuce hearts, cut in half lengthwise (about 24 ounces)
⅓ cup (about 1½ ounces) shaved fresh Parmigiano-Reggiano cheese

1. Preheat grill to high heat.

2. Coat bread slices with cooking spray. Place bread on grill rack coated with cooking spray; grill 1 minute or until golden, turning once. Remove bread from grill. Cut 1 garlic clove in half; rub both sides of bread with cut sides of garlic clove. Discard clove.

3. Pat anchovy fillets dry with a paper towel. Combine 2 garlic cloves, 2 anchovy fillets, juice, mustard, pepper, salt, and egg yolk in a blender; process until smooth. With blender on, add oil, 1 tablespoon at a time; process until smooth.

4. Place lettuce, cut sides down, on grill rack coated with cooking spray; grill 2 minutes. Turn; grill 1 minute. Remove from heat; coarsely chop lettuce. Place lettuce in a large bowl; drizzle with dressing, tossing gently to coat.

5. Cut 5 anchovy fillets in half lengthwise. Arrange about ¾ cup salad on each of 10 plates; top each serving with 1 bread slice and 1 anchovy half. Sprinkle each serving with about 1½ teaspoons Parmigiano-Reggiano.

Serves 10

CALORIES 118; FAT 7g (sat 1.2g, mono 4.4g, poly 0.7g); PROTEIN 3.6g; CARB 10.5g; FIBER 1.2g; CHOL 25mg; IRON 1.5mg; SODIUM 290mg; CALC 66mg

SHRIMP, AVOCADO, AND GRAPEFRUIT SALAD

Clever flavor and texture combinations are the key to salads so good, you close your eyes to savor every bite. Here, creamy avocado mixes with crunchy lettuce, juicy grapefruit, and toothsome shrimp. To test an avocado's ripeness, gently press it, end to end, with your thumb and forefinger; it should give slightly.

Hands-on time: 48 min. ★ **Total time: 48 min.**

2½ tablespoons olive oil, divided

12 ounces peeled and deveined medium shrimp

½ teaspoon salt, divided

¼ teaspoon freshly ground black pepper, divided

1 grapefruit

2 tablespoons chopped fresh tarragon

2 teaspoons brown sugar

1 teaspoon chopped shallots

6 cups chopped romaine lettuce

1 peeled avocado, cut into 12 wedges

1. Heat a large skillet over medium-high heat. Add 1½ teaspoons oil to pan; swirl to coat. Sprinkle shrimp with ¼ teaspoon salt and ⅛ teaspoon pepper. Add shrimp to pan; cook 3 minutes or until shrimp are done, stirring frequently. Remove from pan; keep warm.

2. Peel and section grapefruit over a bowl, reserving 3 tablespoons juice. Combine grapefruit juice, 2 tablespoons oil, ¼ teaspoon salt, ⅛ teaspoon pepper, tarragon, brown sugar, and shallots in a large bowl, stirring well with a whisk. Add lettuce; toss. Arrange 2 cups lettuce mixture on each of 4 plates. Top each serving with 3 avocado wedges; divide shrimp and grapefruit sections evenly among servings.

Serves 4

CALORIES 291; **FAT** 17.7g (sat 2.6g, mono 11.3g, poly 2.5g); **PROTEIN** 19.9g; **CARB** 15.5g; **FIBER** 6g; **CHOL** 129mg; **IRON** 3.4mg; **SODIUM** 433mg; **CALC** 96mg

SOUTHWESTERN-STYLE SHRIMP TACO SALAD

Cilantro, chipotle hot sauce, corn, black beans, and green onions lend fantastic south-of-the-border flavor to this shrimp-topped taco salad.

Hands-on time: 41 min. ★ **Total time: 41 min.**

¼ cup fresh lime juice
2 tablespoons olive oil
1 teaspoon ground cumin
2 teaspoons minced garlic
2 teaspoons maple syrup
2 teaspoons chipotle hot sauce
¾ pound medium shrimp, peeled and deveined
2 ears shucked corn
Cooking spray
1 cup chopped romaine lettuce
½ cup chopped green onions
¼ cup chopped fresh cilantro
3 plum tomatoes, chopped
1 (15-ounce) can black beans, rinsed and drained
2 ounces baked blue corn tortilla chips (about 1½ cups)
⅓ cup light sour cream
¼ cup diced peeled avocado
Lime wedges (optional)

1. Preheat grill to medium-high heat.

2. Combine lime juice, olive oil, cumin, garlic, syrup, and hot sauce in a small bowl, stirring with a whisk. Place shrimp in a shallow bowl. Drizzle 1 tablespoon lime juice mixture over shrimp, tossing gently to coat. Reserve remaining lime juice mixture; set aside. Thread shrimp onto metal skewers. Lightly coat corn with cooking spray. Place shrimp kebabs and corn on grill rack coated with cooking spray. Grill 8 minutes, turning kebabs once and turning corn frequently until browned. Remove from grill; cool slightly.

3. Remove shrimp from skewers, and place in a large bowl. Cut kernels from ears of corn. Add corn, chopped lettuce, green onions, cilantro, plum tomatoes, and black beans to shrimp. Drizzle reserved lime juice mixture over shrimp mixture, and toss gently to combine.

4. Divide tortilla chips evenly among 6 bowls; top each serving with 1 cup shrimp mixture. Combine sour cream and diced avocado in a small bowl; mash with a fork until well blended. Top each serving with about 1 tablespoon sour cream mixture. Serve with a lime wedge, if desired.

Serves 6

CALORIES 228; **FAT** 8.5g (sat 1.8g, mono 4.4g, poly 1.4g); **PROTEIN** 16.2g; **CARB** 25.5g; **FIBER** 4.5g; **CHOL** 91mg; **IRON** 2.7mg; **SODIUM** 327mg; **CALC** 79mg

make it ahead
You can poach the chicken a day or two in advance; allow it to cool, then keep it refrigerated until you're ready to finish making the salad.

CHICKEN AND RICE SALAD

Chicken and rice, together with pecans and cranberries, make this salad reminiscent of popular holiday sides. Goat cheese delivers the finishing touch.

Hands-on time: 30 min. ★ **Total time: 1 hr. 31 min.**

4   cups cold water
2   cups fat-free, lower-sodium chicken broth
3   (6-ounce) skinless, boneless chicken breast halves
1   cup brown and wild rice blend
1   cup chopped carrot
2   tablespoons white wine vinegar
2   tablespoons olive oil
2   teaspoons Dijon mustard
1/2   cup chopped pecans, toasted
1/3   cup sweetened dried cranberries
1/4   cup chopped red onion
3   tablespoons chopped parsley
1/2   teaspoon kosher salt
1/4   teaspoon freshly ground black pepper
1/2   cup (2 ounces) crumbled goat cheese

1. Place 4 cups cold water, chicken broth, and chicken in a saucepan over high heat; bring to a simmer. Reduce heat, and simmer 15 minutes or until chicken is done. Remove chicken from pan, reserving cooking liquid; cool. Shred chicken.

2. Increase heat to medium-high; bring cooking liquid to a boil. Add brown and wild rice blend to pan. Cover, reduce heat, and simmer 28 minutes. Add carrot to rice; cook 7 minutes or until rice is tender. Drain.

3. Combine white wine vinegar, olive oil, and Dijon mustard. Toss dressing with rice mixture. Stir in shredded chicken, pecans, cranberries, red onion, parsley, kosher salt, and black pepper. Spoon rice mixture into each of 6 bowls. Sprinkle evenly with crumbled goat cheese.

Serves 6 (serving size: 1½ cups salad and about 2 teaspoons goat cheese)

CALORIES 359; FAT 18.3g (sat 6.3g, mono 7.4g, poly 3.1g); PROTEIN 27g; CARB 17g; FIBER 2.2g; CHOL 73mg; IRON 1.4mg; SODIUM 655mg; CALC 63mg

MELON SALAD
with prosciutto

Salty cheese and ham accent the sweet summer fruit in this refreshing main-dish salad, a perfect meal on a sweltering summer day.

Hands-on time: 40 min. ★ **Total time: 40 min.**

2 cups sliced seeded watermelon
2 cups sliced seeded honeydew melon
⅓ cup very thinly vertically sliced red onion
2 ripe nectarines, pitted and sliced
1 serrano pepper, very thinly sliced
¼ teaspoon kosher salt
3 tablespoons fresh lemon juice
2 tablespoons olive oil
1½ tablespoons honey
4 cups arugula
¼ cup torn mint leaves
3 ounces prosciutto, very thinly sliced
½ ounce shaved fresh pecorino Romano cheese

1. Combine first 5 ingredients; sprinkle with salt. Combine juice, oil, and honey, stirring well. Drizzle dressing mixture over fruit mixture; toss gently. Arrange 1 cup arugula and 1 tablespoon mint on each of 4 plates; top each serving with about 1¾ cups fruit mixture. Divide prosciutto evenly among plates; top evenly with cheese.

Serves 4

CALORIES 232; **FAT** 10g (sat 2g, mono 5g, poly 0.9g); **PROTEIN** 8.6g; **CARB** 31.5g; **FIBER** 2.8g; **CHOL** 18mg; **IRON** 1.3mg; **SODIUM** 674mg; **CALC** 62mg

GRILLED STEAK PANZANELLA
with pickled vegetables

Use the bottom part of ciabatta for this salad. The crusty, flat surface is easier to grill and provides more crunch. Don't skip the delicious pickled vegetable topping—it's earthy, crunchy, sweet-sour, and welcome in every bite.

Hands-on time: 45 min. ★ **Total time: 45 min.**

¼   **cup red wine vinegar**
1½ **tablespoons sugar**
3   **tablespoons water**
½   **cup thinly sliced red onion**
½   **cup julienne-cut carrot**
½   **cup julienne-cut radishes**
3   **tablespoons extra-virgin olive oil**
1   **tablespoon minced garlic**
2   **teaspoons chopped fresh thyme**
½   **teaspoon salt, divided**
½   **teaspoon freshly ground black pepper, divided**
2   **cups grape or cherry tomatoes, halved**
1   **(4-ounce) piece ciabatta (about 1 inch thick)**
Cooking spray
1   **(1-pound) flat-iron steak, trimmed**
1   **teaspoon paprika**
3   **cups baby spinach and arugula mixture**
¼   **cup chopped basil leaves**

1. Preheat grill to medium-high heat.

2. Combine first 3 ingredients in a medium bowl, stirring with a whisk until sugar dissolves. Add onion, carrot, and radishes; toss well. Let stand 30 minutes; drain.

3. Combine olive oil, garlic, thyme, ¼ teaspoon salt, and ¼ teaspoon pepper in a large bowl, stirring with a whisk. Stir in tomatoes; set aside.

4. Lightly coat bread with cooking spray. Place bread on grill rack, and grill 3 minutes on each side or until crisp. Sprinkle steak evenly with paprika, ¼ teaspoon salt, and ¼ teaspoon black pepper. Place on grill rack coated with cooking spray, and grill 3 minutes on each side or until desired degree of doneness. Let stand 10 minutes. Cut steak diagonally across grain into thin slices. Cut each slice in half.

5. Cut bread into 1-inch cubes. Add bread, greens, steak, and basil to tomato mixture; toss well. Top with carrot mixture.

Serves 4 (serving size: about 1⅔ cups salad and ⅓ cup carrot mixture)

CALORIES 417; **FAT** 22.5g (sat 5.9g, mono 12.9g, poly 1.8g); **PROTEIN** 25.4g; **CARB** 29g; **FIBER** 3.4g; **CHOL** 71mg; **IRON** 4.4mg; **SODIUM** 593mg; **CALC** 60mg

globe-trotting at the table

I was 11 years old when my uncle's sister came to visit from Thailand, and the two of them cooked our family an authentic Thai meal. For a kid who had never been exposed to any international flavors, that meal was a real eye opener: It sparked my love for the sweet and spicy Thai flavors. *Cooking Light*'s Thai Steak Salad is a light version of the spicy beef we ate that evening. Each time I make it, I'm reminded of what a blessing it is to have family members from other cultures.

-Betsy Haley,
San Diego, California

THAI STEAK SALAD

Hands-on time: 31 min. ★ **Total time: 31 min.**

Dressing:
⅓ cup fresh lime juice (about 3 limes)
1½ tablespoons brown sugar
1 tablespoon grated peeled fresh ginger
1 tablespoon Thai fish sauce
1 to 2 teaspoons chile paste with garlic

Steak:
Cooking spray
1 (1½-pound) flank steak, trimmed
1 tablespoon cracked black pepper

Salad:
3 cups trimmed watercress (about 2 bunches)
1 cup thinly sliced red cabbage
1 cup loosely packed basil leaves
1 cup loosely packed mint leaves
½ cup loosely packed cilantro leaves
½ cup julienne-cut carrot
2 tablespoons finely chopped unsalted, dry-roasted peanuts

1. To prepare dressing, combine first 5 ingredients in a bowl; stir well with a whisk.

2. To prepare steak, heat a large nonstick skillet or grill pan coated with cooking spray over medium-high heat. Rub both sides of steak with pepper. Add steak to pan; cook 6 minutes on each side or until desired degree of doneness. Remove from pan; place on a cutting board. Cover loosely with foil; let stand 5 minutes. Cut steak diagonally across grain into thin slices. Place steak in a bowl. Drizzle with half of dressing, and toss well.

3. To prepare salad, combine watercress and next 5 ingredients (through carrot) in a large bowl. Drizzle with remaining dressing, and toss well. Divide salad evenly among 6 plates; arrange 3 ounces steak over each salad. Sprinkle each serving with 1 teaspoon peanuts.

Serves 6

CALORIES 230; FAT 10.3g (sat 4g, mono 4.2g, poly 0.9g); PROTEIN 25.1g; CARB 9.5g; FIBER 2.g; CHOL 57mg; IRON 3.3mg; SODIUM 327mg; CALC 68mg

GRAB A

spoon!

SOUPS

& stews

FRESH PEA AND GARLIC GAZPACHO

Traditionally made with tomatoes, this gazpacho allows you to enjoy a spring version of the room-temp soup, using fresh English peas. Grab them when they're sweetest—peas peak in May. Frozen peas also work well. If you can find fresh pea shoots, add them as a garnish, too.

Hands-on time: 22 min. ★ **Total time: 22 min.**

2½ cups shelled fresh English peas
2¼ cups ice water
1½ cups chopped peeled English cucumber
1 cup (½-inch) cubed French bread
2 tablespoons extra-virgin olive oil
1½ tablespoons sherry vinegar
2 garlic cloves
½ teaspoon kosher salt
½ teaspoon freshly ground black pepper
1 tablespoon small mint leaves
1½ teaspoons extra-virgin olive oil
Fresh pea shoots (optional)

1. Cook peas in boiling water 4 minutes. Drain and rinse with cold water until cool. Set aside ½ cup peas.

2. Place remaining peas, 2¼ cups ice water, cucumber, French bread cubes, 2 tablespoons extra-virgin olive oil, sherry vinegar, and garlic cloves in a blender; process until smooth. Stir in salt and pepper. Ladle 1 cup soup into each of 6 bowls. Top each serving evenly with reserved peas, mint leaves, 1½ teaspoons extra-virgin olive oil, and fresh pea shoots, if desired.

Serves 6

CALORIES 123; FAT 6.3g (sat 0.9g, mono 4.5g, poly 0.7g); PROTEIN 4g; CARB 12.7g; FIBER 3.5g; CHOL 0mg; IRON 1mg; SODIUM 200mg; CALC 25mg

make it ahead
Cook the peas up to a day in advance, and store them in an airtight container in the refrigerator—you'll be able to finish the soup in a few minutes, making this a perfect last-minute first course.

make it ahead

Make a batch or two of this soup ahead: Prepare the soup through step 1, then cool the soup to room temperature. Store it in an airtight container in the refrigerator for up to one week, or in the freezer for up to one month. Heat the soup before adding the cheese, pepper, and green onions for a quick home-cooked dinner.

CHEESY POTATO SOUP

Serve a rich and hearty cheesy soup as part of a comforting cool-weather meal. When making this soup, stir in the cheese and remove from heat as soon as it melts to prevent curdling.

Hands-on time: 20 min. ★ Total time: 30 min.

1	**tablespoon butter**
1	**cup chopped onion**
2½	**tablespoons all-purpose flour**
3	**cups chopped red potato (about 1 pound)**
1¼	**cups 1% low-fat milk**
¾	**cup fat-free, lower-sodium chicken broth**
½	**cup water**
½	**cup (2 ounces) reduced-fat shredded sharp cheddar cheese**
⅛	**teaspoon ground red pepper**
2	**tablespoons diagonally sliced green onion tops**

1. Melt butter in a medium saucepan over medium-high heat. Add onion to pan; sauté 5 minutes or until onion is tender. Sprinkle with flour; cook 1 minute, stirring onion mixture constantly. Add potato, milk, broth, and ½ cup water to pan; bring to a boil. Cover, reduce heat, and simmer 10 minutes.

2. Add cheese and ground red pepper; cook 2 minutes or until cheese melts, stirring frequently. Top each serving evenly with green onions.

Serves 4 (serving size: 1 cup and 1½ teaspoons green onions)

CALORIES 225; FAT 6.9g (sat 4.1g, mono 1g, poly 0.2g); PROTEIN 9.9g; CARB 32.7g; FIBER 2.6g; CHOL 21mg; IRON 1.5mg; SODIUM 250mg; CALC 322mg

CHILLED FRESH CORN SOUP

with king crab

This chilled soup is full of delectably sweet fresh corn and gorgeous pieces of king crab legs.

Hands-on time: 25 min. ★ **Total time: 2 hr. 45 min.**

1   **pound frozen cooked king crab legs, thawed**

6   **cups fresh corn kernels (about 11 ears)**

4 ½ **cups water**

⅛   **teaspoon ground red pepper**

1   **cup 2% reduced-fat milk**

¼   **cup chopped fresh chives**

½   **teaspoon freshly ground black pepper**

1. Cut shells off crab legs with kitchen shears; reserve shells. Coarsely chop crabmeat; chill. Combine shells, corn, 4½ cups water, and red pepper in a saucepan; bring to a boil. Reduce heat; simmer 20 minutes or until corn is very tender. Discard shells.

2. Place half of corn mixture in a blender. Remove center piece of blender lid (to allow steam to escape); secure blender lid on blender. Place a clean towel over opening in blender lid (to avoid splatters). Process until smooth. Press pureed corn mixture through a fine sieve over a bowl, reserving liquid; discard solids. Repeat procedure with remaining corn mixture. Stir in milk, chives, and black pepper. Chill 2 hours. Top with reserved crabmeat.

Serves 8 (serving size: about ⅔ cup soup and about ¼ cup crabmeat)

CALORIES 115; **FAT** 2g (sat 0.6g, mono 0.5g, poly 0.6g); **PROTEIN** 10g; **CARB** 16.2g; **FIBER** 2.2g; **CHOL** 20mg; **IRON** 0.7mg; **SODIUM** 383mg; **CALC** 59mg

TOMATO-BASIL SOUP
with cheese toast

Bright, creamy tomato soup with a grilled cheese sandwich for dunking is a happy and comforting rite of childhood. This version's sure to please adults, too, with cheese toasts to replace the sandwich. Garnish with additional basil and a bit of crème fraîche, if desired.

Hands-on time: 25 min. ★ **Total time: 25 min.**

1	tablespoon extra-virgin olive oil
1½	cups chopped onion
3	garlic cloves, chopped
¾	cup chopped fresh basil
1	(28-ounce) can fire-roasted diced tomatoes, undrained
½	cup (4 ounces) ⅓-less-fat cream cheese, cut into cubes
2	cups 1% low-fat milk
¼	teaspoon salt
¼	teaspoon freshly ground black pepper
12	(½-inch-thick) slices French bread
Cooking spray	
1	garlic clove, halved
1	ounce shredded Asiago cheese

1. Preheat broiler.

2. Heat a saucepan over medium-high heat. Add olive oil to pan; swirl to coat. Add onion; sauté 3 minutes. Stir in chopped garlic; cook 1 minute. Add basil and tomatoes; bring to a boil. Stir in cheese until melted. Place mixture in a blender. Remove center piece of blender lid (to allow steam to escape); secure blender lid on blender. Place a clean towel over opening in blender lid (to avoid splatters). Blend until smooth. Return to pan; stir in milk, salt, and pepper. Return to medium-high heat; cook 2 minutes.

3. Place bread on a baking sheet; lightly coat bread with cooking spray. Broil 1 minute. Rub garlic halves over toasted sides; turn bread over. Top evenly with Asiago cheese; broil 1 minute. Serve toasts with soup.

Serves 4 (serving size: 1¼ cups soup and 3 toasts)

CALORIES 312; **FAT** 13.9g (sat 6.3g, mono 4.5g, poly 0.9g); **PROTEIN** 13.2g; **CARB** 33.8g; **FIBER** 3.4g; **CHOL** 33mg; **IRON** 1.4mg; **SODIUM** 506mg; **CALC** 281mg

CHILLED AVOCADO SOUP
with seared chipotle shrimp

This first-course soup combines smoky chile heat, crisp sweet corn, and silky-rich avocado. Serve it to kick off a dinner party.

Hands-on time: 19 min. ★ **Total time: 30 min.**

Soup:
- 3 cups fat-free, lower-sodium chicken broth
- 1½ cups diced peeled avocado (about 2)
- 2 tablespoons chopped fresh cilantro
- 2 tablespoons lime juice
- ¼ teaspoon kosher salt
- ¼ teaspoon black pepper

Lime Cream:
- ¾ cup reduced-fat sour cream
- 1 tablespoon chopped cilantro
- 1 teaspoon grated lime rind
- ½ teaspoon black pepper

Shrimp:
- ¾ pound peeled and deveined medium shrimp
- ½ teaspoon ground cumin
- ½ teaspoon freshly ground black pepper
- ¼ teaspoon kosher salt
- 1 (7-ounce) can chipotle chiles in adobo sauce

Cooking spray
- 1 cup fresh corn kernels (about 2 ears)
- ¼ cup chopped red onion
- 1 garlic clove, minced
- 1 tablespoon lime juice

1. To prepare soup, place chicken broth and next 5 ingredients (through ¼ teaspoon black pepper) in a blender or food processor, and process until smooth. Cover and chill.

2. To prepare lime cream, combine sour cream and next 3 ingredients (through ½ teaspoon black pepper) in a bowl; stir well. Cover and chill.

3. To prepare shrimp, sprinkle shrimp with cumin, ½ teaspoon pepper, and ¼ teaspoon salt; set aside. Remove 1 chipotle chile and 1 tablespoon adobo sauce from can, and finely chop chile. Reserve remaining chiles and adobo sauce for another use.

4. Heat a large skillet over medium-high heat. Coat pan with cooking spray. Add shrimp, and cook 2 minutes. Turn shrimp over. Add corn, onion, and garlic; sauté 2 minutes. Add chopped chipotle chile, 1 tablespoon adobo sauce, and 1 tablespoon lime juice; sauté 2 minutes or until shrimp are done and vegetables are crisp-tender.

5. Ladle about ½ cup soup into each of 8 bowls. Top with 1½ tablespoons lime cream, one-eighth of shrimp, and about 2 tablespoons corn mixture.

Serves 8

CALORIES 184; FAT 10.5g (sat 2.9g, mono 5.3g, poly 1.3g); PROTEIN 12g; CARB 13g; FIBER 4.6g; CHOL 63mg; IRON 1.7mg; SODIUM 286mg; CALC 28mg

CLAM CHOWDER

No tricks here: Modest amounts of butter, bacon, and a mix of reduced-fat milk and half-and-half for richness enhance this version of a New England classic. Don't forget a few oyster crackers.

Hands-on time: 37 min. ★ **Total time: 67 min.**

1½ cups chopped onion, divided
½ cup unoaked chardonnay or other dry white wine
3½ pounds littleneck clams
1 (8-ounce) bottle clam juice
1 bay leaf
1 tablespoon butter
1 bacon slice, chopped
3 cups diced red potato
½ cup chopped celery
⅛ teaspoon ground red pepper
3 tablespoons all-purpose flour
⅓ cup water
¾ cup half-and-half
¾ cup 2% reduced-fat milk
2 tablespoons chopped chives
1 teaspoon chopped thyme

1. Combine ½ cup onion, wine, and next 3 ingredients (through bay leaf) in a Dutch oven over medium-high heat; bring to a boil. Cover and cook 2 minutes or until clams open; discard any unopened shells. Strain through a cheesecloth-lined sieve over a bowl, reserving cooking liquid and clams. Remove meat from clams; chop. Discard shells.

2. Wipe pan clean. Melt butter in pan. Add bacon; sauté 3 minutes. Stir in 1 cup onion, potato, celery, and red pepper; sauté 4 minutes. Stir in flour; cook 1 minute. Stir in cooking liquid and ⅓ cup water; bring to a boil. Cover and reduce heat; simmer 30 minutes, stirring occasionally. Stir in clams, half-and-half, and milk; cook 1 minute or until heated. Stir in herbs.

Serves 4 (serving size: 1¼ cups)

CALORIES 337; **FAT** 11.1g (sat 6.1g, mono 1.4g, poly 2.1g); **PROTEIN** 24.3g; **CARB** 34.9g; **FIBER** 3.1g; **CHOL** 78mg; **IRON** 20.6mg; **SODIUM** 310mg; **CALC** 204mg

i helped!

I spent summer days at the seashore with my extended family as a child. Everyone, from the young children to elderly aunts, would spend at least some of their time digging clams (called quahogs here in Rhode Island). My aunt taught me her closely guarded technique of finding clams with her feet—a secret other family members had been trying to discover for some time. The insider knowledge made me feel special. At the end of the day, we dragged our harvest home to be made into chowder and clam cakes the next day. We kids probably didn't contribute a whole lot of clams, but we were still proud. Helping to gather the main ingredient somehow made the chowder and clam cakes all the more delicious.

- Robin Gagnon,
Pawtucket, Rhode Island

HOT AND SOUR SOUP

Hands-on time: 37 min. ★ Total time: 1 hr. 22 min.

14 **ounces firm water-packed tofu, drained**
1³⁄₄ **cups water, divided**
¹⁄₂ **ounce dried sliced shiitake mushrooms**
4 **cups fat-free, lower-sodium chicken broth**
¹⁄₄ **cup white vinegar**
2 **tablespoons lower-sodium soy sauce**
1 **tablespoon chopped ginger**
2 **teaspoons sugar**
³⁄₄ **teaspoon white pepper**
1 **garlic clove, minced**
2¹⁄₂ **tablespoons cornstarch**
¹⁄₂ **cup sliced bamboo shoots, drained**
1 **large egg, lightly beaten**
¹⁄₂ **cup thinly sliced green onion tops**

1. Drain tofu, and place on several layers of paper towels. Cover tofu with several more layers of paper towels; top with a cast-iron skillet or other heavy pan. Let stand 30 minutes. Discard paper towels. Cut tofu into 1-inch cubes.

2. Bring 1½ cups water to a boil in a small saucepan; remove from heat. Stir in mushrooms; let stand 30 minutes. Stir in broth and next 6 ingredients (through garlic); bring to a boil. Reduce heat, and simmer 10 minutes, stirring occasionally. Combine ¼ cup water and cornstarch in a small bowl, stirring with a whisk until smooth. Stir cornstarch mixture, tofu, and bamboo shoots into broth mixture; bring to a boil. Cook 1 minute, stirring occasionally; remove from heat. Drizzle egg into broth mixture (do not stir). Place pan over low heat; cook 1 minute. Stir soup gently to combine. Sprinkle with onions.

Serves 6 (serving size: about 1¼ cups)

CALORIES 110; FAT 4.1g (sat 0.6g, mono 3g, poly 0.2g); PROTEIN 8.6g; CARB 10.1g; FIBER 0.8g; CHOL 30mg; IRON 1.4mg; SODIUM 445mg; CALC 141mg

AVGOLEMONO

Whisk constantly as you add the egg mixture to the hot soup so that the egg thickens but doesn't scramble.

Hands-on time: 21 min. ★ **Total time: 37 min.**

2 teaspoons olive oil
½ cup chopped onion
3 garlic cloves, minced
6½ cups fat-free, lower-sodium chicken broth
½ cup uncooked long-grain rice
⅓ cup fresh lemon juice
2 teaspoons cornstarch
½ teaspoon salt
½ teaspoon freshly ground black pepper
1 large egg, lightly beaten
2 cups shredded cooked chicken breast (about 8 ounces)
2 tablespoons chopped parsley
2 tablespoons torn fresh basil

1. Heat a Dutch oven over medium-high heat. Add oil to pan; swirl to coat. Add onion and garlic; sauté 2 minutes. Add broth; bring to a boil. Stir in rice; reduce heat, and simmer 16 minutes. Combine juice, cornstarch, salt, pepper, and egg in a small bowl, stirring with a whisk. Slowly pour egg mixture into broth mixture, stirring constantly with a whisk. Add chicken to broth mixture; cook until mixture thickens and rice is done (about 3 minutes). Top with parsley and basil.

Serves 4 (serving size: about 1½ cups)

CALORIES 269; FAT 7g (sat 1.5g, mono 3.5g, poly 1.1g); PROTEIN 25.4g; CARB 25.7g; FIBER 1.1g; CHOL 116mg; IRON 2.1mg; SODIUM 541mg; CALC 54mg

make it foolproof

The fresh spinach gives this soup its bright color. For best results, add it right before serving; otherwise, the spinach can begin to turn drab.

SPINACH, PASTA, AND PEA SOUP

For a vegetarian version, use organic or lower-sodium vegetable broth in place of chicken broth.

Hands-on time: 16 min. ★ **Total time: 26 min.**

1 tablespoon extra-virgin olive oil
3 garlic cloves, thinly sliced
2 thinly sliced green onions
4 cups fat-free, lower-sodium chicken broth
2 cups water
3/4 cup uncooked orzo
1 tablespoon grated lemon rind
1 (15-ounce) can no-salt-added chickpeas (garbanzo beans), drained
1 tablespoon chopped fresh oregano
1 tablespoon fresh lemon juice
1/2 teaspoon freshly ground black pepper
1/8 teaspoon salt
1 (6-ounce) package fresh baby spinach
1/3 cup (1.5 ounces) shaved fresh Parmesan cheese

1. Heat a large saucepan over high heat. Add olive oil to pan; swirl to coat. Add garlic and onions; sauté 30 seconds, stirring constantly. Add chicken broth and 2 cups water; bring to a boil. Add orzo, lemon rind, and chickpeas. Cover and cook 10 minutes or until orzo is done. Stir in oregano and next 4 ingredients (through spinach). Ladle 1¾ cups soup into each of 4 bowls; top each serving with about 4 teaspoons cheese.

Serves 4

CALORIES 290; FAT 6.7g (sat 1.7g, mono 3.1g, poly 0.5g); PROTEIN 14g; CARB 43.8g; FIBER 7.2g; CHOL 6mg; IRON 2.8mg; SODIUM 648mg; CALC 163mg

LEMON CHICKEN SOUP
with dumplings

Rely on this soup to make gatherings with loved ones extra special. Roasting the bones adds richer, deeper flavor to the stock. Take your time when tempering the egg (used to give the soup body) with the hot broth; the payoff is a smooth, silky texture.

Hands-on time: 20 min. ★ Total time: 4 hr.

2 **pounds chicken bones (such as necks and backs)**
2 **large carrots, cut into 3-inch pieces**
2 **celery stalks, cut into 3-inch pieces**
1 **large onion, halved**
12 **cups water**
1 **bay leaf**
1 **teaspoon ground turmeric**
³/₄ **teaspoon kosher salt, divided**
²/₃ **cup matzo meal**
1 **tablespoon chopped fresh flat-leaf parsley**
2 **tablespoons canola oil**
2 **tablespoons sparkling water**
2 **teaspoons grated lemon rind**
¼ **teaspoon freshly ground black pepper**
3 **large eggs, divided**
½ **pound skinless, boneless chicken breast**
2 **tablespoons fresh lemon juice**
1½ **tablespoons chopped fresh dill**

1. Preheat oven to 425°.

2. Arrange first 4 ingredients on a jelly-roll pan. Bake at 425° for 45 minutes or until browned.

3. Combine chicken bone mixture, 12 cups water, and bay leaf in a stockpot over high heat. Bring to a boil. Reduce heat to low, and simmer gently 2 hours, skimming fat and foam from surface occasionally. Strain stock through a fine sieve into a large bowl; discard solids. Skim fat from surface of stock; discard fat. Return stock to pan; stir in turmeric and ½ teaspoon salt.

4. Combine ¼ teaspoon salt, matzo meal, and next 5 ingredients (through pepper). Lightly beat 2 eggs in a separate bowl. Add 2 eggs to matzo mixture; stir until combined. Cover and refrigerate 30 minutes. With moist hands, shape mixture into 24 (1-inch) balls. Bring stock to a simmer (do not boil). Add dumplings to stock, and cook 15 minutes. Add chicken, and continue cooking 15 minutes or until chicken is done. Remove pan from heat. Remove chicken from stock, and let stand 5 minutes. Cut chicken into thin slices; return to pan. Remove 1 cup hot broth mixture. Lightly beat 1 egg in a medium bowl. Gradually add 1 cup hot broth mixture to egg, stirring constantly with a whisk. Slowly pour beaten egg mixture into pan, stirring constantly with a whisk. Stir in lemon juice, and sprinkle with dill.

Serves 8 (serving size: about 1¼ cups)

CALORIES 138; FAT 5.7g (sat 0.9g, mono 3.1g, poly 1.4g); PROTEIN 10.9g; CARB 10.6g; FIBER 0.6g; CHOL 88mg; IRON 0.9mg; SODIUM 232mg; CALC 18mg

OLD-FASHIONED CHICKEN NOODLE SOUP

Hands-on time: 18 min. ★ **Total time: 66 min.**

8 cups chicken stock or fat-free, lower-sodium chicken broth
2 (4-ounce) skinless, bone-in chicken thighs
12 ounces skinless, boneless chicken breast
2 cups diagonally sliced carrot
2 cups diagonally sliced celery
1 cup chopped onion
6 ounces uncooked egg noodles
½ teaspoon kosher salt
½ teaspoon black pepper
Celery leaves (optional)

1. Combine first 3 ingredients in a Dutch oven over medium-high heat; bring to a boil. Reduce heat; simmer 20 minutes. Remove chicken from pan; let stand 10 minutes. Remove chicken from bones; shred meat into bite-sized pieces. Discard bones.

2. Add carrot, celery, and onion to pan; cover and simmer 10 minutes. Add noodles, and simmer 6 minutes. Add chicken, salt, and black pepper; cook 2 minutes or until noodles are done. Garnish with celery leaves, if desired.

Serves 4 (serving size: about 1½ cups)

CALORIES 423; FAT 7.7 g (sat 2.2g, mono 1.6g, poly 1.4g); PROTEIN 44.4g; CARB 42.2g; FIBER 4.8g; CHOL 171mg; IRON 3.3mg; SODIUM 474mg; CALC 98mg

SPICY ASIAN NOODLE SOUP
with chicken

Hands-on time: 27 min. ★ Total time: 27 min.

1½ cups shredded chicken breast
3 cups fat-free, lower-sodium chicken broth
1½ cups water
½ cup grated carrot
½ cup thinly sliced snow peas
2 teaspoons Sriracha
2 teaspoons lower-sodium soy sauce
1½ teaspoons Thai red curry paste
1 (2-inch) piece peeled ginger
6 cups water
3 ounces uncooked wide rice-flour noodles
1 tablespoon lime juice
¼ cup chopped mint
¼ cup chopped cilantro
¼ cup thinly sliced green onions

1. Bring shredded chicken and next 8 ingredients (through peeled ginger) to a simmer in a medium saucepan; keep warm.

2. Bring 6 cups water to a boil in a large saucepan. Add rice noodles; cook 3 minutes. Drain. Place about ¼ cup rice noodles in each of 4 bowls.

3. Discard ginger from broth mixture. Add juice to broth mixture; stir. Ladle 1⅓ cups broth mixture over each serving of noodles; top with 1 tablespoon each mint, cilantro, and onions.

Serves 4

CALORIES 197; **FAT** 2.1g (sat 0.5g, mono 0.8g, poly 0.3g); **PROTEIN** 19.9g; **CARB** 23.5g; **FIBER** 2.7g; **CHOL** 47mg; **IRON** 2.1mg; **SODIUM** 635mg; **CALC** 53mg

SPICY THAI COCONUT CHICKEN SOUP

Turn dinner into an adventurous trip to Southeast Asia: Coconut milk balances the heat from the ginger, garlic, and sambal oelek. The fish sauce won't make the soup taste fishy; instead, it adds a needed depth of flavor.

Hands-on time: 25 min. ★ **Total time: 35 min.**

2   teaspoons canola oil
1   cup sliced mushrooms
½   cup chopped red bell
     pepper
4   teaspoons minced peeled
     fresh ginger
4   garlic cloves, minced
1   (3-inch) stalk lemongrass,
     halved lengthwise
2   teaspoons sambal oelek
     (ground fresh chile paste)
3   cups fat-free, lower-
     sodium chicken broth
1¼   cups light coconut milk
4   teaspoons fish sauce
1   tablespoon sugar
2   cups shredded cooked
     chicken breast (about 8
     ounces)
½   cup green onion strips
3   tablespoons chopped
     fresh cilantro
2   tablespoons fresh lime
     juice

1. Heat a Dutch oven over medium heat. Add oil to pan; swirl to coat. Add mushrooms and next 4 ingredients (through lemongrass); cook 3 minutes, stirring occasionally. Add sambal oelek; cook 1 minute. Add chicken broth, coconut milk, fish sauce, and sugar; bring to a simmer. Reduce heat to low; simmer 10 minutes. Add chicken to pan; cook 1 minute or until thoroughly heated. Discard lemongrass. Top with onions, cilantro, and juice.

Serves 4 (serving size: about 1⅓ cups)

CALORIES 224; **FAT** 9g (sat 4.5g, mono 2.4g, poly 1.3g); **PROTEIN** 22.7g; **CARB** 15g; **FIBER** 1.1g; **CHOL** 58mg; **IRON** 1.1mg; **SODIUM** 463mg; **CALC** 35mg

PASTA E FAGIOLI

Beans, sausage, and pasta make this a hearty bowl of comfort—no wonder it's a classic. You can switch the seashell pasta for another small shape: Try ditalini or macaroni, for example.

Hands-on time: 11 min. ★ **Total time: 24 min.**

1   tablespoon olive oil
1½   tablespoons minced garlic
6   ounces hot turkey Italian sausage
1   cup water
2   cups fat-free, lower-sodium chicken broth
1   (8-ounce) can no-salt-added tomato sauce
1   cup uncooked small seashell pasta (about 4 ounces)
¼   cup grated Romano cheese
1½   teaspoons dried oregano
¼   teaspoon salt
¼   teaspoon white pepper
2   (15-ounce) cans cannellini beans or other white beans, drained
Minced fresh parsley (optional)
Crushed red pepper (optional)
Grated Romano cheese (optional)

1. Heat a large saucepan over medium-high heat. Add olive oil to pan; swirl to coat. Add garlic and sausage; sauté 2 minutes or until browned, stirring to crumble. Add 1 cup water, broth, and tomato sauce; bring to a boil. Stir in pasta, cheese, oregano, salt, pepper, and beans; bring to a boil. Cover, reduce heat, and simmer 8 minutes or until pasta is done. Let stand 5 minutes. Garnish each serving with parsley, red pepper, and additional Romano cheese, if desired.

Serves 6 (serving size: 1 cup)

CALORIES 265; **FAT** 7.6g (sat 2.4g, mono 2.9g, poly 1.1g); **PROTEIN** 16g; **CARB** 32g; **FIBER** 5.6g; **CHOL** 20mg; **IRON** 3mg; **SODIUM** 632mg; **CALC** 118mg

CHICKEN AND CHORIZO STEW

Saffron and a bit of sherry vinegar lift stew from pedestrian to exciting. Chorizo comes in two forms: Mexican chorizo is a fresh pork sausage; the Spanish type, used to flavor this recipe, is cured and firm.

Hands-on time: 40 min. ★ **Total time: 56 min.**

2   cups fat-free, lower-sodium chicken broth
2   cups water
3   garlic cloves
1   bunch fresh flat-leaf parsley
1   onion, quartered
1   medium carrot, chopped
2   (6-ounce) skinless, boneless chicken breast halves
6   ounces Spanish chorizo sausage, chopped
3   cups cubed red potato
1½ cups chopped onion
1   medium-sized red bell pepper, chopped
1   tablespoon minced garlic
½   teaspoon ground cumin
⅛   teaspoon kosher salt
¼   teaspoon saffron threads
1½ tablespoons sherry vinegar
2   tablespoons chopped fresh flat-leaf parsley

1. Combine first 6 ingredients in a saucepan over medium-high heat. Add chicken to pan; bring mixture to a boil. Reduce heat, and simmer 14 minutes or until chicken is done. Remove chicken, reserving cooking liquid; cool. Shred chicken. Strain cooking liquid through a fine sieve over a bowl; discard solids.

2. Wipe pan with paper towels. Sauté sausage over medium-high heat 2 minutes. Add potato, onion, and bell pepper; sauté 8 minutes, stirring occasionally. Add garlic and next 3 ingredients (through saffron); sauté 2 minutes, stirring constantly. Add reserved cooking liquid; bring to a simmer. Simmer 12 minutes, stirring occasionally. Add shredded chicken; simmer 5 minutes. Remove from heat; stir in vinegar. Ladle about 1 cup stew into each of 4 bowls; top each serving evenly with chopped parsley.

Serves 4

CALORIES 369; **FAT** 12.9g (sat 4.4g, mono 5.7g, poly 1.9g); **PROTEIN** 31g; **CARB** 32g; **FIBER** 4.7g; **CHOL** 54mg; **IRON** 1.9mg; **SODIUM** 436mg; **CALC** 57mg

BACON-CORN CHOWDER
with shrimp

This soup can also serve six as a first course instead of an entrée.

Hands-on time: 20 min. ★ **Total time: 20 min.**

6	center-cut bacon slices, chopped
1	cup prechopped onion
½	cup prechopped celery
1	teaspoon chopped fresh thyme
1	garlic clove, minced
4	cups fresh corn kernels or frozen whole-kernel corn, thawed
2	cups fat-free, lower-sodium chicken broth
¾	pound peeled and deveined medium shrimp
⅓	cup half-and-half
¼	teaspoon black pepper
⅛	teaspoon salt

1. Heat a large Dutch oven over medium-high heat. Add bacon to pan; sauté 4 minutes or until bacon begins to brown. Remove 2 slices bacon. Drain on paper towels. Add onion and next 3 ingredients (through minced garlic) to pan, and sauté 2 minutes. Add corn, and cook 2 minutes, stirring occasionally. Add broth; bring to a boil, and cook 4 minutes.

2. Place 2 cups corn mixture in a blender. Remove center piece of blender lid (to allow steam to escape), and secure lid on blender. Place a clean towel over opening in blender lid (to avoid splatters). Blend until smooth. Return pureed corn mixture to pan. Stir in shrimp; cook 2 minutes or until shrimp are done. Stir in half-and-half, pepper, and salt. Crumble reserved bacon over soup.

Serves 4 (serving size: about 1⅔ cups)

CALORIES 294; **FAT** 7g (sat 2.7g, mono 1.3g, poly 1.2g); **PROTEIN** 26.8g; **CARB** 34.8g; **FIBER** 4.3g; **CHOL** 144mg; **IRON** 3.1mg; **SODIUM** 547mg; **CALC** 94mg

PORK POSOLE

make it special

Offer a range of fresh toppings in small colorful dishes or on a platter when you serve posole for a crowd. Cilantro, thinly sliced radishes, fresh diced onion, lime wedges, shredded lettuce, and cheese are traditional.

Hands-on time: 25 min. ★ Total time: 1 hr. 35 min.

1 tablespoon olive oil
12 ounces boneless pork shoulder, trimmed and cut into ½-inch pieces
1 cup chopped onion
4 garlic cloves, minced
1½ teaspoons ground cumin
½ teaspoon ground red pepper
½ cup beer
1 cup fat-free, lower-sodium chicken broth
1 cup water
½ cup salsa verde
1 (28-ounce) can hominy, drained
¼ cup cilantro leaves
4 radishes, sliced
4 lime wedges

1. Heat a Dutch oven over medium-high heat. Add oil; swirl to coat. Add pork; sauté 5 minutes, turning to brown on all sides. Remove pork from pan. Add onion; sauté 4 minutes, stirring occasionally. Add garlic; sauté 1 minute, stirring constantly. Return pork to pan; stir in cumin and pepper. Add beer; bring to a boil. Cook until liquid almost evaporates (about 9 minutes).

2. Add broth plus 1 cup water, salsa, and hominy; bring to a boil. Cover, reduce heat, and simmer 1 hour and 10 minutes or until pork is very tender, stirring occasionally. Ladle 1½ cups stew into each of 4 bowls. Top each serving with 1 tablespoon cilantro and 1 sliced radish. Serve with lime wedges.

Serves 4

CALORIES 306; FAT 11.3g (sat 2.8g, mono 5.5g, poly 1.6g); PROTEIN 20.1g; CARB 29.7g; FIBER 5.5g; CHOL 57mg; IRON 3.2mg; SODIUM 654mg; CALC 65mg

make it foolproof

French onion soup is such a simple dish that the ingredients and the way they're cooked make all the difference. The bones used in the stock release gelatins that give the soup body and a lip-smacking texture. The flavor is also dependent upon how well the onions are caramelized, so take your time to get them a deep golden brown.

FRENCH ONION SOUP

It's worth the effort to make your own stock for this simple soup, but if you want to save time, you can use store-bought unsalted beef stock or lower-sodium broth. If you use the latter, you'll need to reduce the amount of salt you add to the soup by half.

Hands-on time: 1 hr. 20 min. ★ **Total time: 5 hr. 39 min.**

Stock:

1½	pounds meaty beef bones
1	pound beef shanks
2	large carrots, peeled and coarsely chopped
2	celery stalks, coarsely chopped
1	medium onion, cut into wedges
3	quarts cold water
3	thyme sprigs
1	tablespoon whole black peppercorns
1	bunch fresh flat-leaf parsley
1	bay leaf

Soup:

2	tablespoons olive oil
1	tablespoon butter
5	large onions, vertically sliced (about 13 cups)
1⅛	teaspoons kosher salt
½	teaspoon freshly ground black pepper
1	teaspoon chopped thyme
¼	cup chopped fresh chives
12	(½-ounce) slices French bread baguette
1	cup (4 ounces) shredded Gruyère cheese

1. Preheat oven to 450°.

2. To prepare stock, arrange first 5 ingredients in a single layer on a large baking sheet. Bake at 450° for 35 minutes or until browned. Scrape beef mixture and pan drippings into a large Dutch oven. Stir in 3 quarts cold water and next 4 ingredients (through bay leaf); bring to a boil over medium heat. Reduce heat to low, and simmer 2½ hours, skimming surface as necessary. Strain mixture through a fine sieve lined with a double layer of cheesecloth over a bowl; discard solids. Wipe pan clean with paper towels.

3. To prepare soup, return Dutch oven to medium heat. Add oil to pan; swirl to coat. Melt butter in oil. Add sliced onion to pan; cook 5 minutes, stirring occasionally. Partially cover, reduce heat to medium-low, and cook 15 minutes, stirring occasionally. Add salt and ground pepper; cook, uncovered, until deep golden brown (about 35 minutes), stirring frequently. Add reserved stock and chopped thyme; bring to a boil. Reduce heat, and simmer until reduced to 8 cups (about 50 minutes). Stir in chives.

4. Preheat broiler.

5. Arrange bread slices in a single layer on a jelly-roll pan, and broil 2 minutes or until toasted, turning after 1 minute. Ladle 1⅓ cups soup into each of 6 broiler-safe bowls. Top each serving with 2 bread slices, and sprinkle evenly with cheese. Place bowls on a jelly-roll pan, and broil 4 minutes or until tops are golden brown and cheese bubbles.

Serves 6

CALORIES 346; FAT 14.1g (sat 5.9g, mono 6.2g, poly 1.2g); **PROTEIN** 16.1g; **CARB** 40.5g; **FIBER** 5.3g; **CHOL** 33mg; **IRON** 2.3mg; **SODIUM** 649mg; **CALC** 274mg

ALL-AMERICAN CHILI

Chili is almost an American symbol of winter comfort—or a fun football night. Like most chilis, this one tastes even better the next day, once the flavors have had a chance to mingle and meld.

Hands-on time: 37 min. ★ **Total time: 2 hr. 2 min.**

6   ounces hot turkey Italian sausage
2   cups chopped onion
1   cup chopped green bell pepper
8   garlic cloves, minced
1   pound ground sirloin
1   jalapeño pepper, chopped
2   tablespoons chili powder
2   tablespoons brown sugar
1   tablespoon ground cumin
3   tablespoons tomato paste
1   teaspoon dried oregano
½   teaspoon freshly ground black pepper
¼   teaspoon salt
2   bay leaves
1¼   cups merlot or other fruity red wine
2   (28-ounce) cans no-salt-added whole tomatoes, undrained and coarsely chopped
2   (15-ounce) cans no-salt-added kidney beans, drained
½   cup (2 ounces) reduced-fat shredded sharp cheddar cheese

1. Heat a large Dutch oven over medium-high heat. Remove casings from sausage. Add sausage, onion, and next 4 ingredients (through jalapeño) to pan; cook 8 minutes or until sausage and beef are browned, stirring to crumble.

2. Add chili powder and next 7 ingredients (through bay leaves), and cook 1 minute, stirring constantly. Stir in wine, tomatoes, and kidney beans; bring to a boil. Cover, reduce heat, and simmer 1 hour, stirring occasionally.

3. Uncover and cook 30 minutes, stirring occasionally. Discard bay leaves. Sprinkle each serving with cheddar cheese.

Serves 8 (serving size: 1¼ cups chili and 1 tablespoon cheese)

CALORIES 286; FAT 7.5g (sat 2.1g, mono 1.1g, poly 0.4g); PROTEIN 22.4g; CARB 28.5g; FIBER 6.5g; CHOL 48mg; IRON 5.1mg; SODIUM 460mg; CALC 169mg

ITALIAN BEEF STEW

Red wine helps to both lift and blend the flavors in this beef stew.
Choose a wine that's not heavily oaked, such as a sangiovese or barbera.

Hands-on time: 60 min. ★ Total time: 2 hr. 40 min.

7 teaspoons olive oil,
   divided
1½ cups chopped onion
½ cup chopped carrot
1 tablespoon minced garlic
¼ cup all-purpose flour
2 pounds boneless chuck
   roast, trimmed and cut
   into cubes
¾ teaspoon salt, divided
½ teaspoon black pepper
1 cup dry red wine
3¾ cups chopped seeded
   peeled plum tomato
   (about 2 pounds)
1½ cups fat-free, lower-
   sodium beef broth
½ cup water
2 teaspoons chopped fresh
   oregano
2 teaspoons chopped fresh
   thyme
1 (8-ounce) package
   cremini mushrooms,
   quartered
1 bay leaf
¾ cup (¼-inch-thick) slices
   carrot
2 tablespoons chopped
   fresh basil
1 tablespoon chopped fresh
   parsley

1. Heat a Dutch oven over medium-high heat. Add 1 teaspoon oil to pan; swirl to coat. Add onion and chopped carrot; sauté 8 minutes, stirring occasionally. Add garlic; sauté 45 seconds, stirring constantly. Remove from pan.

2. Add 1 tablespoon oil to pan; swirl to coat. Place ¼ cup flour in a shallow dish. Sprinkle beef with ½ teaspoon salt and pepper; dredge in flour. Add half of beef to pan; sauté 6 minutes, browning on all sides. Remove from pan. Repeat procedure with remaining oil and beef.

3. Add wine to pan, and bring to a boil, scraping pan. Cook until reduced to ⅓ cup (about 5 minutes). Return meat and onion mixture to pan. Add tomato and next 6 ingredients (through bay leaf); bring to a boil. Cover, reduce heat, and simmer 45 minutes, stirring occasionally. Uncover, and stir in sliced carrot. Simmer, uncovered, 1 hour or until meat is very tender, stirring occasionally. Discard bay leaf. Stir in ¼ teaspoon salt, basil, and parsley.

Serves 8 (serving size: 1 cup)

CALORIES 334; **FAT** 13g (sat 3.9g, mono 0.8g, poly 6.6g); **PROTEIN** 40.6g; **CARB** 12.2g; **FIBER** 2.4g; **CHOL** 86mg; **IRON** 4.1mg; **SODIUM** 387mg; **CALC** 51mg

A KITCHEN MEMORY

spices make a dish

The first time I fell in love with lamb was in a spicy stew like Indian-Spiced Lentils and Lamb. I was no stranger to lamb, having eaten it for holidays and festive occasions (if you're thinking along the traditional lines of roast leg of lamb with rosemary and garlic, and mint jelly on the side, you're right on the money). But I'd never had it like this. Paired with the tantalizing flavor of exotic spices, lamb transcends out of the familiar and into the extraordinary. As the dish of lamb, lentils, and Indian spices was cooking, I couldn't help but stand over the pot, deeply inhaling the heady aroma. It was then I knew I'd be retiring the mint jelly in favor of a much more flavorful approach.

- Faith Gorsky,
West Seneca, New York

INDIAN-SPICED LENTILS AND LAMB

A touch of curry powder and jalapeño give the stew a warming flavor that's not overwhelmingly hot from spice.

Hands-on time: 30 min. ★ **Total time: 1 hr. 10 min.**

2	teaspoons olive oil	¾	cup brown lentils
1	teaspoon red curry powder	2	cups fat-free, lower-sodium chicken broth
1	teaspoon ground cumin		
½	teaspoon kosher salt	1	cup water
¼	teaspoon ground red pepper	¾	cup light coconut milk
6	ounces lean ground lamb	1	(15-ounce) can whole peeled tomatoes, drained and coarsely chopped
1½	cups chopped onion		
¾	cup chopped carrot	¼	cup 2% reduced-fat Greek yogurt
1	jalapeño pepper, chopped		
5	garlic cloves, minced	¼	cup cilantro leaves
1	tablespoon tomato paste		

1. Heat a saucepan over medium-high heat. Add oil to pan; swirl to coat. Add curry powder and next 4 ingredients (through lamb); sauté 4 minutes, stirring to crumble. Add onion, carrot, and jalapeño; sauté 4 minutes or until lamb is browned. Add garlic; sauté 1 minute, stirring constantly. Stir in tomato paste; sauté 30 seconds.

2. Add lentils; sauté 30 seconds. Stir in broth and next 3 ingredients (through tomatoes); bring to a boil. Reduce heat, and simmer 40 minutes or until lentils are tender. Ladle about 1 cup lentil mixture into each of 4 bowls; top each serving with 1 tablespoon yogurt and 1 tablespoon cilantro.

Serves 4

CALORIES 371; **FAT** 16g (sat 7.1g, mono 5.8g, poly 1.1g); **PROTEIN** 19.8g; **CARB** 40.5g; **FIBER** 9g; **CHOL** 32mg; **IRON** 4.3mg; **SODIUM** 619mg; **CALC** 107mg

EAT WITH

your fingers!

SANDWICHES

(& OTHER HANDHELD MEALS)

GRILLED VEGGIE AND HUMMUS WRAPS

Creamy hummus, feta cheese, and a mix of grilled veggies make this satisfyingly filling and full of flavor. Wrap these to go for a portable lunch or to take along on a picnic, and serve them with a side salad.

Hands-on time: 20 min. ★ **Total time: 20 min.**

4 (¹⁄₂-inch-thick) slices red onion
1 red bell pepper, quartered
1 (12-ounce) eggplant, cut into ¹⁄₂-inch-thick slices
2 tablespoons olive oil, divided
¹⁄₄ cup chopped fresh flat-leaf parsley
¹⁄₈ teaspoon kosher salt
1 (8-ounce) container plain hummus
4 (1.9-ounce) whole-grain flatbreads
2 ounces crumbled feta cheese (about ¹⁄₂ cup)

1. Heat a large grill pan over medium-high heat. Brush onion, bell pepper, and eggplant with 1 tablespoon oil. Add onion and bell pepper to pan; cook 3 minutes on each side or until grill marks appear. Remove from pan. Add eggplant to pan; cook 3 minutes on each side or until grill marks appear. Remove from pan; coarsely chop vegetables. Combine vegetables, 1 tablespoon oil, parsley, and salt; toss to combine.

2. Spread ¼ cup hummus over each flatbread, leaving a ½-inch border around edges. Divide vegetables evenly among flatbreads; top each serving with 2 tablespoons cheese. Roll up wraps, and cut diagonally in half.

Serves 4 (serving size: 1 wrap)

CALORIES 356; **FAT** 22.7g (sat 3.1g, mono 13.6g, poly 4.4g); **PROTEIN** 16.8g; **CARB** 35.4g; **FIBER** 15.3g; **CHOL** 13mg; **IRON** 3.6mg; **SODIUM** 788mg; **CALC** 156mg

make it ahead
You can grill the veggies a day or two in advance; let them cool and store them in an airtight container until you're ready to make the wraps.

LETTUCE WRAPS
with hoisin-peanut sauce

Lace Asian-inspired lettuce wraps with a homemade tangy, creamy sauce.

Hands-on time: 25 min. ★ **Total time: 39 min.**

Sauce:
- 1 teaspoon canola oil
- 1 tablespoon minced shallots
- 1/3 cup water
- 2 tablespoons creamy peanut butter
- 4 teaspoons hoisin sauce
- 1/8 teaspoon crushed red pepper
- 1 tablespoon fresh lime juice

Filling:
- 1 (14-ounce) package water-packed extra-firm tofu, drained and crumbled
- 1 tablespoon dark sesame oil
- 6 thinly sliced green onions (about 2/3 cup), divided
- 1/2 cup plus 2 tablespoons chopped fresh cilantro, divided
- 3 tablespoons lower-sodium soy sauce
- 2 teaspoons sugar
- 1 teaspoon grated peeled fresh ginger
- 1/2 teaspoon Sriracha (hot chile sauce)
- 1 cup matchstick-cut cucumbers
- 1 cup matchstick-cut carrots
- 2 cups hot cooked sticky rice
- 8 Bibb lettuce leaves

1. To prepare sauce, heat a small saucepan over medium heat. Add canola oil to pan; swirl to coat. Add shallots, and sauté 2 minutes. Add 1/3 cup water and next 3 ingredients (through red pepper), and stir with a whisk. Bring to a boil; cook 1 minute. Remove from heat; stir in lime juice.

2. To prepare filling, spread crumbled tofu in a single layer on several layers of paper towels; cover with additional paper towels. Let stand 20 minutes, pressing down occasionally.

3. Heat a large nonstick skillet over medium-high heat. Add sesame oil to pan; swirl to coat. Add 1/3 cup green onions; sauté 1 minute. Add tofu; sauté 4 minutes, stirring occasionally. Add 2 tablespoons cilantro, soy sauce, sugar, ginger, and Sriracha; sauté 1 minute. Remove from heat; stir in cucumbers, carrots, and 1/3 cup green onions.

4. Spoon 1/4 cup rice into each lettuce leaf. Top with about 1/2 cup tofu mixture; sprinkle with 1 tablespoon cilantro. Serve with sauce.

Serves 4 (serving size: 2 lettuce wraps and 2 tablespoons sauce)

CALORIES 355; **FAT** 15g (sat 2.1g, mono 8.5g, poly 3.7g); **PROTEIN** 16.2g; **CARB** 42.6g; **FIBER** 3.9g; **CHOL** 0mg; **IRON** 4.5mg; **SODIUM** 568mg; **CALC** 224mg

MUSHROOM, CORN, AND POBLANO TACOS

Salsa verde, queso fresco, and black beans help make these vegetarian tacos filling and scrumptious. Keep the tortillas soft by wrapping them in foil and keeping them in a warm oven.

Hands-on time: 21 min. ★ **Total time: 21 min.**

2 tablespoons olive oil, divided
1 (8-ounce) package presliced mushrooms
1 cup prechopped onion
1 teaspoon dried oregano
1 teaspoon minced garlic
3/4 teaspoon chili powder
3/4 teaspoon ground cumin
1 poblano chile, chopped (about 1/2 cup)
1 1/2 cups frozen whole-kernel corn
1 (14.5-ounce) can no-salt-added black beans, rinsed and drained
1/4 cup salsa verde
1 tablespoon fresh lime juice
1 teaspoon hot sauce
1/2 teaspoon salt
8 (6-inch) corn tortillas
3 ounces crumbled queso fresco (about 3/4 cup)
1/4 cup chopped fresh cilantro
1/4 cup light sour cream
8 lime wedges

1. Heat a large nonstick skillet over medium-high heat. Add 1 tablespoon oil to pan; swirl to coat. Add mushrooms to pan; cook 4 minutes, stirring occasionally. Add 1 tablespoon oil to mushrooms. Stir in onion and next 5 ingredients (through poblano); cook 4 minutes, stirring occasionally. Add corn and beans to pan; cook 4 minutes, stirring occasionally. Remove pan from heat; stir in salsa and next 3 ingredients (through salt).

2. Heat tortillas according to package directions. Divide vegetable mixture evenly among tortillas. Top each tortilla with 1½ tablespoons cheese, 1½ teaspoons cilantro, and 1½ teaspoons sour cream. Serve with lime wedges.

Serves 4 (serving size: 2 tacos and 2 lime wedges)

CALORIES 390; FAT 14.4g (sat 4.5g, mono 6.7g, poly 1.7g); PROTEIN 15.6g; CARB 56.6g; FIBER 9.8g; CHOL 20mg; IRON 2mg; SODIUM 553mg; CALC 225mg

make it foolproof

Cooking your own lobsters?
Make sure they're alive when you buy
them by picking them up; the tails should
curl under. Cook them the same day you buy
them. You can steam them or boil them
in salted water. Be sure to either
cook them alive or kill them
right before cooking.

LOBSTER SALAD ROLLS

with shaved fennel and citrus

One bite of a good lobster roll will transport you to a breezy summer day on a boardwalk in Maine. New England–style hot dog buns are top-split.

Hands-on time: 13 min. ★ **Total time: 13 min.**

3   cups coarsely chopped cooked lobster meat (about 3 [1¼-pound] lobsters)

3   tablespoons canola mayonnaise

2   teaspoons chopped fresh tarragon

½   teaspoon kosher salt, divided

2   cups thinly sliced fennel bulb (about 1 medium)

½   teaspoon grated orange rind

1   tablespoon fresh orange juice

1   tablespoon fresh lemon juice

1   tablespoon rice wine vinegar

2   teaspoons extra-virgin olive oil

¼   teaspoon freshly ground black pepper

Cooking spray

6   (1½-ounce) hot dog buns

Tarragon leaves (optional)

1. Combine lobster, mayonnaise, 2 teaspoons tarragon, and ¼ teaspoon salt; cover and refrigerate.

2. Combine fennel, ¼ teaspoon salt, orange rind, and next 5 ingredients (through pepper).

3. Heat a large skillet over medium heat. Coat pan with cooking spray. Add buns to pan; cook 2 minutes on each side or until lightly browned. Place ⅓ cup fennel salad in each bun. Top each serving with ½ cup lobster salad and tarragon leaves, if desired.

Serves 6 (serving size: 1 lobster roll)

CALORIES 238; **FAT** 6.2g (sat 0.8g, mono 3g, poly 1.9g); **PROTEIN** 19.4g; **CARB** 24.9g; **FIBER** 1.9g; **CHOL** 52mg; **IRON** 1.9mg; **SODIUM** 699mg; **CALC** 120mg

TUNA-GUACAMOLE TACOS

Sear the tuna on both sides—but don't cook it all the way through—for the best texture. The guacamole is very creamy and tasty on its own; make extra.

Hands-on time: 15 min. ★ **Total time: 15 min.**

½   **cup thinly sliced red onion**
1   **tablespoon fresh lime juice**
¾   **teaspoon kosher salt, divided**
2   **ripe peeled avocados, mashed**
Cooking spray
2   **(10-ounce) yellowfin tuna steaks (about 1 inch thick)**
8   **(6-inch) corn tortillas**
Lime wedges (optional)
Sliced serrano chiles (optional)
Salsa (optional)

1. Combine onion, lime juice, ¼ teaspoon salt, and avocados in a medium bowl.

2. Heat a grill pan over medium-high heat; coat pan with cooking spray. Sprinkle tuna with ½ teaspoon salt. Add tuna to pan; cook 4 minutes on each side or to desired degree of doneness. Cut tuna into ¼-inch-thick slices. Warm tortillas according to package directions. Divide avocado mixture evenly among tortillas. Divide tuna evenly among tortillas. Top with sliced chiles, if desired, and serve with lime wedges and salsa, if desired.

Serves 4 (serving size: 2 tacos)

CALORIES 402; **FAT** 17.3g (sat 2.5g, mono 10.1g, poly 2.7g); **PROTEIN** 37.3g; **CARB** 28.2g; **FIBER** 9g; **CHOL** 64mg; **IRON** 1.6mg; **SODIUM** 430mg; **CALC** 59mg

TUNA SALAD MELT

Update a nostalgic childhood favorite by adding walnuts and chickpeas to tuna salad. Here, the cheese goes directly on the bread (instead of on top of the sandwich) to help keep the bread from getting soggy.

Hands-on time: 15 min. ★ Total time: 15 min.

¼ cup walnuts, chopped
¼ cup chopped red onion
¼ cup canned chickpeas (garbanzo beans), rinsed and drained
¼ cup canola mayonnaise
1 tablespoon Dijon mustard
1 teaspoon red wine vinegar
¼ teaspoon hot pepper sauce
½ teaspoon salt
½ teaspoon black pepper
1 (12-ounce) can solid white tuna in water, drained and flaked
1 garlic clove, minced
6 (1-ounce) slices multigrain bread
⅓ cup (1½ ounces) shredded Swiss cheese
12 (¼-inch-thick) slices tomato
1 cup bagged baby spinach leaves

1. Preheat broiler.

2. Combine first 11 ingredients (through garlic) in a medium bowl; toss gently to coat.

3. Top bread evenly with cheese; broil 4 minutes or until bubbly. Arrange 2 tomato slices and about ⅓ cup tuna mixture over each bread slice. Top sandwiches evenly with spinach.

Serves 6 (serving size: 1 sandwich)

CALORIES 231; FAT 11.1g (sat 1.9g, mono 2.9g, poly 3.8g); PROTEIN 15.2g; CARB 18g; FIBER 3.9g; CHOL 21mg; IRON 1.4mg; SODIUM 500mg; CALC 94mg

SAVORY SAUSAGE, SPINACH, AND ONION TURNOVERS

Turnovers are making a comeback under the name "hand pies." Flaky crusts encasing savory fillings definitely hit a comfort-food note.

Hands-on time: 16 min. ★ **Total time: 39 min.**

½ teaspoon canola oil
⅔ cup diced peeled red potato
⅓ cup diced red bell pepper
⅓ cup diced yellow onion
2 (3.5-ounce) links hot chicken Italian sausage, casings removed
3 cups bagged prewashed baby spinach leaves
2 tablespoons finely chopped fresh basil
¼ teaspoon salt
¼ teaspoon crushed red pepper
½ (14.1-ounce) package refrigerated pie dough
Cooking spray
2 tablespoons water
1 large egg white, lightly beaten
3 tablespoons grated fresh Parmigiano-Reggiano cheese

1. Preheat oven to 400°.

2. Heat a medium nonstick skillet over medium-high heat. Add oil to pan; swirl to coat. Add potatoes, bell pepper, and onion to pan; sauté 4 minutes or until onion begins to brown, stirring frequently. Add sausage; cook 4 minutes or until browned, stirring to crumble. Stir in spinach; cook 2 minutes or until spinach wilts. Stir in basil, salt, and crushed red pepper. Remove from heat.

3. Cut dough into 4 equal portions. Roll each portion into a 5-inch circle. Spoon about ½ cup potato mixture on half of each circle, leaving a ½-inch border. Fold dough over potato mixture until edges almost meet. Bring bottom edge of dough over top edge; crimp edges of dough to form a rim.

4. Place turnovers on a baking sheet coated with cooking spray. Combine 2 tablespoons water and egg white in a small bowl, stirring with a whisk; brush evenly over dough. Sprinkle about 2 teaspoons cheese over each turnover. Bake at 400° for 18 minutes or until golden brown. Let stand at least 5 minutes before serving.

Serves 4 (serving size: 1 turnover)

CALORIES 323; FAT 16g (sat 6.7g, mono 6.4g, poly 1.7g); PROTEIN 13g; CARB 32g; FIBER 1.8g; CHOL 55mg; IRON 0.9mg; SODIUM 822mg; CALC 79mg

make it ahead
Combine the sauce—the first eight ingredients—up to a day in advance. Keep it covered and chilled until you're ready to add the chicken and proceed with the recipe.

BLACK PEPPER & MOLASSES PULLED CHICKEN SANDWICHES

Make a homemade sauce that delivers great barbecue taste: Chili powder and cumin add smokiness, while ketchup and molasses make it sweet. 'Cue lovers in North Carolina add slaw to this kind of sandwich.

Hands-on time: 10 min. ★ **Total time: 39 min.**

3 tablespoons ketchup
1 tablespoon cider vinegar
1 tablespoon prepared mustard
1 tablespoon molasses
¾ teaspoon chili powder
½ teaspoon ground cumin
¼ teaspoon freshly ground black pepper
⅛ teaspoon ground ginger
12 ounces skinless, boneless chicken thighs, cut into 2-inch pieces
4 (2-ounce) sandwich rolls, cut in half horizontally
12 dill pickle chips

1. Combine first 9 ingredients in a medium saucepan; bring to a boil. Reduce heat to medium-low; cover and cook, stirring occasionally, 23 minutes or until chicken is done and tender. Remove from heat; shred with 2 forks to measure 2 cups meat. Place ½ cup chicken on bottom half of each roll. Top each with 3 pickles and top half of roll.

Serves 4 (serving size: 1 sandwich)

CALORIES 294; **FAT** 6.5g (sat 1.5g, mono 2.6g, poly 1.4g); **PROTEIN** 22g; **CARB** 35.6g; **FIBER** 1.8g; **CHOL** 71mg; **IRON** 3.1mg; **SODIUM** 698mg; **CALC** 105mg

GARLIC-CHIPOTLE CHICKEN TACOS

Fire up the grill (or use a grill pan) to turn weeknight chicken breast cutlets into something exciting. For a heat-balancing side dish, make a salad of orange sections, sliced avocado, thinly sliced red onion, and cherry tomatoes.

Hands-on time: 30 min. ★ Total time: 30 min.

1   **tablespoon chopped fresh garlic**
1   **tablespoon minced chipotle chile, canned in adobo sauce**
2   **tablespoons canola oil, divided**
1   **pound chicken cutlets**
³/₄   **teaspoon kosher salt, divided**
³/₄   **teaspoon freshly ground black pepper, divided**
Cooking spray
2   **teaspoons chili powder**
1   **small red bell pepper, quartered**
1   **small yellow bell pepper, quartered**
1   **small Vidalia onion, cut into ¹/₂-inch rings**
8   **(6-inch) corn tortillas**
¹/₂   **cup shredded green leaf lettuce**

1. Preheat grill to medium-high heat.

2. Combine garlic, chipotle, and 1 tablespoon oil; rub evenly over chicken. Sprinkle with ¼ teaspoon salt and ¼ teaspoon black pepper. Place on grill rack coated with cooking spray; grill 3 minutes on each side or until done. Remove from grill; keep warm.

3. Combine 1 tablespoon oil, ½ teaspoon salt, ½ teaspoon black pepper, and chili powder in a large bowl. Add bell peppers and onion; toss gently to coat. Place vegetables on grill rack; grill 5 minutes on each side or until soft and charred. Remove from grill; slice, and keep warm. Place tortillas on grill rack coated with cooking spray; grill 30 seconds on each side or until lightly charred. Remove from grill; keep warm.

4. Thinly slice chicken. Divide chicken, bell peppers, onion, and lettuce among tortillas.

Serves 4 (serving size: 2 tacos)

CALORIES 312; FAT 9.8g (sat 0.9g, mono 4.8g, poly 2.8g); PROTEIN 29.5g; CARB 27.8g; FIBER 4g; CHOL 66mg; IRON 1.4mg; SODIUM 533mg; CALC 60mg

ROSEMARY-CHICKEN PANINI
with spinach and sun-dried tomatoes

You don't need a panini press. Use a heavy skillet to press the sandwich against the grill pan.

Hands-on time: 40 min. ★ **Total time: 1 hr. 10 min.**

2 tablespoons extra-virgin olive oil, divided
1 teaspoon chopped fresh rosemary
4 (4-ounce) chicken cutlets
¼ cup chopped drained oil-packed sun-dried tomatoes
⅛ teaspoon crushed red pepper
8 garlic cloves, thinly sliced
1 (6-ounce) package fresh baby spinach
³⁄₈ teaspoon salt, divided
Cooking spray
⅛ teaspoon freshly ground black pepper
8 (1-ounce) slices country-style Italian bread
2 ounces shredded fresh mozzarella cheese (about ½ cup)

1. Combine 2 teaspoons olive oil, rosemary, and chicken in a large zip-top plastic bag. Seal and marinate in refrigerator 30 minutes.

2. Heat a large nonstick skillet over medium-high heat. Add 4 teaspoons oil to pan; swirl to coat. Add sun-dried tomato, red pepper, and garlic; sauté 1 minute or until garlic begins to brown. Add spinach; cook 1 minute or until spinach barely wilts. Stir in ⅛ teaspoon salt; set aside.

3. Heat a grill pan over medium-high heat; coat pan with cooking spray. Sprinkle chicken with ¼ teaspoon salt and black pepper. Cook chicken 3 minutes on each side or until done. Remove chicken from pan; keep pan on medium-high heat.

4. Top each of 4 bread slices with 1 tablespoon cheese, 1 chicken cutlet, one-fourth of spinach mixture, 1 additional tablespoon cheese, and 1 bread slice.

5. Recoat pan with cooking spray. Arrange 2 sandwiches in pan. Place a cast-iron or heavy skillet on top of sandwiches; press gently to flatten. Cook 4 minutes on each side (leave skillet on sandwiches while they cook). Repeat procedure with remaining 2 sandwiches. Cut each sandwich in half; serve immediately.

Serves 4 (serving size: 1 sandwich)

CALORIES 414; **FAT** 14.8g (sat 3.9g, mono 6.3g, poly 2.1g); **PROTEIN** 35.5g; **CARB** 33.6g; **FIBER** 3.1g; **CHOL** 77mg; **IRON** 4mg; **SODIUM** 687mg; **CALC** 114mg

SOUTHWEST CRISPY CHICKEN SLIDERS

Hands-on time: 33 min. ★ **Total time: 33 min.**

Muffins:
1   jalapeño pepper
3   ounces all-purpose flour
    (about ²/₃ cup)
²/₃ cup yellow cornmeal
³/₄ teaspoon baking soda
¹/₄ teaspoon baking powder
¹/₄ teaspoon kosher salt
³/₄ cup nonfat buttermilk
2   tablespoons butter, melted
1   large egg, lightly beaten
1¹/₂ ounces shredded sharp
    cheddar cheese (about ¹/₃ cup)

Cooking spray

Chicken:
²/₃ cup panko (Japanese
    breadcrumbs)
¹/₄ cup fat-free milk
1   large egg, lightly beaten
3   (6-ounce) skinless, bone-
    less chicken breast halves
2   tablespoons canola oil,
    divided

Additional ingredients:
2   teaspoons fresh lime juice
1   ripe peeled avocado
2   applewood-smoked
    bacon slices, cooked
12 (¹/₂-inch-thick) slices small
    ripe tomato (about 3 tomatoes)
¹/₄ teaspoon kosher salt
¹/₄ teaspoon black pepper

1. Preheat oven to 350°.

2. To prepare muffins, seed and mince jalapeño; set aside. Weigh or lightly spoon flour into dry measuring cups; level with a knife. Combine flour, cornmeal, baking soda, baking powder, and ¼ teaspoon salt in a medium bowl, stirring well with a whisk. Combine buttermilk, butter, and 1 egg, stirring well. Add buttermilk mixture to flour mixture, stirring just until combined. Stir in cheese and jalapeño. Spoon batter into 12 muffin cups coated with cooking spray. Bake at 350° for 17 minutes or until a wooden pick inserted in centers comes out clean. Cool 5 minutes in pan on a wire rack. Remove muffins from pan; cool on wire rack. Cut muffins in half crosswise.

3. To prepare chicken, place panko in a shallow dish. Combine fat-free milk and 1 egg in a shallow dish, stirring well. Split each chicken breast in half lengthwise to form 2 cutlets; cut pieces in half, crosswise, to form 12 pieces. Heat a large skillet over medium-high heat. Add 1 tablespoon oil to pan; swirl to coat. Dip chicken in egg mixture; dredge in panko. Coat panko lightly with cooking spray. Add 6 chicken cutlets to pan; cook 3 minutes on each side or until golden and done. Repeat procedure with remaining 1 tablespoon oil, remaining 6 chicken cutlets, and cooking spray.

4. To prepare additional ingredients, combine lime juice and avocado; mash to desired consistency. Crumble and stir in bacon. Place 2 muffin bottom halves on each of 6 plates. Divide avocado mixture evenly among muffins; top each slider with 1 chicken cutlet and 1 tomato slice. Sprinkle tomato evenly with ¼ teaspoon salt and black pepper; top with muffin tops.

Serves 6 (serving size: 2 sliders)

CALORIES 402; FAT 18g (sat 5.7g, mono 8.3g, poly 2.6g); PROTEIN 24.5g; CARB 34.3g; FIBER 3.1g; CHOL 106mg; IRON 2.1mg; SODIUM 576mg; CALC 129mg

make it ahead
If you're planning to feed a crowd, you can make the patties ahead and freeze them. Wrap each one tightly in plastic wrap to avoid freezer burn. Thaw them in your refrigerator overnight.

BACON AND CHEDDAR SLIDERS

Pump up a fun party favorite with bacon, cheddar, and pickles. For juicy sliders, form each patty gently—overworking and compressing the mix will give you dense, dry burgers. Resist pressing them with a spatula while they're cooking.

Hands-on time: 20 min. ★ **Total time: 30 min.**

3   **tablespoons minced shallots**
1   **teaspoon Dijon mustard**
12   **ounces ground sirloin**
¾   **teaspoon freshly ground black pepper, divided**
Cooking spray
2   **ounces reduced-fat shredded sharp cheddar cheese (about ½ cup)**
8   **whole-wheat slider buns**
3   **tablespoons canola mayonnaise**
4   **cornichons or other small dill pickles, each cut lengthwise into 4 slices**
4   **small lettuce leaves, each torn in half**
1   **small ripe tomato, cut into 8 slices**
3   **bacon slices, cooked and cut into 1-inch pieces**

1. Preheat grill to medium-high heat.

2. Gently combine first 3 ingredients and ½ teaspoon pepper in a large bowl, being careful not to overmix. Divide beef mixture into 8 equal portions; gently shape each portion into a ¼-inch-thick patty, taking care not to pack mixture down.

3. Arrange patties on grill rack coated with cooking spray; grill 2 minutes on each side or until desired degree of doneness. Top each patty with about 1 tablespoon cheese during last minute of cooking. Lightly coat cut sides of buns with cooking spray. Place buns, cut sides down, on grill rack. Grill 1 minute or until toasted. Spread about 1 teaspoon mayonnaise on bottom half of each bun; top with 1 patty. Top each slider with 2 pickle slices, ½ lettuce leaf, and 1 tomato slice; sprinkle evenly with ¼ teaspoon pepper. Arrange bacon pieces evenly over tomato. Top with bun tops.

Serves 4 (serving size: 2 sliders)

CALORIES 400; FAT 16.9g (sat 4.9g, mono 6.4g, poly 4.2g); PROTEIN 23.8g; CARB 39.8g; FIBER 5.9g; CHOL 48mg; IRON 3.8mg; SODIUM 783mg; CALC 290mg

FRIED EGG BLT SANDWICHES

Gild a classic BLT with a sunny-side-up egg, and it will become the new sandwich of your dreams. Look for focaccia without cheese or herbs, and choose one that doesn't look oily. Share a fruit salad of 1 cup blueberries and 2 cups strawberries to complete the meal.

Hands-on time: 15 min. ★ **Total time: 15 min.**

1   teaspoon olive oil
4   large eggs
4   (1-ounce) slices focaccia bread, toasted
1   cup packed baby arugula
4   applewood-smoked bacon slices, cooked, drained, and halved crosswise
4   (¼-inch-thick) slices tomato
¼   teaspoon kosher salt
¼   teaspoon freshly ground black pepper
Freshly ground black pepper (optional)

1. Heat a large nonstick skillet over medium heat. Add olive oil to pan; swirl to coat. Crack eggs into pan; cook 2 minutes. Cover and cook 2 minutes or until whites are set or until desired degree of doneness. Remove from heat.

2. Place 1 focaccia slice on each of 4 plates; top each serving with ¼ cup arugula, 2 bacon slice halves, and 1 tomato slice. Sprinkle tomatoes evenly with salt and pepper. Top each serving with 1 egg; garnish with additional freshly ground black pepper, if desired.

Serves 4 (serving size: 1 sandwich)

CALORIES 241; FAT 12.7g (sat 3.5g, mono 4.9g, poly 1.2g); PROTEIN 12.7g; CARB 18.3g; FIBER 1g; CHOL 190mg; IRON 2mg; SODIUM 517mg; CALC 38mg

MELTY MONSIEUR

A lighter take on the classic croque monsieur—there's no egg dip, and they're served open-faced—these sandwiches are equally kid friendly and adult pleasing.

Hands-on time: 13 min. ★ **Total time: 13 min.**

4	**(1½-ounce) slices multigrain bread**
8	**teaspoons creamy mustard blend**
8	**Canadian bacon slices (4.8 ounces)**
12	**(¼-inch-thick) slices tomato**
3	**ounces shaved Gruyère cheese (about ¾ cup)**

1. Preheat broiler.

2. Place bread in a single layer on a baking sheet; broil 1½ minutes on each side or until lightly toasted. Spread 2 teaspoons mustard blend on each bread slice. Top each serving with 2 bacon slices, 3 tomato slices, and about 3 tablespoons cheese. Broil 3 minutes or until cheese melts.

Serves 4 (serving size: 1 sandwich)

CALORIES 312; FAT 16.5g (sat 6.6g, mono 6.6g, poly 2.2g); PROTEIN 19.7g; CARB 21.9g; FIBER 4.5g; CHOL 48mg; IRON 1.4mg; SODIUM 692mg; CALC 320mg

CHEESY PIGS IN BLANKETS

Treat your kids to this childhood fave, made lighter with turkey hot dogs, part-skim mozzarella, and pizza dough in place of a more buttery pastry dough. Serve steamed broccoli and apple wedges on the side.

Hands-on time: 15 min. ★ Total time: 47 min.

1 **(6-ounce) portion fresh pizza dough**
1½ **ounces shredded part-skim mozzarella cheese (about ⅓ cup)**
4 **turkey hot dogs, halved crosswise**
Cooking spray
2 **tablespoons ketchup**
1 **tablespoon barbecue sauce**
1 **teaspoon prepared mustard**

1. Preheat oven to 425°.

2. Let dough stand, covered, 20 minutes. On a lightly floured surface, roll dough into a 12 x 4–inch rectangle. Cut rectangle into 4 (4 x 3–inch) rectangles; cut each rectangle in half diagonally to form 8 triangles. Divide cheese evenly among triangles; place in center of wide ends. Place ½ hot dog at wide end of each triangle; roll up, pinching ends to seal. Arrange rolls on a baking sheet coated with cooking spray. Bake at 425° for 12 minutes. Combine ketchup, barbecue sauce, and mustard. Serve with rolls.

Serves 4 (serving size: 2 rolls and 2½ teaspoons sauce)

CALORIES 215; FAT 6.4g (sat 2.1g, mono 0.5g, poly 0.8g); PROTEIN 13.5g; CARB 27.5g; FIBER 0.8g; CHOL 32mg; IRON 1.4mg; SODIUM 825mg; CALC 85mg

BEEF AND MUSHROOM SLOPPY JOES

Hands-on time: 20 min. ★ Total time: 20 min.

1   tablespoon olive oil
12 ounces ground sirloin
2   (8-ounce) packages
    presliced cremini
    mushrooms
1   cup prechopped onion
3   garlic cloves, minced
½   cup no-salt-added
    tomato paste
1   tablespoon minced fresh
    oregano

2   tablespoons red wine
    vinegar
2   tablespoons
    Worcestershire sauce
1   tablespoon molasses
¼   teaspoon salt
¾   teaspoon freshly ground
    black pepper
½   teaspoon hot sauce
4   (2-ounce) Kaiser rolls or
    hamburger buns, toasted

1. Heat a large nonstick skillet over medium-high heat. Add
oil; swirl to coat. Add beef; cook 4 minutes or until browned,
stirring to crumble.

2. While beef cooks, place mushrooms in a food processor;
pulse 10 times or until finely chopped. Add mushrooms, onion,
and garlic to pan; cook 3 minutes or until onion is tender. Add
tomato paste and next 5 ingredients (through salt) to pan; cook
5 minutes or until mushrooms are tender and liquid evaporates.
Stir in pepper and hot sauce. Spoon about 1 cup beef mixture
on bottom half of each bun; top with top halves of buns.

Serves 4 (serving size: 1 sandwich)

CALORIES 439; **FAT** 14.7g (sat 4.6g, mono 6.8g, poly 1.9g); **PROTEIN** 27.3g; **CARB** 49.2g;
FIBER 4g; **CHOL** 55mg; **IRON** 6.1mg; **SODIUM** 618mg; **CALC** 160mg

make it ahead

Give yourself a head start on a hearty weeknight dinner: Prepare a batch of the beef mixture, cool it, store it in an airtight container (or a zip-top freezer bag), and then freeze it.

what-burgers?

Every Halloween my mom would make beef Sloppy Joes for our family to eat before we went trick-or-treating. Yet we never knew them as Sloppy Joes. Being supercreative and fun, my mom would insert a paper bat–topped toothpick into each bun top, and we called them "Batburgers." For years, I thought this was actually the name of the sandwich! When dinnertime rolled around on October 31st, my four siblings and I would eagerly devour our delicious "Batburgers," trying hard not to spill the saucy filling on our costumes, and then we'd go hit the neighborhood for treats. It became a favorite family tradition that we enjoyed almost as much as getting a plastic pumpkin full of candy. Almost.

-Megan Murphy,
New York City, New York

CABERNET-BALSAMIC BURGERS

with sautéed mushrooms and onions

Grilled cheeseburgers get an irresistible upgrade with creamy blue cheese and caramelized onions spiked with jammy red wine and tart-sweet vinegar. A portion of the tender onions mixes with the lean beef to keep the patties moist.

Hands-on time: 57 min. ★ **Total time: 57 min.**

5 teaspoons olive oil, divided
4 cups thinly sliced red onion
1½ teaspoons chopped fresh thyme
½ cup cabernet sauvignon or other dry red wine
2 tablespoons balsamic vinegar
¾ teaspoon salt, divided
1 (8-ounce) package sliced mushrooms
1½ pounds ground sirloin
Cooking spray
⅓ cup light mayonnaise
1 ounce crumbled blue cheese (about ¼ cup)
1 garlic clove, minced
6 (1½-ounce) whole-wheat hamburger buns
1½ cups baby arugula

1. Heat a large nonstick skillet over medium-low heat. Add 2 teaspoons olive oil to pan; swirl to coat. Add onion and thyme; cook 17 minutes or until golden and very tender, stirring occasionally. Increase heat to medium-high; add wine, vinegar, and ¼ teaspoon salt. Cook 6 minutes or until liquid almost evaporates, stirring occasionally. Remove onion mixture from pan.

2. Wipe pan clean with paper towels. Heat pan over medium-high heat. Add 3 teaspoons oil; swirl to coat. Add mushrooms and ¼ teaspoon salt; sauté 8 minutes or until mushrooms brown and liquid mostly evaporates.

3. Preheat grill to medium-high heat.

4. Coarsely chop 1 cup onion mixture, and stir chopped onion mixture into beef. Divide beef mixture into 6 equal portions, gently shaping each into a 1-inch-thick patty. Press a nickel-sized indentation in center of each patty. Sprinkle patties with ¼ teaspoon salt. Place patties on grill rack coated with cooking spray, and grill 4 minutes on each side or until done.

5. Combine mayonnaise, blue cheese, and garlic in a bowl, and mash well with a fork. Spread top halves of buns evenly with mayonnaise mixture. Arrange ¼ cup arugula on bottom half of each bun; top with 1 patty, about 2 tablespoons onion mixture, about ¼ cup mushrooms, and top half of bun.

Serves 6 (serving size: 1 burger)

CALORIES 395; **FAT** 17.1 (sat 4.6g, mono 6.8g, poly 4.3g); **PROTEIN** 29.2g; **CARB** 33g; **FIBER** 5g; **CHOL** 69mg; **IRON** 3.4mg; **SODIUM** 756mg; **CALC** 106mg

THAI BEEF CABBAGE CUPS

In Thailand, the spicy ground beef mixture that's folded inside these cabbage cups is called larb. Serve these fun-to-eat cups with lime wedges.

Hands-on time: 27 min. ★ **Total time: 27 min.**

2½ teaspoons dark sesame oil, divided
2 teaspoons minced peeled fresh ginger
3 garlic cloves, minced
1 pound ground sirloin
1 tablespoon sugar
2 tablespoons fresh lime juice
1½ tablespoons fish sauce
1 tablespoon water
¼ teaspoon crushed red pepper
½ cup vertically sliced red onion
½ cup chopped fresh cilantro
8 large green cabbage leaves
2 tablespoons finely chopped unsalted, dry-roasted peanuts

1. Heat a large nonstick skillet over medium-high heat. Add 2 teaspoons oil to pan; swirl to coat. Add ginger and garlic; cook 1 minute, stirring constantly. Add beef; cook 5 minutes or until browned, stirring to crumble.

2. Combine ½ teaspoon oil, sugar, and next 4 ingredients (through pepper) in a large bowl. Add beef mixture, onion, and cilantro; toss well. Place 2 cabbage leaves on each of 4 plates; divide beef mixture evenly among leaves. Top each serving with 1½ teaspoons peanuts.

Serves 4 (serving size: 2 filled cabbage leaves)

CALORIES 292; FAT 16.7g (sat 5.4g, mono 7.3g, poly 2.4g); PROTEIN 25.4g; CARB 10.9g; FIBER 2.4g; CHOL 74mg; IRON 3.1mg; SODIUM 516mg; CALC 51mg

make it foolproof

Be sure to use a large skillet for this recipe. A smaller skillet will crowd the pan, and the ground beef will steam and boil in its own juices, making it hard to get the beef properly browned.

KOREAN-STYLE BEEF TACOS

Hands-on time: 28 min. ★ **Total time: 1 hr. 28 min.**

1/3 cup sugar

5 tablespoons lower-sodium soy sauce

1 1/2 tablespoons sambal oelek (ground fresh chile paste)

1 tablespoon fresh lime juice

1 tablespoon dark sesame oil

4 garlic cloves, minced

12 ounces flank steak, sliced against grain into thin strips

1/8 teaspoon salt

Cooking spray

8 (6-inch) corn tortillas

Quick Pickled Cabbage

3 tablespoons sliced green onion tops

1. Combine first 6 ingredients in a shallow dish. Add steak to dish; cover. Marinate in refrigerator 1 hour, turning after 30 minutes.

2. Preheat grill to medium-high heat.

3. Remove steak from marinade, and discard marinade. Thread steak onto 8 (8-inch) skewers; sprinkle with salt. Place skewers on grill rack coated with cooking spray. Grill 2 minutes on each side or until desired degree of doneness. Grill tortillas 30 seconds on each side or until lightly charred; keep warm. Place 2 tortillas on each of 4 plates, and divide steak evenly among tortillas. Divide Quick Pickled Cabbage evenly among tacos; sprinkle with onions.

Serves 4 (serving size: 2 tacos)

CALORIES 270; FAT 6.3g (sat 1.6g, mono 2g, poly 1.4g); PROTEIN 18.1g; CARB 37.1g; FIBER 3g; CHOL 21mg; IRON 1.3mg; SODIUM 568mg; CALC 95mg

quick pickled cabbage

Hands-on time: 6 min. ★ **Total time: 36 min.**

3 cups chopped napa (Chinese) cabbage

2 garlic cloves, crushed

1/2 cup rice vinegar

1 tablespoon sugar

2 tablespoons lower-sodium soy sauce

2 teaspoons chile paste

1. Place cabbage and garlic in a medium bowl. Bring vinegar, sugar, soy sauce, and chile paste to a boil. Pour hot vinegar mixture over cabbage mixture; toss. Let stand at least 30 minutes.

Serves 4 (serving size: 1/2 cup)

CALORIES 33; FAT 0g (sat 0g, mono 0g, poly 0g); PROTEIN 1.4g; CARB 6.9g; FIBER 0.8g; CHOL 0mg; IRON 0mg; SODIUM 204mg; CALC 49mg

LAMB FAJITAS

The inspiration for these fajitas is the gyro, the Greek lamb-filled pita sandwich. Make the sauce first so it can chill while the lamb marinates.

Hands-on time: 16 min. ★ **Total time: 36 min.**

¾   **pound lean boneless leg of lamb**
1   **teaspoon olive oil**
½   **teaspoon dried oregano**
¼   **teaspoon salt**
¼   **teaspoon freshly ground pepper**
2   **garlic cloves, minced**
4   **(8-inch) flour tortillas**
1   **teaspoon olive oil**
¼   **cup thinly sliced fresh mint leaves**
Cucumber-Dill Sauce

1. Trim fat from lamb, and cut into thin strips. Combine lamb and next 5 ingredients (through garlic) in a heavy-duty zip-top plastic bag; seal bag, and shake well to coat. Marinate in refrigerator 20 minutes.

2. Heat tortillas according to package directions.

3. Heat a nonstick skillet over medium-high heat. Add 1 teaspoon oil; swirl to coat. Add lamb; sauté 6 minutes. Divide lamb evenly among tortillas; sprinkle with mint, and roll up. Serve with Cucumber-Dill Sauce.

Serves 4 (serving size: 1 fajita and 6 tablespoons sauce)

CALORIES 324; FAT 9.6g (sat 2.3g, mono 4.6g, poly 1.9g); PROTEIN 25.3g; CARB 32.8g; FIBER 1.8g; CHOL 56mg; IRON 3.5mg; SODIUM 471mg; CALC 193mg

cucumber-dill sauce

Don't make this more than a few hours in advance; the cucumber will make the sauce watery.

Hands-on time: 5 min. ★ **Total time: 5 min.**

1   **cup diced seeded peeled cucumber**
1   **cup plain fat-free yogurt**
¼   **teaspoon dried dill**
1   **garlic clove, minced**

1. Combine all ingredients in a small bowl; stir well. Cover and chill.

Serves 4 (serving size: 6 tablespoons)

CALORIES 38; FAT 0.1g (sat 0.1g, mono 0g, poly 0g); PROTEIN 3.5g; CARB 5.7g; FIBER 0.2g; CHOL 1mg; IRON 0.2mg; SODIUM 45mg; CALC 121mg

WEEKNIGHT

comforts:

SPEEDY

dinners

MUSHROOM FETTUCCINE
with hazelnuts

Look for blanched hazelnuts, which should have most or all of their skins removed.

Hands-on time: 17 min. ★ Total time: 17 min.

1 **(9-ounce) package refrigerated fresh fettuccine**
1 **tablespoon butter**
¼ **cup chopped blanched hazelnuts**
1 **tablespoon olive oil**
4 **garlic cloves, thinly sliced**
3 **(4-ounce) packages presliced exotic mushroom blend**
½ **teaspoon salt, divided**
¼ **teaspoon freshly ground black pepper**
2 **teaspoons chopped fresh sage**
2 **ounces shaved Parmigiano-Reggiano cheese (about ½ cup)**
2 **tablespoons finely chopped chives**

1. Cook pasta according to package directions, omitting salt and fat. Drain in a colander over a bowl, reserving ¾ cup cooking liquid.

2. While water for pasta comes to a boil, melt butter in a large nonstick skillet over medium-high heat. Add hazelnuts to pan; sauté 3 minutes or until toasted and fragrant. Remove from pan with a slotted spoon. Add oil to pan, and swirl to coat. Add garlic and mushrooms to pan; sprinkle with ¼ teaspoon salt and black pepper. Sauté mushroom mixture 5 minutes; stir in sage. Add pasta, reserved cooking liquid, and ¼ teaspoon salt to pan; toss well to combine. Remove from heat; top with cheese, toasted hazelnuts, and chives.

Serves 4 (serving size: about 1½ cups pasta mixture, about 2 tablespoons cheese, and 1 tablespoon hazelnuts)

CALORIES 364; **FAT** 16.5g (sat 5.7g, mono 7.6g, poly 1.2g); **PROTEIN** 16.8g; **CARB** 40.2g; **FIBER** 3.2g; **CHOL** 56mg; **IRON** 2.4mg; **SODIUM** 563mg; **CALC** 204mg

WALNUT-BREADCRUMB PASTA
with a soft egg

Hands-on time: 37 min. ★ **Total time: 42 min.**

4   large eggs
1   (2-ounce) piece French bread
     baguette, torn into small pieces
¼   cup walnuts
3   tablespoons olive oil
4   garlic cloves, minced
½   teaspoon kosher salt
½   teaspoon freshly ground black
     pepper
8   ounces uncooked fresh linguine
⅓   cup chopped fresh flat-leaf
     parsley
2   tablespoons finely chopped
     fresh chives
1½   ounces crumbled goat cheese
     (about ⅓ cup)

1. Bring 3 inches of water to a boil in a medium saucepan. Add eggs to pan; boil 5½ minutes. Drain. Plunge eggs into ice water, and let stand 5 minutes. Drain and peel.

2. Place bread in a food processor; process until finely ground. Add nuts to bread; pulse until finely ground. Heat a large skillet over medium-high heat. Add olive oil to pan, and swirl to coat. Add garlic, and sauté 30 seconds, stirring constantly. Add breadcrumb mixture, salt, and pepper to pan; sauté 5 minutes or until toasted, stirring frequently.

3. Cook pasta according to package directions, omitting salt and fat; drain. Add pasta to breadcrumb mixture; toss to combine. Sprinkle with parsley and chives; toss to combine. Divide pasta mixture among 4 bowls, and top each serving with 1 egg and 1½ tablespoons cheese. Serve immediately.

Serves 4

CALORIES 492; FAT 23.2g (sat 5.3g, mono 10.5g, poly 5.4g); PROTEIN 19.2g; CARB 53.3g; FIBER 3g; CHOL 216mg; IRON 4.1mg; SODIUM 448mg; CALC 80mg

CRAB CAKES
with spicy mustard sauce

Panko (Japanese breadcrumbs) in these lightened crab cakes give them a crisper, airier texture compared to regular breadcrumbs. Serve a simple green salad on the side.

Hands-on time: 39 min. ★ Total time: 39 min.

⅓ **cup prechopped red bell pepper**

2 **tablespoons canola mayonnaise**

¼ **teaspoon kosher salt**

¼ **teaspoon freshly ground black pepper**

2 **green onions, chopped**

1 **large egg, lightly beaten**

1 **large egg yolk, lightly beaten**

1⅓ **cups panko (Japanese breadcrumbs), divided**

1 **pound lump crabmeat, drained and shell pieces removed**

2 **tablespoons olive oil, divided**

2 **tablespoons canola mayonnaise**

2 **tablespoons reduced-fat sour cream**

2 **teaspoons chopped fresh parsley**

2 **teaspoons Dijon mustard**

1 **teaspoon white wine vinegar**

⅛ **teaspoon ground red pepper**

1. Combine first 7 ingredients. Add ⅓ cup panko and crab; toss gently. Divide crab mixture into 8 equal portions; shape each into a ¾-inch-thick patty. Place remaining panko in a shallow dish. Gently dredge patties in panko.

2. Heat a large skillet over medium-high heat. Add 1 tablespoon oil to pan; swirl to coat. Add 4 crab cakes to pan; cook 4 minutes on each side. Remove from pan; keep warm. Repeat procedure with remaining oil and crab cakes.

3. Combine 2 tablespoons mayonnaise and next 5 ingredients (through ground red pepper); serve with crab cakes.

Serves 4 (serving size: 2 crab cakes and 1½ tablespoons sauce)

CALORIES 404; FAT 23.7g (sat 3.1g, mono 13.5g, poly 5.4g); PROTEIN 2g; CARB 16.3g; FIBER 1.2g; CHOL 219mg; IRON 1.6mg; SODIUM 670mg; CALC 149mg

LINGUINE WITH CLAMS AND FRESH HERBS

Hands-on time: 23 min. ★ Total time: 23 min.

8 ounces uncooked linguine
⅓ cup flat-leaf parsley leaves
1 tablespoon chopped fresh oregano
2 teaspoons grated lemon rind
2 tablespoons olive oil
2 cups vertically sliced red onion
¼ teaspoon crushed red pepper
4 garlic cloves, sliced
½ cup white wine
1½ pounds littleneck clams
2 tablespoons butter
¾ teaspoon salt
½ teaspoon freshly ground black pepper

1. Cook pasta according to package directions, omitting salt and fat; drain pasta well.

2. Finely chop parsley. Combine parsley, oregano, and rind.

3. Heat a large skillet over medium-high heat. Add olive oil to pan; swirl to coat. Add onion, red pepper, and garlic; sauté 4 minutes. Add wine and clams; cover and simmer 5 minutes or until shells open. Discard any unopened shells.

4. Combine clam mixture, pasta, butter, salt, and black pepper in a large bowl; toss until butter melts. Sprinkle with parsley mixture; toss well.

Serves 4 (serving size: 1½ cups pasta mixture and 6 clams)

CALORIES 373; **FAT** 14.2g (sat 5g, mono 6.6g, poly 1.4g); **PROTEIN** 15g; **CARB** 47.5g; **FIBER** 2.5g; **CHOL** 32mg; **IRON** 9.5mg; **SODIUM** 521mg; **CALC** 61mg

SHRIMP PAD THAI

Hands-on time: 23 min. ★ **Total time: 23 min.**

8   **ounces uncooked flat rice noodles (pad Thai noodles)**
2   **tablespoons dark brown sugar**
2   **tablespoons lower-sodium soy sauce**
1½ **tablespoons fish sauce**
1½ **tablespoons fresh lime juice**
1   **tablespoon Sriracha (hot chile sauce)**
3   **tablespoons canola oil**
1   **cup (2-inch) green onion pieces**
8   **ounces peeled and deveined large shrimp**
5   **garlic cloves, minced**
1   **cup fresh bean sprouts**
¼   **cup chopped unsalted, dry-roasted peanuts**
3   **tablespoons fresh basil**
Lime wedges (optional)

1. Cook noodles according to package directions; drain.

2. While water comes to a boil, combine sugar and next 4 ingredients (through Sriracha) in a small bowl.

3. Heat a large skillet or wok over medium-high heat. Add oil to pan; swirl to coat. Add onion pieces, shrimp, and garlic; stir-fry 2 minutes or until shrimp are almost done. Add cooked noodles; toss to combine. Stir in sauce; cook 1 minute, stirring constantly to combine. Arrange about 1 cup noodle mixture on each of 4 plates; top each serving with ¼ cup bean sprouts, 1 tablespoon peanuts, and 2 teaspoons basil. Serve with lime wedges, if desired.

Serves 4

CALORIES 462; **FAT** 16.1g (sat 1.6g, mono 9.1g, poly 4.8g); **PROTEIN** 15.8g; **CARB** 64.3g; **FIBER** 2.6g; **CHOL** 86mg; **IRON** 3.7mg; **SODIUM** 779mg; **CALC** 90mg

SHRIMP VODKA PASTA

Vodka doesn't contribute much flavor on its own, but when it mingles with tomatoes, it releases their alcohol-soluble flavors. Don't skip it.

Hands-on time: 18 min. ★ Total time: 18 min.

1   (9-ounce) package refrigerated fresh fettuccine
1   tablespoon olive oil, divided
12 ounces peeled and deveined large shrimp
3   garlic cloves, thinly sliced
1/3 cup vodka
1 1/3 cups lower-sodium marinara sauce
1/3 cup chopped fresh basil, divided
1/4 cup heavy whipping cream
1/2 teaspoon kosher salt
1/4 teaspoon freshly ground black pepper

1. Cook pasta according to package directions, omitting salt and fat.

2. Heat a large skillet over medium-high heat. Add 1½ teaspoons oil to pan; swirl to coat. Add shrimp; sauté 4 minutes or until done. Remove shrimp from pan.

3. Add 1½ teaspoons oil and garlic to pan; sauté 1 minute. Carefully add vodka; cook 1 minute. Add marinara, ¼ cup basil, cream, salt, and pepper; bring to a simmer. Stir in pasta and shrimp. Sprinkle with remaining basil.

Serves 4 (serving size: 1¼ cups)

CALORIES 427; **FAT** 12.6g (sat 4.9g, mono 4.8g, poly 1.4g); **PROTEIN** 24.6g; **CARB** 60.1g; **FIBER** 2.4g; **CHOL** 184mg; **IRON** 2.2mg; **SODIUM** 632mg; **CALC** 65mg

SHRIMP WITH LEMON-SAFFRON RICE

This recipe combines all the flavors of a traditional paella in a weeknight-friendly dish. Put some flamenco tunes on to complete this culinary journey to Spain.

Hands-on time: 30 min. ★ **Total time: 30 min.**

1 tablespoon extra-virgin olive oil
½ cup chopped onion
½ cup chopped green bell pepper
1 teaspoon minced fresh garlic
1 pound peeled and deveined large shrimp
2 cups uncooked instant rice
½ cup water
1½ teaspoons chopped fresh oregano
¼ teaspoon salt
¼ teaspoon saffron threads, crushed
¼ teaspoon paprika
¼ teaspoon freshly ground black pepper
1 (14-ounce) can fat-free, lower-sodium chicken broth
1 cup frozen green peas, thawed
2½ tablespoons fresh lemon juice

1. Heat a large Dutch oven over medium-high heat. Add oil to pan; swirl to coat. Add onion and bell pepper; sauté 3 minutes or until vegetables are tender, stirring frequently. Add garlic; cook 30 seconds, stirring constantly. Add shrimp to pan; cook 30 seconds, stirring frequently. Add rice and next 7 ingredients (through broth). Bring rice mixture to a boil; cover pan. Reduce heat, and simmer 5 minutes or until rice is done. Remove from heat; stir in peas and lemon juice.

Serves 4 (serving size: 1 cup)

CALORIES 394; **FAT** 6.5g (sat 0.9g, mono 2.9g, poly 1.3g); **PROTEIN** 29.9g; **CARB** 51.8g; **FIBER** 3.7g; **IRON** 6.6mg; **SODIUM** 517mg; **CALC** 97mg

make it foolproof

Saffron lends a beautiful golden color and distinct, subtle floral note to dishes. Buy saffron threads; you'll miss out on flavor with ground saffron (and some may have been adulterated with other ingredients). Crush saffron with a mortar and pestle. Some cooks mix it with a little water to better distribute it in a dish.

make it special
When you have extra time, seek out stone-ground, whole-corn grits. They will take up to 40 minutes to cook, but the payoff is that you'll get the flavor and health benefits of a whole grain.

SPICY SHRIMP AND GRITS

Crank up the heat and serve this spicy version of a Southern favorite.

Hands-on time: 35 min. ★ **Total time: 35 min.**

3	**cups 1% low-fat milk**
1	**cup water**
1	**tablespoon butter**
1/2	**teaspoon salt, divided**
1/4	**teaspoon black pepper, divided**
1	**cup uncooked quick-cooking grits**
2	**ounces grated fresh Parmesan cheese (about 1/2 cup)**
2	**applewood-smoked bacon slices**
1	**pound peeled and deveined large shrimp**
1	**cup thinly vertically sliced white onion**
2	**cups grape tomatoes, halved**
1	**teaspoon hot pepper sauce or chopped chipotle chile, canned in adobo sauce**
1/8	**teaspoon ground or crushed red pepper**
1/4	**cup green onion strips**

1. Combine milk, 1 cup water, butter, 1/4 teaspoon salt, and 1/8 teaspoon black pepper in a saucepan over medium-high heat. Bring to a simmer; gradually add grits, stirring constantly with a whisk. Reduce heat to medium; cook 4 minutes or until thick, stirring occasionally. Remove from heat; stir in cheese.

2. While grits cook, cook bacon in a large nonstick skillet over medium heat until crisp. Remove bacon from pan, reserving 2 teaspoons drippings; crumble bacon. Add shrimp to drippings in pan; cook 2 minutes on each side or until done. Remove shrimp from pan. Add white onion to pan; sauté 1 minute. Stir in bacon, tomatoes, 1/4 teaspoon salt, and 1/8 teaspoon black pepper; sauté 2 minutes, stirring occasionally. Add shrimp, pepper sauce, and red pepper; cook 1 minute or until shrimp are heated. Serve over grits; sprinkle with green onions.

Serves 4 (serving size: 1 cup grits, about 1½ cups shrimp mixture, and 1 tablespoon green onions)

CALORIES 481; FAT 13.5g (sat 6.2g, mono 3.4g, poly 1.2g); PROTEIN 34.9g; CARB 54.5g; FIBER 3.7g; CHOL 175mg; IRON 2mg; SODIUM 804mg; CALC 516mg

CHIP-CRUSTED FISH FILLETS

The tang in the salt and vinegar chips mellows as the fish bakes in the oven, creating a crunchy spin on fish and chips. Look to hook-and-line–caught Atlantic or Pacific cod for the most sustainable choice.

Hands-on time: 4 min. ★ **Total time: 14 min.**

4   **(6-ounce) cod fillets (or other firm white fish)**
2   **teaspoons canola mayonnaise**
1/8   **teaspoon salt**
1   **(2-ounce) package salt and vinegar kettle-style potato chips, crushed**
1/2   **cup light ranch dressing**

1. Preheat oven to 400°.

2. Arrange fillets on a parchment-lined baking sheet. Brush ½ teaspoon mayonnaise over top of each fillet; sprinkle with salt. Gently press about 2 tablespoons crushed chips on top of each fillet. Bake fish at 400° for 10 minutes or until desired degree of doneness. Serve with ranch dressing.

Serves 4 (serving size: 1 fillet and 2 tablespoons ranch dressing)

CALORIES 291; **FAT** 11.3g (sat 1.2g, mono 5.7g, poly 2.8g); **PROTEIN** 31.7g; **CARB** 14.5g; **FIBER** 0.8g; **CHOL** 79mg; **IRON** 1.4mg; **SODIUM** 549mg; **CALC** 49mg

CHEESY CHICKEN BAGEL PIZZAS

Bagel halves are a quick, kid-friendly stand-in for traditional pizza crust.

Hands-on time: 6 min. ★ **Total time: 6 min.**

2   (4½-inch, 2¼-ounce)
    plain bagels, sliced in half
½   cup lower-sodium
    marinara sauce
1   cup shredded rotisserie
    chicken breast (about 5
    ounces)
1   cup preshredded part-
    skim mozzarella cheese

1. Preheat broiler.

2. Place bagel halves, cut sides up, on a baking sheet. Broil 2 minutes or until lightly toasted.

3. Spread 2 tablespoons marinara on cut side of each bagel half. Top each half with ¼ cup chicken, and sprinkle with ¼ cup cheese. Broil bagel halves 2 minutes or until cheese melts.

Serves 4 (serving size: 1 bagel pizza)

CALORIES 268; **FAT** 8g (sat 4.2g, mono 2.4g, poly 0.6g); **PROTEIN** 22.1g; **CARB** 32.7g; **FIBER** 1g; **CHOL** 47mg; **IRON** 2.9mg; **SODIUM** 516mg; **CALC** 251mg

CREAMY SPRING PASTA

This dish is luxuriously creamy, but the pasta soaks up the sauce quickly. Be sure to serve it right away. Use refrigerated pasta to cut several minutes off the cooking time. Some simple roasted carrots round out the meal.

Hands-on time: 30 min. ★ **Total time: 30 min.**

3 quarts water
2 ounces French bread baguette, torn into pieces
1 tablespoon butter
3 garlic cloves, minced and divided
1½ cups (2-inch) diagonally cut asparagus
1 cup frozen green peas
6 ounces uncooked fettuccine
2 teaspoons olive oil
⅓ cup finely chopped sweet onion
1 tablespoon all-purpose flour
¼ cup fat-free, lower-sodium chicken broth
1 cup 1% low-fat milk
3 ounces ⅓-less-fat cream cheese (about ⅓ cup)
1 ounce grated fresh Parmigiano-Reggiano cheese (about ¼ cup)
½ teaspoon kosher salt
¼ teaspoon freshly ground black pepper
2 tablespoons chopped fresh tarragon

1. Bring 3 quarts water to a boil in a Dutch oven.

2. Place torn bread in a food processor; process until coarse crumbs form. Melt butter in a large skillet over medium-high heat. Add 1 garlic clove to pan; sauté 1 minute. Add breadcrumbs; sauté 3 minutes or until golden brown and toasted. Remove breadcrumb mixture from pan; wipe pan clean with paper towels.

3. Add asparagus and peas to boiling water; cook 3 minutes or until crisp-tender. Remove from pan with a slotted spoon. Rinse under cold water; drain.

4. Add pasta to boiling water; cook 10 minutes or until al dente. Drain and keep warm.

5. Heat pan over medium heat. Add olive oil; swirl to coat. Add onion and 2 garlic cloves; cook 3 minutes or until tender, stirring frequently. Place flour in a small bowl; gradually whisk in chicken broth. Add broth mixture and milk to pan, stirring constantly with a whisk; bring to a boil. Reduce heat; cook 1 minute or until thick. Remove from heat; add cheeses, salt, and pepper, stirring until cheeses melt. Add pasta, asparagus, and peas; toss well. Sprinkle with breadcrumbs and tarragon.

Serves 4 (serving size: about 1¼ cups)

CALORIES 408; FAT 13.8g (sat 6.7g, mono 4.5g, poly 1.1g); PROTEIN 17.6g; CARB 54g; FIBER 4.6g; CHOL 33mg; IRON 3.9mg; SODIUM 625mg; CALC 225mg

CHICKEN FRIED RICE

Stir-fries come together fast, making them perfect for a weeknight supper. But because cooking happens so quickly, have all your ingredients ready to go and within reach before you heat up your wok.

Hands-on time: 24 min. ★ **Total time: 24 min.**

2   (3¹/₂-ounce) bags boil-in-bag long-grain white rice
7   teaspoons lower-sodium soy sauce, divided
1   teaspoon cornstarch
12   ounces skinless, boneless chicken breast, cut into ¹/₂-inch pieces
2   tablespoons hoisin sauce
2   tablespoons rice wine vinegar
2   tablespoons fresh lime juice
1   teaspoon chili paste with garlic
2   tablespoons canola oil, divided
2   large eggs, lightly beaten
1   cup chopped white onion
1   teaspoon grated peeled fresh ginger
3   garlic cloves, minced
1   cup frozen green peas, thawed
¹/₂   cup chopped green onions

1. Cook rice according to package directions, omitting salt and fat.

2. Combine 1 tablespoon soy sauce, cornstarch, and chicken in a bowl; toss well. Combine 4 teaspoons soy sauce, hoisin sauce, and next 3 ingredients (through chili paste) in a small bowl.

3. Heat a wok or large nonstick skillet over medium-high heat. Add 1 tablespoon oil; swirl to coat. Add chicken mixture; stir-fry 4 minutes or until lightly browned. Push chicken to 1 side of skillet; add eggs to open side of pan. Cook 45 seconds, stirring constantly; stir eggs and chicken mixture together. Remove chicken mixture from pan; keep warm. Return pan to medium-high heat. Add 1 tablespoon oil to pan. Add white onion, ginger, and garlic; cook 2 minutes or until fragrant. Add rice; cook 1 minute. Add peas; cook 1 minute. Add chicken mixture and soy sauce mixture; cook 2 minutes or until thoroughly heated. Remove pan from heat; stir in green onions.

Serves 4 (serving size: about 1½ cups)

CALORIES 477; **FAT** 11.7g (sat 1.7g, mono 5.7g, poly 2.7g); **PROTEIN** 30.2g; **CARB** 58.3g; **FIBER** 3.5g; **CHOL** 139mg; **IRON** 3.5mg; **SODIUM** 488mg; **CALC** 58mg

COCONUT CHICKEN FINGERS

Kids love the sweetness that the coconut adds to the coating of these chicken fingers. This recipe uses rice flour instead of wheat flour for the coating, making it allergy free.

Hands-on time: 27 min. ★ **Total time: 27 min.**

1½ **pounds skinless, boneless chicken breast halves, cut into ½-inch-thick strips**
½ **teaspoon salt**
¼ **teaspoon ground red pepper**
1 **cup rice flour**
1 **cup whole buttermilk**
1 **large egg**
1½ **cups flaked unsweetened coconut**
3 **tablespoons canola oil**
Sweet chile sauce (optional)

1. Sprinkle chicken with salt and pepper. Place flour in a shallow dish. Combine buttermilk and egg in a shallow dish, stirring well. Place coconut in a shallow dish. Dredge chicken in flour; shake off excess. Dip chicken in egg mixture; dredge in coconut.

2. Heat a large skillet over medium-high heat. Add oil to pan; swirl to coat. Add chicken to pan; cook 6 minutes or until done, turning to brown. Serve with chile sauce, if desired.

Serves 6 (serving size: about 4.5 ounces)

CALORIES 298; **FAT** 12.7g (sat 4.1g, mono 5.4g, poly 2.6g); **PROTEIN** 28.7g; **CARB** 15.9g; **FIBER** 1.7g; **CHOL** 102mg; **IRON** 1.4mg; **SODIUM** 318mg; **CALC** 20mg

GREEK-STYLE SKEWERS

Hands-on time: 17 min. ★ **Total time: 17 min.**

1 **pound skinless, boneless chicken breast, cut into 32 cubes**
24 **cherry tomatoes (optional)**
¾ **teaspoon salt, divided**
¼ **teaspoon freshly ground black pepper**
Cooking spray
1 **lemon**
2 **garlic cloves**
¼ **cup oregano leaves**
3 **tablespoons extra-virgin olive oil**

1. Preheat grill to medium-high heat.

2. Thread 4 chicken cubes alternately with 3 tomatoes, if desired, onto each of 8 (12-inch) skewers. Sprinkle skewers with ½ teaspoon salt and pepper; coat with cooking spray. Place skewers on grill rack coated with cooking spray; grill 3 minutes. Turn skewers over; grill 2 minutes or until chicken is done.

3. Grate 1½ teaspoons rind from 1 end of lemon; cut lemon in half crosswise. Cut ungrated lemon half into quarters; reserve remaining lemon half for another use. Place ¼ teaspoon salt, lemon rind, garlic, and oregano in a food processor; process until finely ground, scraping sides. With motor running, slowly drizzle oil through food chute; process until well blended. Brush oregano mixture over skewers; serve with lemon wedges.

Serves 4 (serving size: 2 skewers and 1 lemon wedge)

CALORIES 221; **FAT** 13.3g (sat 2.3g, mono 8.4g, poly 2.1g); **PROTEIN** 23.2g; **CARB** 19g; **FIBER** 0.3g; **CHOL** 63mg; **IRON** 0.9mg; **SODIUM** 498mg; **CALC** 36mg

SPRING RISOTTO

An Italian dish based on creamy rice, risotto is perfect when you want to curl up with a bowl of something warm and soothing.

Hands-on time: 36 min. ★ **Total time: 36 min.**

6   cups water, divided
1   pound asparagus, trimmed and cut into ³/₄-inch pieces
1³/₄ cups fat-free, lower-sodium chicken broth
2   tablespoons olive oil
1¹/₂ cups chopped onion
2   garlic cloves, minced
1   cup uncooked Arborio rice
1   cup frozen shelled edamame
¹/₂ teaspoon kosher salt
2   ounces ¹/₃-less-fat cream cheese (about ¹/₄ cup)
¹/₂ teaspoon freshly ground black pepper
1   ounce shaved fresh Parmesan cheese (about ¹/₄ cup)
2   tablespoons chopped fresh thyme

1. Bring 4 cups water to a boil in a saucepan. Add asparagus, and cook 2 minutes. Drain. Bring 2 cups water and chicken broth to a simmer in a saucepan.

2. Heat a large saucepan over medium heat. Add olive oil, and swirl to coat. Add onion; cook 4 minutes. Add garlic, and cook 2 minutes, stirring constantly. Stir in rice, edamame, and salt; cook 1 minute. Stir in 1 cup broth mixture; cook 4 minutes or until liquid is nearly absorbed, stirring constantly. Add remaining broth mixture, ½ cup at a time, stirring constantly until liquid is absorbed before adding more (about 20 minutes total).

3. Stir in asparagus, cream cheese, and pepper; cook 1 minute. Spoon 1 cup risotto into each of 4 bowls. Top each serving with 1 tablespoon Parmesan cheese; sprinkle with thyme.

Serves 4

CALORIES 394; **FAT** 14g (sat 3.6g, mono 6.6g, poly 1.8g); **PROTEIN** 17g; **CARB** 54g; **FIBER** 7.6g; **CHOL** 14mg; **IRON** 4.5mg; **SODIUM** 623mg; **CALC** 171mg

LEMONY CHICKEN SALTIMBOCCA

Hands-on time: 17 min. ★ **Total time: 17 min.**

4	**(4-ounce) chicken cutlets**
¹⁄₈	**teaspoon salt**
12	**sage leaves**
2	**ounces very thinly sliced prosciutto, cut into 8 thin strips**
4	**teaspoons extra-virgin olive oil, divided**
¹⁄₃	**cup fat-free, lower-sodium chicken broth**
¹⁄₄	**cup fresh lemon juice**
¹⁄₂	**teaspoon cornstarch**
Lemon wedges (optional)	

1. Sprinkle chicken with salt. Place 3 sage leaves on each cutlet; wrap 2 prosciutto slices around each cutlet, securing sage leaves in place.

2. Heat a large skillet over medium heat. Add 1 tablespoon oil to pan, and swirl to coat. Add chicken to pan; cook 2 minutes on each side or until done. Remove chicken from pan; keep warm.

3. Combine broth, lemon juice, and cornstarch in a small bowl; stir with a whisk until smooth. Add cornstarch mixture and 1 teaspoon olive oil to pan; bring to a boil, stirring constantly. Cook 1 minute or until slightly thick, stirring constantly with a whisk. Spoon sauce over chicken. Serve with lemon wedges, if desired.

Serves 4 (serving size: 1 cutlet and 2 tablespoons sauce)

CALORIES 202; **FAT** 7.5g (sat 1.5g, mono 4.3g, poly 0.9g); **PROTEIN** 30.5g; **CARB** 2.3g; **FIBER** 0.2g; **CHOL** 77mg; **IRON** 1.1mg; **SODIUM** 560mg; **CALC** 18mg

make it ahead
You can prepare the pimiento cheese up to three days in advance, but to keep the bacon crisp, stir it in just before you prepare the chicken.

PIMIENTO CHEESE CHICKEN

Instead of using pimiento cheese as a sandwich spread (a Southern tradition), try using it as a filling for skillet-cooked chicken breasts.

Hands-on time: 15 min. ★ **Total time: 32 min.**

1   **applewood-smoked bacon slice**
3   **ounces shredded cheddar cheese (about ¾ cup)**
2   **tablespoons minced green onions**
1½ **tablespoons diced pimientos**
1   **tablespoon canola mayonnaise**
2   **teaspoons fresh lemon juice**
½   **teaspoon hot sauce**
½   **teaspoon salt, divided**
4   **(6-ounce) skinless, boneless chicken breast halves**
½   **teaspoon freshly ground black pepper**
1   **tablespoon canola oil**

1. Preheat oven to 350°.

2. Cook bacon in a large ovenproof skillet until crisp. Remove bacon, reserving drippings in pan; crumble bacon. Combine bacon, next 6 ingredients (through hot sauce), and ¼ teaspoon salt. Cut a 1-inch-wide slit in thick end of each breast half; carefully cut down to center to form a deep pocket. Divide cheese mixture among pockets. Secure with wooden picks. Sprinkle chicken with ¼ teaspoon salt and pepper.

3. Heat pan over medium-high heat. Add oil to drippings. Add chicken to pan; sauté 4 minutes. Turn chicken over. Bake at 350° for 12 minutes; let stand 5 minutes.

Serves 4

CALORIES 299; **FAT** 16g (sat 5.8g, mono 6.1g, poly 2.3g); **PROTEIN** 36.8g; **CARB** 1.3g; **FIBER** 0.2g; **CHOL** 100mg; **IRON** 1.2mg; **SODIUM** 606mg; **CALC** 171mg

SZECHUAN CHICKEN STIR-FRY

Chile paste and fresh ginger add just the right amount of heat to this dish.

Hands-on time: 25 min. ★ Total time: 25 min.

1 tablespoon dark sesame oil, divided

½ cup fat-free, lower-sodium chicken broth

2 tablespoons lower-sodium soy sauce

1 tablespoon rice vinegar

2 teaspoons sambal oelek (ground fresh chile paste)

2 teaspoons cornstarch

¼ teaspoon salt

2 tablespoons canola oil, divided

1 pound skinless, boneless chicken breast, cut into bite-sized pieces

1 yellow bell pepper, cut into strips

1 red bell pepper, cut into strips

1 cup diagonally cut snow peas

½ cup vertically sliced onion

1 tablespoon grated ginger

1 tablespoon minced garlic

2 cups hot cooked long-grain white rice

¼ cup (1-inch) sliced green onions

¼ cup chopped unsalted, dry-roasted peanuts

1. Combine 2 teaspoons sesame oil and next 6 ingredients (through salt) in a small bowl. Heat a wok or large skillet over medium-high heat. Add 1 teaspoon sesame oil and 1 tablespoon canola oil; swirl to coat. Add chicken; stir-fry 2 minutes. Remove chicken from pan.

2. Add 1 tablespoon canola oil; swirl. Add bell peppers and next 4 ingredients (through garlic); stir-fry 1 minute. Add broth mixture; cook 30 seconds or until thick. Return chicken to pan; cook 4 minutes or until chicken is done. Spoon ½ cup rice onto each of 4 plates; top each with 1 cup chicken mixture, green onions, and peanuts.

Serves 4

CALORIES 420; **FAT** 16.7g (sat 2g, mono 8.2g, poly 5.1g); **PROTEIN** 32.3g; **CARB** 32.3g; **FIBER** 2.7g; **CHOL** 66mg; **IRON** 2.7mg; **SODIUM** 478mg; **CALC** 45mg

BACON AND BROCCOLI MAC AND CHEESE

This one-dish meal will win over adults and children alike. Substitute English peas or fresh spinach for the broccoli, if you prefer.

Hands-on time: 36 min. ★ **Total time: 36 min.**

3   cups broccoli florets
8   ounces uncooked rigatoni
1   tablespoon butter
1½ tablespoons all-purpose flour
1¼ cups 2% reduced-fat milk
2   ounces reduced-fat processed American cheese, cut into pieces (about ½ cup)
2   ounces shredded extra-sharp cheddar cheese (about ½ cup)
¼   cup thinly sliced green onions
½   teaspoon salt
¼   teaspoon freshly ground black pepper
2   center-cut bacon slices, cooked and crumbled

1. Steam broccoli 5 minutes or until crisp-tender; drain. Pat dry, and keep warm. Cook pasta in boiling water in a large saucepan 8 minutes or until al dente; drain and keep warm. Wipe pan with paper towels, and return to medium heat.

2. Melt butter in pan. Sprinkle flour over melted butter; cook 1 minute, stirring constantly with a whisk. Gradually add milk to flour mixture in pan, and bring to a boil, stirring constantly with a whisk. Cook 1 minute or until slightly thick; and remove from heat. Add American cheese; stir until smooth. Stir in cheddar cheese and next 4 ingredients (through bacon). Stir in broccoli and pasta; serve immediately.

Serves 4 (serving size: 1½ cups)

CALORIES 413; FAT 13.3g (sat 7.5g, mono 3.4g, poly 0.9g); PROTEIN 19.6g; CARB 53.4g; FIBER 3.8g; CHOL 39mg; IRON 2.8mg; SODIUM 772mg; CALC 317mg

POTATO, CHORIZO, AND GREEN CHILE BURRITOS

Hands-on time: 36 min. ★ **Total time: 36 min.**

10	ounces red potatoes, cut into ½-inch cubes
1	cup chopped tomato
2	tablespoons diced white onion
1	tablespoon chopped fresh cilantro
2	teaspoons fresh lime juice
6	ounces Mexican raw chorizo
1	cup chopped white onion
⅓	cup thinly sliced poblano chile
2	teaspoons olive oil
⅛	teaspoon salt
4	(7- to 8-inch) whole-wheat flour tortillas
2	ounces crumbled queso fresco (about ½ cup)

1. Place potato in a saucepan, and cover with cold water. Bring to a boil. Remove pan from heat, and let stand 5 minutes. Drain; pat potato dry.

2. Combine 1 cup tomato, 2 tablespoons diced onion, cilantro, and lime juice.

3. Heat a large skillet over medium-high heat. Add chorizo; cook 3 minutes, stirring to crumble. Add 1 cup chopped onion and poblano to pan; cook 2 minutes or until chorizo is done. Remove chorizo mixture from pan. Add oil to pan, and swirl to coat. Add potato; cook 8 minutes or until browned, stirring occasionally. Remove pan from heat. Stir in chorizo mixture and salt.

4. Heat tortillas according to package directions. Divide potato mixture among tortillas, and top with salsa and cheese. Roll up each burrito.

5. Heat a large nonstick skillet over medium heat. Add 2 burritos to pan, seams down; cook 1 minute on each side. Repeat with remaining burritos.

Serves 4 (serving size: 1 burrito)

CALORIES 349; **FAT** 15.4g (sat 4.6g, mono 7g, poly 1.8g); **PROTEIN** 14.5g; **CARB** 39.6g; **FIBER** 5.8g; **CHOL** 77mg; **IRON** 1.4mg; **SODIUM** 669mg; **CALC** 135mg

PASTA PORK BOLOGNESE

Who says Bolognese sauce has to take hours? Here, refrigerated fresh pasta and a jar of marinara sauce make quick work of a perfect dish for pasta night.

Hands-on time: 14 min. ★ **Total time: 14 min.**

1	**(9-ounce) package refrigerated fresh fettuccine**
2	**teaspoons olive oil**
1/2	**cup grated carrot**
12	**ounces lean ground pork**
3	**garlic cloves, minced**
1/3	**cup red wine**
1 2/3	**cups lower-sodium marinara sauce**
1/2	**cup thinly sliced fresh basil, divided**
1/2	**teaspoon kosher salt**
1/4	**teaspoon freshly ground black pepper**

1. Cook pasta according to package directions, omitting salt and fat.

2. Heat a large skillet over medium-high heat. Add olive oil to pan; swirl to coat. Add carrot, pork, and garlic; sauté 4 minutes or until pork is done. Add wine; cook 1 minute. Add marinara, 1/4 cup basil, salt, and pepper; bring to a simmer. Pour sauce over pasta. Sprinkle with 1/4 cup basil.

Serves 4 (serving size: 1 1/4 cups)

CALORIES 412; **FAT** 13.1g (sat 4.6g, mono 5.1g, poly 1g); **PROTEIN** 24.9g; **CARB** 67.6g; **FIBER** 2.1g; **CHOL** 102mg; **IRON** 1.7mg; **SODIUM** 468mg; **CALC** 35mg

CARAMEL PORK

Give pork tenderloin an Asian twist by cooking it in a sweet and spicy sauce. Serve alongside a mixture of rice and green peas for a complete meal.

Hands-on time: 35 min. ★ **Total time: 45 min.**

1   cup water
³/₄   cup uncooked sushi or short-grain rice
¹/₂   teaspoon kosher salt, divided
¹/₂   cup frozen green peas, thawed
1   tablespoon rice vinegar
Cooking spray
1   (1-pound) pork tenderloin, trimmed and cut into 1-inch pieces
¹/₂   cup chopped Vidalia or other sweet onion
3   garlic cloves, minced
¹/₂   cup fat-free, lower-sodium chicken broth
3   tablespoons dark brown sugar
1   tablespoon lower-sodium soy sauce
1   teaspoon bottled ground fresh ginger
¹/₂   teaspoon crushed red pepper
2   canned anchovy fillets, rinsed and minced
8   lime wedges

1. Combine 1 cup water, rice, and ¼ teaspoon salt in a small saucepan; bring to a boil. Cover, reduce heat, and simmer 15 minutes; remove from heat. Let stand 10 minutes; gently stir in peas and vinegar.

2. Heat a medium skillet over high heat. Coat pan with cooking spray. Add pork; sauté 5 minutes. Sprinkle with ¼ teaspoon salt. Add onion and garlic; stir-fry 2 minutes. Stir in broth and next 5 ingredients (through anchovy fillets); bring to a boil. Reduce heat; simmer 5 minutes or until slightly thick. Spoon ½ cup rice on each of 4 plates; top each serving with ½ cup pork mixture. Serve with lime wedges.

Serves 4

CALORIES 295; FAT 2.9g (sat 0.9g, mono 1g, poly 0.5g); PROTEIN 27.8g; CARB 37.3g; FIBER 2.1g; CHOL 75mg; IRON 2.7mg; SODIUM 577mg; CALC 31mg

PORK CHOPS

with Caribbean rub and mango salsa

Let allspice, ginger, and a fruity salsa take you on a weeknight island adventure.

Hands-on time: 16 min. ★ **Total time: 16 min.**

1½ teaspoons ground coriander
1½ teaspoons ground cumin
¾ teaspoon sugar
¾ teaspoon ground ginger
½ teaspoon salt
¼ teaspoon ground allspice
⅛ teaspoon ground red pepper
4 (6-ounce) bone-in center-cut pork chops (about ½ inch thick)
Cooking spray
½ cup diced peeled mango
½ cup diced plum tomato
½ cup chopped cilantro
1 tablespoon red wine vinegar
2 teaspoons extra-virgin olive oil

1. Combine first 7 ingredients in a small bowl. Rub pork chops with spice mixture.

2. Heat a grill pan over medium-high heat. Coat pan with cooking spray. Add pork to pan; grill 3 minutes on each side or until a thermometer registers 145° (slightly pink).

3. Combine mango and next 4 ingredients (through olive oil) in a small bowl; toss gently. Serve salsa with pork.

Serves 4 (serving size: 1 chop and ¼ cup salsa)

CALORIES 192; FAT 7g (sat 1.6g, mono 3.2g, poly 0.7g); PROTEIN 24.9g; CARB 6.3g; FIBER 1.4g; CHOL 76mg; IRON 1.2mg; SODIUM 363mg; CALC 38mg

PORK TENDERLOIN
with red and yellow peppers

Hands-on time: 13 min. ★ **Total time: 20 min.**

1	(1-pound) pork tenderloin, trimmed and cut crosswise into 1-inch-thick medallions
½	teaspoon kosher salt
½	teaspoon freshly ground black pepper
1	tablespoon extra-virgin olive oil
1½	teaspoons chopped fresh rosemary, divided
4	canned anchovy fillets, drained and mashed
3	garlic cloves, thinly sliced
1	red bell pepper, cut into 1½-inch strips
1	yellow bell pepper, cut into 1½-inch strips
2	teaspoons balsamic vinegar

1. Heat a large skillet over medium-high heat. Sprinkle pork with salt and pepper. Add oil to pan; swirl to coat. Add pork to pan; cook 5 minutes. Reduce heat to medium; turn pork over. Add 1 teaspoon rosemary, anchovies, garlic, and bell peppers; cook 7 minutes or until peppers are tender and pork is done. Drizzle with vinegar. Top with ½ teaspoon rosemary.

Serves 4 (serving size: 3 ounces pork and about ½ cup bell pepper mixture)

CALORIES 215; FAT 10.1g (sat 2.7g, mono 5.4g, poly 1.2g); PROTEIN 25.2g; CARB 5g; FIBER 1.4g; CHOL 78mg; IRON 2mg; SODIUM 441mg; CALC 26mg

ALL-AMERICAN MEAT LOAF

Meat loaf showed up in American cookbooks in 1899, and it's been a national weeknight staple since, enjoyed hot or cold. This version includes sharp cheddar cheese and tangy buttermilk.

Hands-on time: 15 min. ★ Total time: 1 hr. 20 min.

1½ ounces French bread, torn into pieces
1 cup coarsely chopped onion
2 ounces diced sharp cheddar cheese (about ½ cup)
½ cup ketchup, divided
5 tablespoons chopped fresh flat-leaf parsley, divided
¼ cup nonfat buttermilk
1 tablespoon minced garlic (about 3 cloves)
1 tablespoon Dijon mustard
½ teaspoon freshly ground black pepper
¼ teaspoon kosher salt
2 large eggs, lightly beaten
1 pound ground sirloin
Cooking spray

1. Preheat oven to 350°.

2. Place bread in a food processor; pulse 10 times or until coarse crumbs measure 1 cup. Arrange breadcrumbs in an even layer on a baking sheet. Bake at 350° for 6 minutes or until lightly toasted; cool. Combine toasted breadcrumbs, onion, cheese, ¼ cup ketchup, 3 tablespoons parsley, and next 7 ingredients (through beef) in a bowl; gently mix until just combined.

3. Transfer mixture to a 9 x 5–inch loaf pan coated with cooking spray; do not pack. Bake at 350° for 30 minutes. Brush top of loaf with ¼ cup ketchup. Bake an additional 25 minutes or until a thermometer registers 160°. Let stand 10 minutes, and cut into 6 slices. Sprinkle with remaining parsley.

Serves 6 (serving size: 1 slice)

CALORIES 258; FAT 12.6g (sat 5.8g, mono 4g, poly 0.6g); PROTEIN 21.2g; CARB 14g; FIBER 0.8g; CHOL 119mg; IRON 2.6mg; SODIUM 557mg; CALC 104mg

CHILI-CHEESE MAC

Meaty, cheesy, and delicious—kids will love this comforting dinner. Parents will love it, too—it's quick.

Hands-on time: 10 min. ★ **Total time: 20 min.**

1 teaspoon canola oil
¾ pound ground round
2 teaspoons chili powder
1 teaspoon garlic powder
1 teaspoon ground coriander
1 teaspoon ground cumin
2 cups fat-free, lower-sodium beef broth
1 cup water
1 (10-ounce) can mild diced tomatoes and green chiles, undrained
8 ounces uncooked elbow macaroni
½ cup fat-free milk
4 ounces ⅓-less-fat cream cheese (about ½ cup)
4½ ounces reduced-fat finely shredded sharp cheddar cheese (about 1⅛ cups)

1. Heat a Dutch oven over medium-high heat. Add oil; swirl to coat. Add beef and next 4 ingredients (through cumin); cook 3 minutes. Add broth, 1 cup water, and tomatoes; bring to a boil. Stir in macaroni; cover and cook 10 minutes or until macaroni is done.

2. Heat milk and cream cheese in a saucepan over medium heat. Cook 4 minutes or until cheese melts, stirring frequently. Remove from heat. Stir in cheddar. Add cheese sauce to macaroni mixture; toss well to coat.

Serves 6 (serving size: 1 cup)

CALORIES 342; **FAT** 12.3g (sat 6g, mono 3.7g, poly 1.1g); **PROTEIN** 25.7g; **CARB** 32.7g; **FIBER** 1.8g; **CHOL** 60mg; **IRON** 2.3mg; **SODIUM** 652mg; **CALC** 363mg

A KITCHEN MEMORY

on your mark, get set, slurp!

Growing up, I counted the days until our annual beach trip. Not only was I excited about sandcastles and seashells, I was also thrilled about our family's famous "noodle slurping contest." Tolerant of bad manners only once a year, Mama would make her famous spaghetti sauce, rich with vegetables and ground beef. We would take our places at the table, scoping out the competition while we drooled over the smells coming from the boiling pot. Once Mama put plates of pasta and sauce on the table, we each chose our noodle, and the slurping began. The person who could slurp a whole noodle the fastest earned bragging rights for an entire year. My older sister typically won, but eventually I learned her ways and won my own proud title as the family noodle slurping champion.

-Emily Robinson,
Macon, Georgia

GARLICKY MEATBALL PASTA

In about 30 minutes, you can have a bowl of this dish on your table, homemade meatballs included. Serve with a simple green salad.

Hands-on time: 31 min. ★ **Total time: 31 min.**

1   (9-ounce) package refrigerated fresh fettuccine
12 ounces ground sirloin
½   cup panko (Japanese breadcrumbs)
⅓   cup chopped fresh basil
⅜   teaspoon kosher salt
¼   teaspoon freshly ground black pepper
2   garlic cloves, minced
1   large egg, lightly beaten
2   teaspoons olive oil
1¾ cups lower-sodium marinara sauce
1   ounce grated fresh Parmesan cheese (about ¼ cup)

1. Cook pasta according to package directions, omitting salt and fat. Drain over a bowl, and reserve ⅓ cup pasta water.

2. While pasta cooks, combine beef and next 6 ingredients (through egg); shape mixture into 16 meatballs. Heat a large skillet over medium-high heat. Add oil; swirl to coat. Add meatballs; cook 5 minutes, browning on all sides. Reduce heat to medium-low. Add marinara and ⅓ cup pasta water. Cover and cook 11 minutes or until meatballs are done. Divide pasta evenly among 4 plates; top evenly with sauce, meatballs, and cheese.

Serves 4

CALORIES 489; FAT 16.6g (sat 6.1g, mono 6.9g, poly 1g); PROTEIN 29.1g; CARB 71.6g; FIBER 2.6g; CHOL 147mg; IRON 2.4mg; SODIUM 688mg; CALC 110mg

CHILI—CORN CHIP PIE

Hands-on time: 40 min. ★ Total time: 40 min.

Cooking spray
1   **pound ground sirloin**
1¼   **cups chopped onion**
6   **garlic cloves, minced**
½   **teaspoon ground cumin**
½   **teaspoon ground red pepper**
⅛   **teaspoon kosher salt**
1   **tablespoon no-salt-added tomato paste**
1   **cup fat-free, lower-sodium beef broth**
⅓   **cup water**
1   **(10-ounce) can diced tomatoes and green chiles, undrained**
4   **ounces lightly salted corn chips**
1½   **ounces shredded sharp cheddar cheese (about ⅓ cup)**
¼   **cup fat-free sour cream**
½   **cup green onion strips**

1. Heat a large skillet over medium-high heat. Coat pan with cooking spray. Add beef to pan; sauté 5 minutes, stirring to crumble. Remove beef; drain. Wipe pan clean with paper towels. Add onion to pan; sauté 4 minutes, stirring occasionally. Add garlic; sauté 1 minute, stirring constantly. Stir in beef, cumin, pepper, and salt.

2. Stir in tomato paste; cook 1 minute, stirring occasionally. Add broth, ⅓ cup water, and tomatoes; bring to a boil. Reduce heat to medium, and simmer 15 minutes or until slightly thick, stirring occasionally. Remove from heat.

3. Place 1 ounce chips in each of 4 bowls, and top each serving with about ⅔ cup beef mixture, about 1½ tablespoons cheese, and 1 tablespoon sour cream. Sprinkle each serving with 2 tablespoons green onions.

Serves 4

CALORIES 414; **FAT** 21.9g (sat 7g, mono 7.6g, poly 5.5g); **PROTEIN** 24.5g; **CARB** 29.2g; **FIBER** 3.2g; **CHOL** 68mg; **IRON** 2.6mg; **SODIUM** 682mg; **CALC** 160mg

GRILLED FLANK STEAK
with onions, avocado, and tomatoes

Use colorful in-season heirloom tomatoes for a pretty presentation.

Hands-on time: 20 min. ★ Total time: 30 min.

2　medium-sized red onions, cut into ½-inch-thick slices
Cooking spray
1½　pounds flank steak, trimmed
1　teaspoon kosher salt, divided
1　teaspoon freshly ground black pepper, divided
2　cups cherry tomatoes, halved
¼　cup balsamic vinegar
1　ripe peeled avocado, cut into 8 wedges

1. Preheat grill to high heat.

2. Lightly coat onions with cooking spray. Place onions on grill rack; grill 10 minutes on each side or until tender. Place onions in a medium bowl; cover tightly with foil. Keep warm. Lightly coat steak with cooking spray; sprinkle steak with ¾ teaspoon kosher salt and ¾ teaspoon black pepper. Place steak on grill rack; grill 6 minutes on each side or until desired degree of doneness. Let stand 3 minutes. Cut steak diagonally across grain into thin slices.

3. Add tomatoes, balsamic vinegar, ¼ teaspoon kosher salt, and ¼ teaspoon black pepper to onions; toss gently to combine. Divide steak evenly among 6 plates; top with ½ cup tomato mixture. Cut avocado wedges in thirds crosswise. Top each serving with 4 avocado pieces.

Serves 6

CALORIES 262; **FAT** 13.6g (sat 4g, mono 7.7g, poly 1g); **PROTEIN** 24.3g; **CARB** 10.3g; **FIBER** 3.6g; **CHOL** 50mg; **IRON** 2.9mg; **SODIUM** 393mg; **CALC** 31mg

FEASTS:
dinners for a
CROWD
(or just two)

BIBIMBOP

Hands-on time: 50 min. ★ Total time: 66 min.

- 8 ounces water-packed extra-firm tofu, drained
- ⅓ cup water
- ¼ cup apple cider vinegar
- 2 teaspoons sugar, divided
- 2 teaspoons minced garlic, divided
- 1 teaspoon minced peeled fresh ginger, divided
- ¼ teaspoon crushed red pepper
- 1 cup julienne-cut carrot
- 2 tablespoons lower-sodium soy sauce
- 3 tablespoons plus 2 teaspoons dark sesame oil, divided
- 3 cups hot cooked short-grain rice
- 1 cup fresh bean sprouts
- 1 (5-ounce) package sliced shiitake mushroom caps
- 1 (9-ounce) package fresh baby spinach
- 1 teaspoon unsalted butter
- 4 large eggs
- 4 teaspoons gochujang (Korean chili paste)
- ¼ teaspoon kosher salt

1. Cut tofu into ¾-inch-thick slices. Place tofu in a single layer on several layers of paper towels; cover with additional paper towels. Let stand 30 minutes, pressing down occasionally.

2. Combine ⅓ cup water, vinegar, 1 teaspoon sugar, ½ teaspoon garlic, ½ teaspoon ginger, and crushed red pepper in a small saucepan. Bring to a boil. Add carrot, and remove from heat; let stand 30 minutes. Drain.

3. Remove tofu from paper towels; cut into ¾-inch cubes. Place tofu in a medium bowl. Combine 1 teaspoon sugar, ½ teaspoon garlic, ½ teaspoon ginger, soy sauce, and 1 tablespoon oil, stirring with a whisk. Add 1 tablespoon soy sauce mixture to tofu; toss gently. Let stand 15 minutes.

4. Heat a 10-inch cast-iron skillet over high heat 4 minutes. Add 1 tablespoon sesame oil; swirl to coat. Add rice to pan in a single layer; cook 1 minute (do not stir). Remove from heat; let stand 20 minutes.

5. Heat a large nonstick skillet over medium-high heat. Add 1 teaspoon oil; swirl to coat. Add 1½ teaspoons soy sauce mixture and bean sprouts to pan; sauté 1 minute. Remove sprouts from pan; keep warm. Add 1 teaspoon oil to pan. Add mushrooms to pan; sauté 2 minutes. Stir in 1½ teaspoons soy sauce mixture; sauté 1 minute. Remove mushrooms from pan; keep warm. Add 2 teaspoons oil to pan. Add tofu to pan; sauté 7 minutes or until golden brown. Remove tofu from pan; keep warm. Add 1 teaspoon oil to pan. Add 1 teaspoon garlic and 1 tablespoon soy sauce mixture; sauté 30 seconds. Add spinach to pan; sauté 1 minute or until spinach wilts. Remove spinach from pan; keep warm. Reduce heat to medium. Melt butter in pan. Crack eggs into pan; cook 4 minutes or until whites are set. Remove from heat.

6. Place ¾ cup rice in each of 4 bowls. Top each serving evenly with carrots, sprouts, mushrooms, tofu, and spinach. Top each serving with 1 egg and 1 teaspoon chili paste. Sprinkle evenly with salt.

Serves 4 (serving size: 1 bowl)

CALORIES 502; FAT 23.4g (sat 4.5g, mono 9.9g, poly 7.1g); PROTEIN 20.9g; CARB 56.4g; FIBER 6.1g; CHOL 214mg; IRON 6.8mg; SODIUM 698mg; CALC 199mg

BUTTERNUT SQUASH AND SPINACH LASAGNA

Hands-on time: 1 hr. 15 min. ★ **Total time: 2 hr.**

6   cups (½-inch) cubed peeled butternut squash
2   tablespoons extra-virgin olive oil, divided
2   tablespoons chopped fresh sage
1   teaspoon kosher salt, divided
½   teaspoon black pepper
12 garlic cloves, unpeeled (about 1 head)
Cooking spray
1   large onion, vertically sliced
2   tablespoons water
2   (9-ounce) packages fresh spinach
5   cups 1% low-fat milk, divided
1   bay leaf
1   thyme sprig
5   tablespoons all-purpose flour
6   ounces shredded fontina cheese (about 1½ cups), divided
3/8 teaspoon ground red pepper
¼   teaspoon grated whole nutmeg
9   no-boil lasagna noodles

1. Preheat oven to 425°.

2. Combine squash, 1 tablespoon oil, sage, ½ teaspoon salt, black pepper, and garlic in a large bowl; toss to coat. Arrange squash mixture on a baking sheet coated with cooking spray. Bake at 425° for 30 minutes. Cool slightly; peel garlic. Place squash and garlic in a bowl; partially mash with a fork.

3. Heat 1 tablespoon oil in a large Dutch oven over medium-high heat. Add onion, sauté 4 minutes. Reduce heat to medium-low; cook 20 minutes or until golden brown, stirring frequently. Place in a bowl.

4. Add 2 tablespoons water and spinach to Dutch oven; increase heat to high. Cover and cook 2 minutes or until spinach wilts. Drain in a colander; cool. Squeeze liquid from spinach. Add to onions.

5. Heat 4½ cups milk, bay leaf, and thyme in a medium saucepan over medium-high heat. Bring to a boil; remove from heat. Let stand 10 minutes. Discard bay leaf and thyme. Return pan to medium heat. Combine ½ cup milk and flour in a small bowl. Add to pan, stirring with a whisk. Bring to a boil; reduce heat, and simmer 5 minutes, stirring constantly. Remove from heat; stir in ½ teaspoon salt, 1¼ cups cheese, red pepper, and nutmeg.

6. Spread ½ cup milk mixture in bottom of a 13 x 9–inch glass or ceramic baking dish coated with cooking spray. Arrange 3 noodles over milk mixture; top with half of squash mixture, half of spinach mixture, and ¾ cup milk mixture. Repeat layers, ending with noodles. Spread remaining milk mixture over noodles. Bake at 425° for 30 minutes, and remove from oven. Sprinkle with ¼ cup cheese.

7. Preheat broiler. Broil 2 minutes or until cheese melts and is lightly browned. Let stand 10 minutes before serving.

Serves 8 (serving size: 1 piece)

CALORIES 360; FAT 11.9g (sat 5.4g, mono 4.7g, poly 1g); PROTEIN 16.6g; CARB 50g; FIBER 6.5g; CHOL 31mg; IRON 4mg; SODIUM 576mg; CALC 406mg

CHILES RELLENOS MADE EASY

A favorite at Mexican restaurants, this homemade version is easier and lighter, and delivers plenty of wow with a homemade sauce and creamy goat cheese.

Hands-on time: 43 min. ★ **Total time: 66 min.**

Cooking spray
1¼ cups coarsely chopped onion
2 cups chopped tomatoes
½ cup lower-sodium salsa verde
¼ teaspoon salt
¼ cup fresh cilantro
4 poblano chiles
4 ounces reduced-fat shredded Monterey Jack cheese (about 1 cup)
2 tablespoons goat cheese
3 large egg yolks
3 large egg whites
1.1 ounces all-purpose flour (about ¼ cup)
¼ teaspoon freshly ground black pepper
3 tablespoons cornmeal
¼ cup canola oil

1. Preheat broiler.

2. Heat a large skillet over medium-high heat. Coat pan with cooking spray. Add onion; sauté 4 minutes or until tender. Stir in chopped tomatoes, salsa verde, and ¼ teaspoon salt; cook 15 minutes or until thick, stirring frequently. Place tomato mixture in a food processor; add cilantro. Process mixture until smooth. Set aside.

3. Place poblanos on a foil-lined baking sheet; broil 3 inches from heat 8 minutes or until blackened and charred, turning after 6 minutes. Place in a paper bag; fold to close tightly. Let stand 15 minutes. Peel and discard skins. Cut a lengthwise slit in each chile; discard seeds, leaving stems intact. Spoon ¼ cup Jack cheese and 1½ teaspoons goat cheese in cavity of each chile.

4. Reduce oven temperature to 350°.

5. Lightly beat egg yolks in a small bowl. Place egg whites in a medium bowl; beat with a mixer at high speed until stiff peaks form. Fold egg yolks into egg whites. Combine flour and black pepper in a shallow dish. Place cornmeal in another shallow dish. Dredge poblanos in flour mixture, and dip into egg mixture. Dredge in cornmeal.

6. Heat a large stainless steel skillet over medium-high heat until hot. Add oil to pan; swirl to coat. Reduce to medium heat. Add coated poblanos to oil; cook 6 minutes or until crisp, turning to cook on all sides. Place chiles on a baking sheet, and bake at 350° for 8 minutes or until cheese melts. Serve with tomato sauce.

Serves 4 (serving size: 1 chile and about ⅓ cup sauce)

CALORIES 297; **FAT** 14.8g (sat 5.8g, mono 4.1g, poly 1.8g); **PROTEIN** 16.1g; **CARB** 25.6g; **FIBER** 2.7g; **CHOL** 159mg; **IRON** 1.9mg; **SODIUM** 562mg; **CALC** 254mg

CREAMY FOUR-CHEESE MACARONI

There's something about the way plain old macaroni cooks to a soft, silky texture that enhances the creaminess of this dish. Each hollow noodle gets coated inside and out with luscious sauce. Although we rarely use processed cheese, here it's the key to a supercreamy texture that does not rely on heavy cream. The result is a mac and cheese with half the fat and calories of traditional versions with no loss of richness.

Hands-on time: 29 min. ★ **Total time: 59 min.**

1.5 ounces all-purpose flour (about ⅓ cup)

2 ⅔ cups 1% low-fat milk

2 ounces shredded fontina or Swiss cheese (about ½ cup)

2 ounces grated fresh Parmesan cheese (about ½ cup)

2 ounces shredded extra-sharp cheddar cheese (about ½ cup)

3 ounces light processed cheese

6 cups cooked elbow macaroni (about 3 cups uncooked)

½ teaspoon salt

¼ teaspoon freshly ground black pepper

Cooking spray

⅓ cup crushed melba toasts (about 12 pieces)

1 tablespoon canola oil

1 garlic clove, minced

1. Preheat oven to 375°.

2. Weigh or lightly spoon flour into a dry measuring cup; level with a knife. Place flour in a large saucepan. Gradually add milk, stirring with a whisk until blended. Cook over medium heat until thick (about 8 minutes), stirring constantly with a whisk. Remove from heat; let stand 4 minutes or until sauce cools to 155°. Add cheeses, and stir until cheeses melt. Stir in cooked macaroni, salt, and black pepper.

3. Spoon mixture into a 2-quart glass or ceramic baking dish coated with cooking spray. Combine crushed toasts, oil, and garlic in a small bowl; stir until well blended. Sprinkle over macaroni mixture. Bake at 375° for 30 minutes or until bubbly.

Serves 8 (serving size: about 1 cup)

CALORIES 347; FAT 11.5g (sat 5.9g, mono 3.4g, poly 1.4g); PROTEIN 17.4g; CARB 43.8g; FIBER 1.9g; CHOL 29mg; IRON 1.7mg; SODIUM 607mg; CALC 346mg

make it ahead
You can make the tomato sauce up to a week in advance; keep it refrigerated in an airtight container. You can also broil the eggplant slices up to a few hours in advance.

EGGPLANT INVOLTINI

Ciao down on the flavors of Italy with this cheesy, fun vegetarian entrée.

Hands-on time: 1 hr. 8 min. ★ **Total time: 1 hr. 33 min.**

1 tablespoon extra-virgin olive oil

2 pounds tomatoes, seeded and coarsely chopped (about 3 large)

½ teaspoon kosher salt, divided

4 garlic cloves, crushed and divided

12 (¼-inch-thick) lengthwise slices eggplant (about 2 medium)

¼ teaspoon freshly ground black pepper

Cooking spray

2 tablespoons pine nuts, lightly toasted

1 ounce whole-wheat French bread, toasted and torn into pieces

8 ounces part-skim ricotta cheese

1 teaspoon grated lemon rind

1 large egg

¾ cup chopped fresh basil leaves, divided

2 ounces grated fresh Parmigiano-Reggiano cheese (about ½ cup), divided

1. Combine oil and tomatoes in a medium saucepan; stir in ¼ teaspoon salt and 2 garlic cloves. Bring to a boil over medium-high heat; reduce heat, and simmer 15 minutes or until reduced to 2 cups. Cool 10 minutes. Place mixture in a food processor; process until smooth. Set aside.

2. Preheat broiler.

3. Sprinkle eggplant slices with ¼ teaspoon salt and pepper; arrange slices in a single layer on a foil-lined baking sheet. Lightly coat eggplant with cooking spray. Broil 4 minutes on each side or until lightly browned. Cool 10 minutes.

4. Preheat oven to 375°.

5. Place 2 garlic cloves in a mini food processor; pulse until chopped. Add nuts and bread; pulse 10 times or until coarse crumbs form. Add ricotta, rind, and egg; process until smooth. Stir in ½ cup basil and ¼ cup Parmigiano-Reggiano.

6. Spread 1½ cups tomato sauce over the bottom of an 8-inch square glass or ceramic baking dish coated with cooking spray. Spread 2 tablespoons ricotta mixture onto each eggplant slice; roll up jelly-roll fashion. Place rolls, seam sides down, over sauce in dish. Spoon remaining sauce over rolls. Sprinkle with ¼ cup Parmigiano-Reggiano. Bake at 375° for 25 minutes or until bubbly. Sprinkle with remaining basil.

Serves 4 (serving size: 3 eggplant rolls)

CALORIES 323; **FAT** 16.2g (sat 6g, mono 5.2g, poly 2.6g); **PROTEIN** 18.3g; **CARB** 32.3g; **FIBER** 12.4g; **CHOL** 79mg; **IRON** 2.3mg; **SODIUM** 442mg; **CALC** 374mg

GNOCCHI WITH BROWNED BUTTER

If you like, add some fresh or fried sage leaves to this simple, comforting dish.

Hands-on time: 35 min. ★ Total time: 1 hr. 52 min.

2   (12-ounce) baking potatoes, unpeeled
1   teaspoon kosher salt
4.5 ounces all-purpose flour (about 1 cup)
¼   cup chopped fresh chives, divided
¼   teaspoon freshly ground black pepper
2   large eggs, lightly beaten
6   quarts boiling water
3   tablespoons butter
1   large garlic clove, crushed
¼   cup coarsely chopped walnut halves
2   tablespoons grated fresh Parmigiano-Reggiano or Grana Padano cheese

1. Place potatoes in a saucepan; cover with water. Bring to a boil over medium-high heat. Cook 40 minutes; drain. Cool; peel. Press potato flesh through a ricer. Spread potatoes on a baking sheet; sprinkle with salt. Cool.

2. Scoop potatoes into a large bowl. Weigh or lightly spoon flour into a dry measuring cup. Add flour, and toss. Form a well in center. Add 2 tablespoons chives, pepper, and eggs; stir. Turn dough out onto a lightly floured surface. Gently knead just until dough comes together (about 1 minute).

3. Cut dough into 4 equal portions, and roll each into a 22-inch-long rope. Cut each rope into 22 pieces. Score gnocchi with a fork. Cook half of gnocchi 3 minutes in 6 quarts boiling water. Repeat with remaining gnocchi; drain.

4. Melt butter in a large skillet over medium heat. Add garlic; cook 2 minutes. Add nuts; cook 2 minutes or until butter browns. Discard garlic. Set aside half of butter mixture. Add half of gnocchi to pan; toss. Cook 1 minute or until browned. Repeat with remaining butter and gnocchi. Divide gnocchi among 4 bowls. Sprinkle evenly with 2 tablespoons chives and cheese.

Serves 4 (serving size: about 22 gnocchi)

CALORIES 398; **FAT** 15.2g (sat 6.8g, mono 3.5g, poly 3.7g); **PROTEIN** 10.6g; **CARB** 56.4g; **FIBER** 3.6g; **CHOL** 78mg; **IRON** 3.4mg; **SODIUM** 606mg; **CALC** 73mg

SPINACH AND RICOTTA PIZZA

Hands-on time: 11 min. ★ **Total time: 1 hr. 28 min.**

12 ounces refrigerated fresh pizza dough

Cooking spray

1 tablespoon extra-virgin olive oil

3/4 cup New York–Style Pizza Sauce

1 tablespoon grated fresh Parmesan cheese

1½ cups loosely packed baby spinach leaves

1 teaspoon minced garlic

4 ounces fresh mozzarella cheese, sliced

1/3 cup part-skim ricotta cheese

2 plum tomatoes, cored and thinly sliced

1. Remove dough from refrigerator; let stand at room temperature 1 hour.

2. Preheat oven to 500°.

3. Coat a 12-inch perforated pizza pan with cooking spray.

4. Place dough on a lightly floured surface; roll into a 12-inch circle. Transfer dough to prepared pan, shaking off excess flour. Brush dough with oil. Spread New York–Style Pizza Sauce over dough, leaving a ¼-inch border. Sprinkle with Parmesan; top with spinach and garlic. Scatter mozzarella over spinach. Spoon teaspoonfuls of ricotta over mozzarella. Bake at 500° for 12 minutes or until mozzarella melts and crust browns. Let stand 5 minutes; top with tomato slices. Cut into 8 wedges.

Serves 6 (serving size: 1 wedge)

CALORIES 388; FAT 12.1g (sat 4.2g, mono 5.9g, poly 1.2g); PROTEIN 16.4g; CARB 52.5g; FIBER 3.2g; CHOL 20mg; IRON 1.4mg; SODIUM 458mg; CALC 261mg

New York–style pizza sauce

Hands-on time: 3 min. ★ **Total time: 3 min.**

7 tablespoons water

2 tablespoons chopped fresh basil

1½ tablespoons olive oil

2 teaspoons dried oregano

1½ teaspoons sugar

1 teaspoon minced garlic

1 (14.5-ounce) can petite-cut diced tomatoes, undrained

1 (6-ounce) can tomato paste

1. Combine all ingredients in a medium bowl; stir with a whisk.

Serves 10 (serving size: about ¼ cup)

CALORIES 40; FAT 1.9g (sat 0.3g, mono 1.4g, poly 0.2g); PROTEIN 1g; CARB 5.6g; FIBER 1.4g; CHOL 0mg; IRON 0.7mg; SODIUM 170mg; CALC 17mg

SEARED SCALLOPS
with Meyer lemon beurre blanc

Ask for "dry" scallops—this means they haven't soaked in a salty brine. They'll release less moisture in the pan as they cook, making it easier to get a gorgeous crust—and a perfect entrée for a romantic dinner.

Hands-on time: 32 min. ★ **Total time: 40 min.**

2/3   cup fresh Meyer lemon juice (about 6 lemons)
1/3   cup dry white wine
3   tablespoons minced shallots
2   thyme sprigs
3   tablespoons chilled butter, cut into pieces
3/4   teaspoon sugar
1/2   teaspoon salt, divided
1/4   teaspoon freshly ground black pepper, divided
Cooking spray
1 1/2   pounds dry sea scallops
1 1/2   teaspoons chopped fresh thyme (optional)

1. Combine first 4 ingredients in a small heavy saucepan over medium-high heat; bring to a boil. Cook until reduced to about ¼ cup (about 8 minutes). Remove from heat; discard thyme sprigs. Add butter, 1 piece at a time, stirring constantly with a whisk until butter is thoroughly incorporated. Strain mixture through a fine sieve over a bowl, pressing to release all of the sauce; discard solids. Stir in sugar, ¼ teaspoon salt, and ⅛ teaspoon pepper.

2. Heat a large cast-iron skillet over high heat. Coat pan with cooking spray. Sprinkle both sides of scallops with ¼ teaspoon salt and ⅛ teaspoon pepper. Add scallops to pan; cook 2 minutes. Turn scallops over; cook 1 minute or until desired degree of doneness. Serve scallops with sauce; sprinkle with chopped thyme, if desired.

Serves 4 (serving size: 4½ ounces scallops and 2 tablespoons sauce)

CALORIES 247; **FAT** 10g (sat 5.6g, mono 2.3g, poly 0.8g); **PROTEIN** 29g; **CARB** 10g; **FIBER** 0.2g; **CHOL** 79mg; **IRON** 0.7mg; **SODIUM** 633mg; **CALC** 52mg

STEAMED CLAMS
with white wine and tomatoes

This is a great dish to serve for a cozy night with friends—put the pot on the table and pass around a baguette. Cook clams within 24 hours of purchasing in order to ensure freshness. Be sure to throw out any clams that don't open after steaming.

Hands-on time: 24 min. ★ **Total time: 24 min.**

4   (½-inch-thick) slices diagonally cut French bread baguette
1½ cups dry white wine
½   cup fat-free, lower-sodium chicken broth
¼   teaspoon freshly ground black pepper
1   (14.5-ounce) can diced tomatoes, undrained
1   teaspoon olive oil
½   cup prechopped onion
1   teaspoon chopped fresh oregano
1   teaspoon chopped fresh rosemary
1   teaspoon chopped fresh thyme
48 littleneck clams in shells, scrubbed (about 3 pounds)
1   tablespoon chopped fresh parsley

1. Preheat broiler.

2. Arrange baguette slices on a baking sheet. Broil 5 inches from heat 2 minutes or until toasted.

3. Combine white wine and next 3 ingredients (through tomatoes) in a microwave-safe bowl. Microwave at HIGH 1 minute. Heat a Dutch oven over medium-high heat. Add oil to pan; swirl to coat. Add onion and next 3 ingredients (through thyme); sauté 2 minutes. Add wine mixture to pan; bring to a boil. Stir in clams; cover and cook 5 minutes or until clams open. Discard any unopened shells. Sprinkle with parsley, and serve with toasted baguette slices.

Serves 4 (serving size: about ⅓ cup broth, about 12 clams, and 1 toast slice)

CALORIES 237; **FAT** 2.8g (sat 0.4g, mono 1g, poly 0.6g); **PROTEIN** 17.8g; **CARB** 27.2g; **FIBER** 3.1g; **CHOL** 34mg; **IRON** 17.2mg; **SODIUM** 457mg; **CALC** 98mg

GRILLED MAINE LOBSTER TAILS
with miso butter

Lobster makes for a popular and great Valentine's Day dinner. Put a fresh twist on a romantic dish: Miso brings salty umami notes to the sweet, succulent lobster.

Hands-on time: 25 min. ★ **Total time: 25 min.**

3   tablespoons butter
2   teaspoons red miso (soybean paste)
4   (8-ounce) lobster tails, halved lengthwise
Cooking spray
Lemon wedges

1. Preheat grill to high heat.

2. Place butter and miso in a microwave-safe dish. Microwave at HIGH 30 seconds or until butter melts. Stir to combine.

3. Coat lobster tails with cooking spray. Place tails, flesh sides down, on grill rack coated with cooking spray; grill 4 minutes. Turn tails over; brush with butter mixture. Grill 3 minutes or until done, brushing occasionally with butter mixture. Serve with remaining butter mixture and lemon wedges.

Serves 4 (serving size: 1 lobster tail and about 1 tablespoon miso butter)

CALORIES 336; **FAT** 12.3g (sat 6g, mono 2.9g, poly 1.8g); **PROTEIN** 47.1g; **CARB** 6g; **FIBER** 0g; **CHOL** 182mg; **IRON** 2.8mg; **SODIUM** 586mg; **CALC** 114mg

SIMPLE LOBSTER RISOTTO

Risotto develops creaminess as the rice releases its starch during cooking. Lobster adds decadence, making this dish one that calls to you when you need to unwind and treat yourself. Simmering the shells infuses the broth with lobster flavor.

Hands-on time: 58 min. ★ **Total time: 63 min.**

4   cups fat-free, lower-sodium chicken broth
1½ cups water
3   (5-ounce) American lobster tails
3   tablespoons butter, divided
1   cup uncooked Arborio rice or other medium-grain rice
¾   cup frozen green peas, thawed

1. Bring broth and 1½ cups water to a boil in a saucepan. Add lobster; cover and cook 4 minutes. Remove lobster from pan; cool 5 minutes. Remove meat from cooked lobster tails, reserving shells. Chop meat.

2. Place shells in a large zip-top plastic bag. Coarsely crush shells using a meat mallet or heavy skillet. Return crushed shells to broth mixture. Reduce heat to medium-low. Cover and cook 20 minutes. Strain shell mixture through a sieve over a bowl, reserving broth; discard solids. Return broth mixture to saucepan; keep warm over low heat.

3. Heat 1 tablespoon butter in a medium saucepan over medium-high heat. Add rice to pan; cook 2 minutes, stirring constantly. Stir in 1 cup broth mixture, and cook 5 minutes or until liquid is nearly absorbed, stirring constantly. Reserve 2 tablespoons broth mixture. Add remaining broth mixture, ½ cup at a time, stirring constantly until each portion is absorbed before adding the next (about 22 minutes total).

4. Remove from heat, and stir in lobster, reserved 2 tablespoons broth mixture, 2 tablespoons butter, and green peas.

Serves 4 (serving size: 1 cup)

CALORIES 374; **FAT** 10.7g (sat 5.8g, mono 2.6g, poly 0.9g); **PROTEIN** 24.7g; **CARB** 44.4g; **FIBER** 4.1g; **CHOL** 80mg; **IRON** 2mg; **SODIUM** 620mg; **CALC** 63mg

make it foolproof

Toasting the rice in the butter for a few minutes before adding any liquid not only enhances the flavor of the rice, it also coaxes the rice to release its starch once you start adding broth. The starch, along with careful stirring, is what gives risotto its signature texture.

make it foolproof

Leeks can often be sandy. To clean them, slice the leek down the middle, but not all the way through. Rinse them under running water, fanning the layers apart to wash sand and grit away.

ARCTIC CHAR AND VEGETABLES
in parchment hearts

Seafood in parchment hearts is great for a dinner for two, not only because of the heart-shaped envelope, but also because you can prepare the packets a few hours in advance, leaving you free to set the scene for a romantic evening.

Hands-on time: 10 min. ★ Total time: 25 min.

1 tablespoon unsalted butter, softened
1 teaspoon grated lemon rind
1 tablespoon fresh lemon juice
1 teaspoon chopped fresh dill
2 (6-ounce) Arctic char fillets (about 1 inch thick)
¼ teaspoon kosher salt
⅛ teaspoon freshly ground black pepper
¼ cup julienne-cut leek
¼ cup julienne-cut red bell pepper
¼ cup julienne-cut carrot
¼ cup julienne-cut snow peas

1. Preheat oven to 450°.

2. Combine first 4 ingredients in a small bowl; stir until blended.

3. Cut 2 (15 x 24–inch) pieces of parchment paper. Fold in half crosswise. Draw a large heart half on each piece, with the fold of the paper along the center of the heart. Cut out the heart, and open. Sprinkle both sides of fillets with salt and pepper. Place 1 fillet near fold of each parchment heart. Top each fillet with half of vegetables and half of butter mixture. Start at top of heart and fold edges of parchment, sealing edges with narrow folds. Twist end tip to secure tightly. Place packets on a baking sheet. Bake at 450° for 15 minutes. Place on plates; cut open. Serve immediately.

Serves 2 (serving size: 1 fillet, ½ cup vegetables, and about 1 tablespoon sauce)

CALORIES 316; FAT 15g (sat 5.6g, mono 4.7g, poly 3.6g); PROTEIN 37g; CARB 5.5g; FIBER 1.4g; CHOL 105mg; IRON 1.3mg; SODIUM 445mg; CALC 39mg

CEDAR PLANK GRILLED SALMON
with mango-kiwi salsa

Serve this for a lively outdoor dinner party. Purchase wild Alaskan salmon for a sustainable seafood choice.

Hands-on time: 25 min. ★ **Total time: 40 min.**

1   **large cedar plank**
1   **cup finely diced peeled ripe mango**
½   **cup diced peeled kiwifruit**
2   **tablespoons chopped fresh cilantro**
1   **teaspoon extra-virgin olive oil**
1   **teaspoon fresh lime juice**
1   **serrano chile, finely chopped**
½   **teaspoon kosher salt, divided**
½   **teaspoon freshly ground black pepper, divided**
4   **(6-ounce) skinless salmon fillets**

1. Soak plank in water 25 minutes.

2. Preheat grill to medium-high heat.

3. Combine mango and next 5 ingredients (through chile). Add ¼ teaspoon salt and ¼ teaspoon pepper; set aside.

4. Sprinkle salmon with ¼ teaspoon salt and ¼ teaspoon pepper. Place plank on grill rack; grill 3 minutes or until lightly charred. Turn plank over; place fish on charred side. Cover; grill 8 minutes or until desired degree of doneness. Place 1 fillet on each of 4 plates; top each serving with ⅓ cup mango salsa.

Serves 4

CALORIES 267; **FAT** 7.5g (sat 1.2g, mono 2.5g, poly 2.6g); **PROTEIN** 34.7g; **CARB** 14.8g; **FIBER** 2.2g; **CHOL** 88mg; **IRON** 1.6mg; **SODIUM** 356mg; **CALC** 42mg

FANTASTIC BOURBON-SMOKED CHICKEN

Hands-on time: 20 min. ★ **Total time: 20 hr. 35 min.**

2	quarts water
9	tablespoons bourbon, divided
¼	cup packed dark brown sugar
3	tablespoons kosher salt
2	quarts ice water
1	tablespoon black peppercorns
1	tablespoon coriander seeds
3	bay leaves
3	garlic cloves, peeled
1	small onion, quartered
1	small Fuji apple, cored and quartered
1	lemon, quartered
1	(4-pound) whole chicken
2	cups applewood chips
½	teaspoon freshly ground black pepper
	Cooking spray
1	tablespoon butter, melted

1. Combine 2 quarts water, ½ cup bourbon, sugar, and kosher salt in a large Dutch oven, and bring to a boil, stirring until salt and sugar dissolve. Add 2 quarts ice water and next 7 ingredients (through lemon), and cool to room temperature. Add chicken to brine; cover and refrigerate 18 hours, turning chicken occasionally.

2. Soak wood chips in water 1 hour; drain.

3. Remove chicken from brine; pat chicken dry with paper towels. Strain brine through a sieve; discard brine, and reserve 2 apple quarters, 2 lemon quarters, 2 onion quarters, and garlic. Discard remaining solids. Sprinkle chicken cavity with pepper; add reserved solids to chicken cavity. Lift wing tips up and over back; tuck under chicken. Tie legs.

4. Remove grill rack, and set aside. Prepare grill for indirect grilling, heating one side to high and leaving one side with no heat. Pierce the bottom of a disposable foil pan several times with the tip of a knife. Place pan on heat element on heated side of grill; add 1 cup wood chips to pan. Place another disposable foil pan (do not pierce pan) on unheated side of grill. Pour 2 cups water in pan. Let chips stand 15 minutes or until smoking; reduce heat to medium-low. Maintain temperature at 275°.

5. Coat grill rack with cooking spray; place on grill. Place chicken, breast side up, on grill rack over foil pan on unheated side. Combine 1 tablespoon bourbon and butter; baste chicken with bourbon mixture. Close lid, and cook 2 hours at 275° or until a thermometer inserted into meaty part of thigh registers 165°. Add 1 cup wood chips halfway through cooking time. Place chicken on a platter; cover with foil. Let stand 15 minutes. Discard skin before serving.

Serves 4 (serving size: 5 ounces)

CALORIES 299; **FAT** 12.6g (sat 4.4g, mono 4.3g, poly 2.3g); **PROTEIN** 35.8g; **CARB** 6.2g; **FIBER** 1g; **CHOL** 114mg; **IRON** 1.8mg; **SODIUM** 560mg; **CALC** 30mg

MUSHROOM & SAUSAGE RAGÙ
with polenta

Cream cheese and butter stirred into polenta creates an inviting base for a savory, chunky sauce.

Hands-on time: 39 min. ★ **Total time: 39 min.**

1½ tablespoons olive oil, divided
8 ounces hot turkey Italian sausage
½ cup chopped onion
1 pound cremini mushrooms, sliced
2 large garlic cloves, minced
¼ teaspoon kosher salt, divided
1 (14.5-ounce) can no-salt-added diced tomatoes, undrained
2½ cups fat-free, lower-sodium chicken broth
1½ cups water
1 cup uncooked polenta
½ cup (4 ounces) ⅓-less-fat cream cheese
1 tablespoon unsalted butter

1. Heat a skillet over medium-high heat. Add 1½ teaspoons oil to pan; swirl to coat. Remove sausage from casings. Add sausage to pan; sauté 3 minutes or until browned, stirring to crumble. Remove sausage from pan.

2. Add remaining 1 tablespoon oil to pan; swirl to coat. Add onion; sauté 3 minutes, stirring occasionally. Add mushrooms; sauté 4 minutes, stirring occasionally. Add garlic; sauté 1 minute, stirring constantly. Stir in sausage, ⅛ teaspoon salt, and tomatoes; bring to a simmer. Reduce heat to medium; simmer 15 minutes.

3. Bring broth and 1½ cups water to a boil in a medium sauce-pan. Add polenta to pan, stirring well. Reduce heat to medium; simmer 20 minutes or until thick, stirring occasionally. Stir in remaining ⅛ teaspoon salt, cream cheese, and butter. Serve with sausage mixture.

Serves 4 (serving size: 1 cup polenta and 1 cup ragù)

CALORIES 428; **FAT** 18.7g (sat 8.4g, mono 8.5g, poly 1.4g); **PROTEIN** 18.2g; **CARB** 46g; **FIBER** 4.6g; **CHOL** 53mg; **IRON** 3.3mg; **SODIUM** 796mg; **CALC** 74mg

a good catch every hunting trip

My teenage son and I share a hobby that allows us to spend time together: hunting for wild mushrooms. Nothing is better than an outdoor adventure, chatting with my boy while searching for that rare windfall. Sometimes we are fortunate enough to find a coveted handful of mushrooms to add to the evening meal and a dish like Mushroom & Sausage Ragù. But even the times when we come back empty-handed, I return with a full heart, having shared meaningful time with my son.

- Elizabeth Cowie,
St. Louis, Missouri

TANDOORI GRILLED CHICKEN
with mint raita

Barbecued chicken, a backyard summer favorite, marinates here in an exciting, heady Indian spice blend and tangy yogurt. A cool, herby raita complements it perfectly.

Hands-on time: 1 hr. 50 min. ★ **Total time: 5 hr. 50 min.**

Marinade:
- ¾ **cup plain fat-free Greek yogurt**
- 2 **tablespoons chopped peeled fresh ginger**
- 1 **tablespoon paprika**
- 1 **tablespoon fresh lime juice**
- 1 **teaspoon chili powder**
- ¾ **teaspoon salt**
- ½ **teaspoon ground turmeric**
- ½ **teaspoon ground cumin**
- ⅛ **teaspoon ground red pepper**
- 3 **garlic cloves, chopped**
- 4 **(12-ounce) bone-in chicken leg-thigh quarters, skinned**

Raita:
- ¾ **cup plain fat-free Greek yogurt**
- ¾ **cup chopped seeded cucumber**
- 2 **tablespoons chopped fresh mint**
- ½ **teaspoon ground cumin**
- ¼ **teaspoon salt**

Cooking spray

1. To prepare marinade, place first 10 ingredients (through garlic) in a blender; process until smooth. Pour into a large zip-top plastic bag. Add chicken; turn to coat. Marinate chicken in refrigerator at least 4 hours or overnight.

2. To prepare raita, combine ¾ cup yogurt and next 4 ingredients (through ¼ teaspoon salt) in a small bowl; cover and refrigerate.

3. Remove chicken from refrigerator, and let stand at room temperature 45 minutes.

4. Prepare grill for indirect grilling. If using a gas grill, heat one side to medium-high and leave one side with no heat. If using a charcoal grill, arrange hot coals on either side of charcoal grate, leaving an empty space in the middle.

5. Remove chicken from marinade, and discard remaining marinade. Place chicken on unheated part of grill rack coated with cooking spray. Close lid, and grill 90 minutes or until a thermometer inserted into meaty part of thigh registers 165°, turning chicken every 20 minutes. Serve with raita.

Serves 4 (serving size: 1 chicken quarter and about ⅓ cup raita)

CALORIES 284; **FAT** 7.9g (sat 2g, mono 2.4g, poly 2g); **PROTEIN** 45.7g; **CARB** 4.9g; **FIBER** 0.7g; **CHOL** 161mg; **IRON** 2.5mg; **SODIUM** 502mg; **CALC** 76mg

QUINOA-STUFFED SQUASH

Sausage and cheese baked in small winter squash make a cold-weather comfort dish that you might want to eat with a spoon. Quinoa has a natural, bitter coating—be sure to rinse it thoroughly under cool water before cooking it.

Hands-on time: 37 min. ★ **Total time: 1 hr. 47 min.**

4 **(1-pound) golden nugget squash**
Cooking spray
2 **(4-ounce) links hot turkey Italian sausage, casings removed**
½ **cup finely chopped carrot**
½ **cup finely chopped onion**
2 **garlic cloves, minced**
½ **cup water**
2 **cups cooked quinoa**
2 **tablespoons chopped fresh parsley**
½ **teaspoon chopped fresh thyme**
¼ **teaspoon kosher salt**
¼ **teaspoon freshly ground black pepper**
3 **ounces reduced-fat shredded Monterey Jack cheese (about ¾ cup), divided**

1. Cut top quarter off each squash; reserve tops. Discard seeds. Arrange squash, cut sides down, in 2 (11 x 7–inch) glass or ceramic baking dishes. Fill each dish with 1 inch water; microwave 1 dish at HIGH 15 minutes. Remove dish; repeat with remaining dish. Cool.

2. Preheat oven to 350°.

3. Heat a large skillet over medium-high heat. Coat pan with cooking spray. Add sausage; sauté 5 minutes or until browned, stirring to crumble. Remove sausage with a slotted spoon. Add carrot, onion, and garlic to drippings in pan; sauté 2 minutes, stirring frequently. Stir in ½ cup water; bring to a boil. Reduce heat to medium; cover and cook 8 minutes or until carrot is tender.

4. Combine sausage, carrot mixture, quinoa, parsley, thyme, salt, and pepper; stir in ½ cup cheese. Stuff about 1 cup quinoa mixture in each squash, and top each serving with 1 tablespoon cheese. Arrange stuffed squash in a broiler-safe glass or ceramic baking dish, and place tops in dish. Bake at 350° for 20 minutes or until thoroughly heated. Remove from oven.

5. Preheat broiler.

6. Broil squash 4 minutes or until cheese is golden.

Serves 4 (serving size: 1 stuffed squash)

CALORIES 362; **FAT** 14.6g (sat 4.4g, mono 5.4g, poly 1.8g); **PROTEIN** 21.5g; **CARB** 39.4g; **FIBER** 4.7g; **CHOL** 53mg; **IRON** 4.6mg; **SODIUM** 620mg; **CALC** 238mg

make it ahead
You can cook the squash, prepare the filling, and refrigerate up to two days ahead. Then assemble and bake just before serving.

MAPLE-BRINED TURKEY

Hands-on time: 40 min. ★ **Total time: 20 hr. 40 min.**

Brine:
- 2   quarts apple cider
- ½   cup kosher salt
- ½   cup maple syrup
- 1   teaspoon allspice berries
- ¾   teaspoon whole black peppercorns
- ½   teaspoon whole cloves
- 6   (2-inch) strips orange rind
- 2   rosemary sprigs
- 2   bay leaves

Turkey:
- 1   (12-pound) fresh or frozen turkey, thawed
- 3   tablespoons butter, softened
- 2   teaspoons chopped fresh rosemary
- 2   teaspoons chopped sage
- ½   teaspoon black pepper
- 1   apple, cut into wedges
- 6   garlic cloves
- 1   rosemary sprig
- 1   sage sprig
- ½   orange, cut into wedges
- ½   onion, cut into wedges

Cooking spray

Gravy:
- 1   tablespoon butter
- 1   tablespoon chopped thyme
- 1   shallot, finely chopped
- ½   cup apple cider
- ¼   cup bourbon
- 1¼   cups fat-free, lower-sodium chicken broth, divided
- 3   tablespoons all-purpose flour
- 1   tablespoon chopped parsley
- 1   tablespoon cider vinegar

1. To prepare brine, combine first 9 ingredients (through bay leaves) in a large stockpot over high heat; cook 6 minutes or until salt dissolves, stirring occasionally. Remove from heat; add 1 gallon cold water. Cool to room temperature.

2. To prepare turkey, remove giblets and neck from turkey; reserve neck. Trim excess fat; add turkey to brine. Refrigerate 18 to 24 hours, turning occasionally.

3. Preheat oven to 375°. Remove turkey from brine; discard brine. Pat turkey dry. Starting at neck cavity, loosen skin from breast and drumsticks by inserting fingers, gently pushing between skin and meat. Combine 3 tablespoons butter and next 3 ingredients (through ½ teaspoon pepper) in a small bowl; rub butter mixture under loosened skin and over breast and drumsticks. Lift wing tips up and over back; tuck under turkey. Place apple and next 5 ingredients (through onion) in body cavity. Secure legs with kitchen twine. Place turkey on rack of a roasting pan coated with cooking spray. Place neck in bottom of roasting pan; place rack with turkey in pan. Bake at 375° for 1 hour and 15 minutes. Cover turkey loosely with foil; bake an additional 45 minutes or until a thermometer inserted into thickest part of thigh registers 165°. Remove from oven; place turkey on a cutting board. Let stand, covered, 20 minutes; discard neck and skin.

4. To prepare gravy, place a zip-top plastic bag inside a 2-cup glass measure. Pour pan drippings into bag; let stand 10 minutes. Seal bag; carefully snip off 1 bottom corner of bag. Drain drippings into a small bowl, stopping before fat layer reaches opening; discard fat.

5. Melt 1 tablespoon butter in a medium saucepan over medium-high heat. Add thyme and shallots; sauté 2 minutes. Add ½ cup cider and bourbon; boil 3 minutes or until liquid is reduced by half. Combine ¼ cup broth and flour, stirring with a whisk. Add flour mixture, 1 cup broth, and drippings to pan; bring to a boil. Reduce heat, and simmer 4 minutes or until thick. Stir in parsley and vinegar.

Serves 12 (serving size: 6 ounces turkey and 2½ tablespoons gravy)

CALORIES 326; FAT 8.4g (sat 3.9g, mono 2g, poly 1.5g); PROTEIN 51g; CARB 7g; FIBER 0.2g; CHOL 177mg; IRON 3.6mg; SODIUM 566mg; CALC 42mg

TEX-MEX HASH BROWN CASSEROLE

This fun skillet supper uses shredded potatoes as a base. The potato mixture cooks on the stovetop first to get it browned and crisp on the bottom.

Hands-on time: 45 min. ★ **Total time: 1 hr. 15 min.**

4 teaspoons canola oil, divided
4 ounces Mexican chorizo
3 garlic cloves, minced
1 cup enchilada sauce
⅓ cup grated white onion
½ teaspoon freshly ground black pepper
¼ teaspoon kosher salt
3 pounds Yukon gold or baking potatoes, peeled and shredded
1 large egg, lightly beaten
4 ounces shredded sharp cheddar cheese (about 1 cup)
½ cup sliced avocado
1½ teaspoons fresh lemon juice
¼ cup cilantro leaves
¼ cup thinly sliced white onion
6 thinly sliced radishes

1. Preheat oven to 450°.

2. Heat a 10-inch cast-iron skillet over medium-high heat. Add 1 teaspoon canola oil to pan, and swirl to coat. Remove casings from chorizo. Add chorizo to pan; sauté 3 minutes, stirring to crumble. Add garlic, and sauté 30 seconds. Remove sausage mixture from pan. Combine sausage mixture and enchilada sauce.

3. Add 1 tablespoon oil to pan; swirl to coat. Combine grated onion, pepper, salt, potato, and egg; toss. Add potato mixture to pan, pressing gently; cook 10 minutes (do not stir). Spread enchilada sauce mixture over potato mixture; sprinkle with cheese. Bake at 450° for 20 minutes. Remove from oven; let stand 10 minutes. Cut into 6 wedges.

4. Combine avocado and juice; toss gently. Stir in cilantro, onion, and radishes. Serve avocado mixture with casserole.

Serves 6 (serving size: 1 wedge)

CALORIES 432; FAT 20.2g (sat 7.5g, mono 9.2g, poly 2.1g); PROTEIN 17g; CARB 47.1g; FIBER 4.9g; CHOL 72mg; IRON 2.9mg; SODIUM 686mg; CALC 152mg

MAPLE-MUSTARD GLAZED FRESH HAM

Fresh ham is different from the cured ham you may be used to. It's juicy, full of rich pork flavor, and much less salty—a wonderful special-occasion roast. Serve with roasted Brussels sprouts and mashed sweet potatoes for a festive meal.

Hands-on time: 50 min. ★ **Total time: 13 hr. 25 min.**

2   teaspoons garlic powder
2   teaspoons ground cumin
2   teaspoons ground coriander
2   teaspoons Hungarian sweet paprika
1¼ teaspoons kosher salt
½   teaspoon freshly ground black pepper
1   (10-pound) shank portion, bone-in fresh ham, skin removed
Cooking spray
⅓   cup maple syrup
3   tablespoons Dijon mustard
2   tablespoons unsalted butter, melted

1. Combine first 6 ingredients in a small bowl. Score outside of ham in a diamond pattern; rub with spice mixture. Cover and chill overnight.

2. Remove ham from refrigerator; let stand at room temperature 1 hour.

3. Preheat oven to 425°.

4. Arrange ham, fat side up, on the rack of a roasting pan coated with cooking spray, and place rack in pan. Bake at 425° for 30 minutes. Reduce oven temperature to 350° (do not remove ham from oven); bake at 350° for 1½ hours.

5. Combine maple syrup, Dijon mustard, and butter. Turn ham, fat side down. Bake an additional 40 minutes, basting with syrup mixture every 20 minutes. Turn ham again. Baste with remaining syrup mixture, and bake an additional 35 minutes or until a thermometer inserted close to bone registers 145°. Let stand 20 minutes; remove excess fat, and slice.

Serves 16 (serving size: 3 ounces)

CALORIES 358; **FAT** 14.3g (sat 5.3g, mono 6.1g, poly 1.5g); **PROTEIN** 46.9g; **CARB** 7.3g; **FIBER** 0.2g; **CHOL** 140mg; **IRON** 2.4mg; **SODIUM** 381mg; **CALC** 26mg

SPANISH PORK
with apple-citrus salsa

Pimentón is a Spanish paprika made from peppers that have been slowly smoked and dried over oak fires. If pimentón is not available, use Spanish smoked paprika. Serve this smoky pork with lime wedges and cilantro leaves, if desired.

Hands-on time: 25 min. ★ **Total time: 59 min.**

1½ teaspoons chili powder
½ teaspoon dried oregano
½ teaspoon ground cumin
⅛ teaspoon pimentón
¾ teaspoon kosher salt, divided
½ teaspoon freshly ground black pepper, divided
2 tablespoons olive oil, divided
1 (1-pound) pork tenderloin, trimmed
2 cups diced Granny Smith apple
2 tablespoons chopped fresh cilantro
2 tablespoons apple juice
½ teaspoon grated lime rind
1½ teaspoons fresh lime juice
2 green onions, thinly sliced
½ jalapeño pepper, thinly sliced
Cooking spray

1. Combine first 4 ingredients. Stir in ½ teaspoon salt and ¼ teaspoon black pepper. Brush 1 tablespoon olive oil over pork, and sprinkle with chili powder mixture. Let stand 30 minutes at room temperature.

2. Preheat grill to medium-high heat.

3. Combine 1 tablespoon olive oil, ¼ teaspoon salt, ¼ teaspoon black pepper, apple, and next 6 ingredients (through jalapeño) in a medium bowl; toss.

4. Place pork on grill rack coated with cooking spray; grill 6 minutes on each side or until a thermometer registers 145°. Remove pork from grill; let stand 5 minutes. Slice pork crosswise; serve with salsa.

Serves 4 (serving size: 3 ounces pork and ½ cup salsa)

CALORIES 227; FAT 9.6g (sat 1.8g, mono 5.8g, poly 1.2g); PROTEIN 24.2g; CARB 10.7g; FIBER 2g; CHOL 74mg; IRON 1.5mg; SODIUM 453mg; CALC 21mg

make it foolproof

Don't skip the five minutes of standing time before cutting the tenderloin. Allowing meat to rest before cutting it will help it stay juicy—important when you're serving a lean cut like tenderloin.

BEEF AND BLACK BEAN ENCHILADAS

Hands-on time: 1 hr. ★ **Total time: 1 hr. 30 min.**

Sauce:

2   dried ancho chiles, stemmed
3   cups fat-free, lower-sodium chicken broth
1   (6-inch) corn tortilla, torn
1/3   cup cilantro leaves
2   teaspoons minced garlic
2   green onions, chopped

Enchiladas:

8   ounces ground sirloin
2   teaspoons olive oil
2   cups chopped onion
4   teaspoons minced garlic
1   teaspoon dried oregano
1/2   teaspoon ground cumin
1/4   teaspoon kosher salt
1   tablespoon no-salt-added tomato paste
2/3   cup rinsed and drained organic black beans
1/2   cup fat-free, lower-sodium chicken broth
1   tablespoon fresh lime juice
12   (6-inch) corn tortillas, at room temperature
   Cooking spray
2 1/2   ounces shredded sharp cheddar cheese (about 2/3 cup)
2   ounces shredded Monterey Jack cheese (about 1/2 cup)
3   green onions, thinly sliced
6   tablespoons Mexican crema

1. Preheat oven to 400°.

2. To prepare sauce, place ancho chiles in a medium saucepan. Add 3 cups broth; bring to a boil. Reduce heat, and simmer 5 minutes. Stir in 1 torn tortilla; simmer 5 minutes. Pour chile mixture into a blender; let stand 10 minutes. Add cilantro, 2 teaspoons garlic, and 2 chopped green onions to blender; process until smooth. Return mixture to pan; bring to a boil over medium heat. Cook until reduced to 2 cups (about 7 minutes). Remove sauce from heat.

3. To prepare enchiladas, heat a large skillet over medium-high heat. Add beef; sauté 5 minutes or until browned. Remove beef from pan using a slotted spoon; drain on paper towels. Wipe pan. Return pan to medium heat. Add oil to pan; swirl to coat. Add onion; cook 8 minutes or until tender. Add garlic and next 3 ingredients (through salt); cook 2 minutes, stirring constantly. Stir in tomato paste; cook 1 minute, stirring frequently. Stir in beef, beans, and 1/2 cup broth; bring to a boil, scraping pan to loosen browned bits. Cook 1 minute. Remove from heat; stir in juice.

4. Place 4 cups water in a saucepan over medium-high heat; bring to a simmer. Working with 1 tortilla at a time, dip tortillas in simmering water 2 to 3 seconds each or until softened. Place 1 tortilla on a flat work surface; spoon 3 tablespoons beef mixture onto 1 end of each tortilla. Roll up enchiladas, jelly-roll fashion. Repeat procedure with remaining tortillas and beef mixture. Spread 1/2 cup sauce in the bottom of a 13 x 9–inch baking dish coated with cooking spray. Arrange enchiladas, seam sides down, in dish. Pour remaining sauce over enchiladas. Top with cheeses. Bake at 400° for 20 minutes or until lightly browned and bubbly. Let stand 10 minutes. Sprinkle with 3 sliced green onions; serve with crema.

Serves 6 (serving size: 2 enchiladas and 1 tablespoon crema)

CALORIES 343; FAT 15.4g (sat 5.8g, mono 5.1g, poly 1.4g); PROTEIN 18.2g; CARB 35.7g; FIBER 6.9g; CHOL 48mg; IRON 2.6mg; SODIUM 540mg; CALC 236mg

LEBANESE PEPPERS

*The Lebanese often use ground lamb, but this version calls for ground beef.
The rice is precooked to ensure there are no crunchy bits in the flavorful meat
mixture. Take a bite—you'll see why this is a globetrotter's comfort food.*

Hands-on time: 50 min. ★ **Total time: 1 hr. 10 min.**

4	medium-sized red bell peppers
1	cup cooked long-grain white rice, cooled
½	cup fat-free, lower-sodium beef broth, divided
1	teaspoon freshly ground black pepper, divided
½	teaspoon ground allspice
½	teaspoon salt
¼	teaspoon ground cinnamon
¾	pound ground sirloin
2	cups water
½	cup chopped fresh parsley, divided
2	teaspoons olive oil
¾	cup chopped onion
1	teaspoon minced garlic
1	cup canned crushed tomatoes
¼	cup water
¼	teaspoon sugar
¼	teaspoon dried oregano
⅛	teaspoon crushed red pepper
2	tablespoons plain 2% reduced-fat Greek yogurt
4	lemon wedges

1. Preheat oven to 400°.

2. Cut tops off bell peppers; reserve. Discard seeds. Place peppers in a microwave-safe glass or ceramic baking dish; cover with damp paper towels. Microwave at HIGH 6 minutes. Let stand 5 minutes.

3. Combine rice, ¼ cup broth, ½ teaspoon black pepper, and next 4 ingredients (through beef). Divide beef mixture among peppers; top with tops. Pour 2 cups water into dish; cover. Bake at 400° for 45 minutes. Sprinkle peppers with ¼ cup parsley.

4. Heat a medium skillet over medium-high heat. Add oil to pan; swirl to coat. Add onion; sauté 8 minutes, stirring occasionally. Add garlic; sauté 30 seconds. Add ½ teaspoon black pepper, ¼ cup broth, tomatoes, and next 4 ingredients (through crushed red pepper); bring to a boil. Reduce heat; simmer 30 minutes. Stir in ¼ cup parsley and yogurt. Serve with lemon wedges.

Serves 4 (serving size: 1 stuffed pepper, about 3 tablespoons sauce, and 1 lemon wedge)

CALORIES 454; **FAT** 12.1g (sat 4.1g, mono 5.5g, poly 0.9g); **PROTEIN** 25.2g; **CARB** 60g; **FIBER** 6.2g; **CHOL** 56mg; **IRON** 5.8mg; **SODIUM** 507mg; **CALC** 90mg

COFFEE-RUBBED TEXAS-STYLE BRISKET

Coffee has long been used in barbecue sauces and gravies for the depth and nuanced flavor it adds. Here, it's mixed with salt, brown sugar, and spices for a rub that pairs perfectly with beef.

Hands-on time: 60 min. ★ **Total time: 8 hr. 45 min.**

6 cups oak or hickory wood chips
1 tablespoon ground coffee
1 tablespoon kosher salt
1 tablespoon dark brown sugar
2 teaspoons smoked paprika
2 teaspoons ancho chile powder
1 teaspoon garlic powder
1 teaspoon onion powder
1 teaspoon ground cumin
1 teaspoon freshly ground black pepper
1 (4½-pound) flat-cut brisket (about 3 inches thick)

1. Soak wood chips in water at least 1 hour; drain.

2. Combine coffee and next 8 ingredients (through pepper) in a bowl. Pat brisket dry; rub with coffee mixture.

3. Remove grill rack, and set aside. Prepare grill for indirect grilling, heating one side to high and leaving one side with no heat. Pierce bottom of a disposable foil pan several times with the tip of a knife. Place pan on heat element on heated side of grill; add 1½ cups wood chips to pan. Place another disposable foil pan (do not pierce pan) on unheated side of grill. Pour 2 cups water in pan on unheated side. Let chips stand 15 minutes or until smoking; reduce heat to medium-low. Maintain temperature at 225°. Place grill rack on grill. Place brisket in a small roasting pan, and place pan on grill rack on unheated side. Close lid; cook 6 hours or until a thermometer registers 195°. Add 1½ cups wood chips every hour for first 4 hours; cover pan with foil for remaining 2 hours. Remove from grill. Let stand, covered, 30 minutes.

4. Uncover brisket, reserving juices; trim and discard fat. Place a large zip-top plastic bag inside a 4-cup glass measure. Pour juices through a sieve into bag; discard solids. Let drippings stand 10 minutes (fat will rise to the top). Seal bag; carefully snip off 1 bottom corner of bag. Drain drippings into a bowl, stopping before fat reaches opening; discard fat. Cut brisket across grain into thin slices; serve with juices.

Serves 18 (serving size: 3 ounces)

CALORIES 156; **FAT** 4.4g (sat 1.6g, mono 1.8g, poly 0.2g); **PROTEIN** 24.9g; **CARB** 2.3g; **FIBER** 0.2g; **CHOL** 47mg; **IRON** 2.4mg; **SODIUM** 414mg; **CALC** 25mg

ROSEMARY-DIJON CRUSTED STANDING RIB ROAST

A standing rib roast is a bone-in prime rib roast. Serve with roasted potatoes and steamed haricots verts. If you cannot find pinot noir, substitute another dry red wine.

Hands-on time: 15 min. ★ Total time: 3 hr. 5 min.

1   **(5-pound) standing rib roast, trimmed**
1   **teaspoon salt**
1   **teaspoon freshly ground black pepper**
5   **garlic cloves**
¼   **cup Dijon mustard**
1½ **tablespoons chopped fresh thyme**
1   **tablespoon chopped fresh rosemary**
1   **tablespoon extra-virgin olive oil**
    Cooking spray
1½ **cups fat-free, lower-sodium beef broth**
⅔   **cup pinot noir**

1. Let beef stand 1 hour at room temperature. Sprinkle beef with salt and pepper.

2. Preheat oven to 400°.

3. Place garlic in a mini chopper, and pulse until finely chopped. Add Dijon mustard, thyme, rosemary, and oil; pulse to combine. Rub Dijon mixture over beef. Place roast on the rack of a roasting pan coated with cooking spray; place rack in pan. Bake at 400° for 30 minutes. Reduce oven temperature to 350° (do not remove roast from oven); bake at 350° for 30 minutes. Add broth to pan. Bake 30 minutes or until a thermometer registers 135° or until desired degree of doneness. Remove roast from oven, and let stand 20 minutes before slicing.

4. Heat roasting pan over medium-high heat; bring broth mixture to a boil, scraping pan to loosen browned bits. Stir in wine; boil 6 minutes or until reduced to ⅔ cup (about 6 minutes). Serve with beef.

Serves 12 (serving size: about 3 ounces beef and about 2½ teaspoons sauce)

CALORIES 255; **FAT** 15.4g (sat 5.7g, mono 6.7g, poly 0.7g); **PROTEIN** 23g; **CARB** 1.9g; **FIBER** 0.1g; **CHOL** 107mg; **IRON** 1.6mg; **SODIUM** 417mg; **CALC** 20mg

HERB AND CITRUS ROAST LEG OF LAMB

Orange and lemon in the marinade make for a bright counterpoint to the earthy cumin. Stuff leftovers into pitas, and drizzle with yogurt.

Hands-on time: 11 min. ★ **Total time: 10 hr. 46 min.**

3 tablespoons chopped fresh flat-leaf parsley
3 tablespoons chopped shallots
2 tablespoons chopped fresh oregano
2 tablespoons minced garlic (about 6 medium cloves)
2 tablespoons extra-virgin olive oil
2 tablespoons balsamic vinegar
1 tablespoon grated lemon rind
1 tablespoon grated orange rind
2 tablespoons fresh lemon juice
2 tablespoons fresh orange juice
1 teaspoon ground cumin
1 (6-pound) bone-in leg of lamb, trimmed
1 teaspoon salt
1 teaspoon freshly ground black pepper
Cooking spray

1. Combine first 11 ingredients (through cumin) in a small bowl, stirring well. Place lamb in a roasting pan; rub with garlic mixture. Cover with plastic wrap, and refrigerate 8 hours or overnight.

2. Remove lamb from refrigerator. Sprinkle lamb with 1 teaspoon salt and black pepper. Place lamb on the rack of a roasting pan coated with cooking spray, and place rack in pan. Let lamb stand 1 hour at room temperature.

3. Preheat oven to 425°.

4. Roast lamb at 425° for 30 minutes. Reduce oven temperature to 375° (do not remove lamb from oven); bake an additional 45 minutes or until a thermometer inserted into thickest portion of roast registers 135° or until desired degree of doneness. Let stand 20 minutes; slice.

Serves 16 (serving size: about 3 ounces)

CALORIES 241; FAT 9.4g (sat 3g, mono 4.3g, poly 0.9g); PROTEIN 35.2g; CARB 1.8g; FIBER 0.2g; CHOL 109mg; IRON 3.3mg; SODIUM 255mg; CALC 20mg

SLOW-BRAISED LAMB SHANKS

Tender lamb, lovingly prepared, will speak volumes to your dinner guests. Serve over mashed potatoes, polenta, or couscous.

Hands-on time: 30 min. ★ **Total time: 2 hr. 45 min.**

4　(12-ounce) lamb shanks, trimmed
¼　teaspoon freshly ground black pepper
1　teaspoon olive oil
1　cup chopped onion
1　teaspoon chopped fresh thyme
3　garlic cloves, minced
½　cup red wine
3　cups lower-sodium marinara sauce
½　cup fat-free, lower-sodium chicken broth
¼　cup thinly sliced fresh basil
2　teaspoons grated lemon rind

1. Heat a large Dutch oven over medium-high heat. Sprinkle lamb with pepper. Add oil to pan; swirl to coat. Add lamb to pan; cook 8 minutes, browning on all sides. Remove lamb from pan. Add onion, thyme, and garlic to pan; cook 2 minutes, stirring occasionally. Add wine to pan, scraping pan to loosen browned bits; cook until liquid evaporates (about 2 minutes). Stir in marinara sauce and broth; cook 4 minutes, stirring occasionally. Return lamb to pan. Cover; reduce heat to low, and simmer 2 hours or until very tender and meat pulls easily from the bone. Remove lamb from pan; skim any fat from surface of sauce, and discard. Increase heat to medium-high; bring sauce to a boil, and cook until sauce thickens (about 6 minutes). Add lamb; cook 2 minutes or until thoroughly heated. Remove pan from heat; stir in basil and rind.

Serves 4 (serving size: 1 shank and ¾ cup sauce)

CALORIES 426; FAT 18.7g (sat 7.3g, mono 7.3g, poly 1.2g); PROTEIN 33g; CARB 60.3g; FIBER 0.9g; CHOL 120mg; IRON 2.8mg; SODIUM 422mg; CALC 46mg

TOTALLY
perfect
MORNINGS:
breakfast & brunch

ANGEL BISCUITS

These angel biscuits are light, fluffy, and oh-so-delicious. Serve with bacon, scrambled eggs, and cheese for a homemade breakfast sandwich, or with supper for a tasty side.

Hands-on time: 10 min. ★ Total time: 1 hr. 23 min.

1 package dry yeast (about 2¼ teaspoons)
½ cup warm water (100° to 110°)
22.5 ounces all-purpose flour (about 5 cups)
¼ cup sugar
1 teaspoon baking powder
1 teaspoon baking soda
1 teaspoon salt
½ cup vegetable shortening
2 cups low-fat buttermilk
Cooking spray
1 tablespoon butter, melted

1. Dissolve yeast in ½ cup warm water in a small bowl; let stand 5 minutes.

2. Weigh or lightly spoon flour into dry measuring cups; level with a knife. Combine flour and next 4 ingredients (through salt) in a large bowl. Cut in shortening with a pastry blender or 2 knives until mixture resembles coarse meal. Add yeast mixture and buttermilk; stir just until moist. Cover and chill 1 hour.

3. Preheat oven to 450°.

4. Turn dough out onto a heavily floured surface; knead lightly 5 times. Roll dough to ½-inch thickness; cut with a 3-inch biscuit cutter. Place on a baking sheet coated with cooking spray. Brush melted butter over biscuit tops. Bake at 450° for 13 minutes or until golden.

Serves 24 (serving size: 1 biscuit)

CALORIES 150; **FAT** 4.6g (sat 1.2g, mono 1.5g, poly 1.3g); **PROTEIN** 3.6g; **CARB** 23.1g; **FIBER** 0.8g; **CHOL** 0mg; **IRON** 1.3mg; **SODIUM** 183mg; **CALC** 41mg

banana-lime jam

This jam is a great way to use overripe bananas, and it's supersimple to make.

Hands-on time: 5 min. ★ Total time: 50 min.

¾ cup packed brown sugar
½ cup granulated sugar
¼ cup fresh lime juice
3 overripe sliced bananas
2 tablespoons butter

1. Combine sugars and lime juice in a saucepan; bring to a boil. Add bananas, reduce heat to medium-low, and cook 45 minutes or until slightly thick, mashing banana occasionally with the back of a spoon. Stir in 2 tablespoons butter. The mixture will thicken as it cools. Store jam in an airtight container in refrigerator for up to 1 week.

Serves 16 (serving size: 2 tablespoons)

CALORIES 97; **FAT** 1.5g (sat 0.9g, mono 0.4g, poly 0.1g); **PROTEIN** 0.3g; **CARB** 21.8g; **FIBER** 0.6g; **CHOL** 4mg; **IRON** 0.1mg; **SODIUM** 16mg; **CALC** 11mg

ASPARAGUS QUICHE

Hands-on time: 40 min. ★ **Total time: 1 hr. 30 min.**

Crust:
- 3.9   ounces all-purpose flour (about ¾ cup plus 2 tablespoons)
- ¼   teaspoon salt
- 3   tablespoons chilled butter, cut into small pieces
- 1   tablespoon ice water

Cooking spray

Filling:
- 2   tablespoons butter
- 12   ounces asparagus, chopped
- ½   teaspoon salt, divided
- ¼   teaspoon freshly ground black pepper, divided
- 1   cup sliced green onions
- 3   ounces crumbled goat cheese (about ¾ cup)
- ¾   cup 2% reduced-fat milk
- 3   large eggs
- 1   large egg yolk

Dash of grated fresh nutmeg

1. To prepare crust, weigh or lightly spoon flour into dry measuring cups; level with a knife. Place flour and ¼ teaspoon salt in a food processor; pulse 2 times or until combined. Add ¼ cup chilled butter; pulse 4 times or until mixture resembles coarse meal. With processor on, add 1 tablespoon ice water through food chute, processing just until combined (do not form a ball).

2. Preheat oven to 425°.

3. Press dough gently into a 4-inch circle on plastic wrap. Cover and chill 20 minutes. Slightly overlap 2 sheets of plastic wrap on a slightly damp surface. Unwrap and place chilled dough on plastic wrap. Cover with 2 additional sheets of overlapping plastic wrap. Roll dough, still covered, into an 11-inch circle. Place dough in freezer 5 minutes or until plastic wrap can be easily removed.

4. Remove 2 sheets of wrap; let stand 1 minute or until pliable. Fit dough, plastic-wrap side up, into a 9-inch pie plate lightly coated with cooking spray. Remove remaining wrap. Press dough into bottom and up sides of pan; fold edges under and flute. Line pastry with foil; place pie weights or dried beans on foil. Bake at 425° for 15 minutes or until lightly browned. Remove weights and foil. Reduce oven temperature to 350°. Bake an additional 5 minutes or until golden. Remove pan from oven; cool on a wire rack.

5. To prepare filling, melt 2 tablespoons butter in a large skillet over medium-high heat. Add asparagus to pan. Sprinkle ¼ teaspoon salt and ⅛ teaspoon pepper over asparagus; sauté 8 minutes or until crisp-tender, stirring frequently. Add onions; sauté 2 minutes or until asparagus just begin to brown. Remove from heat. Spoon asparagus mixture into prepared shell in an even layer. Arrange goat cheese in an even layer over asparagus mixture.

6. Combine milk, eggs, and egg yolk. Stir in ¼ teaspoon salt, ⅛ teaspoon pepper, and nutmeg. Pour custard into pie plate. Bake at 350° for 30 minutes or until quiche is almost set in center. Remove from heat, and cool 5 minutes on wire rack before slicing.

Serves 8 (serving size: 1 wedge)

CALORIES 187; **FAT** 10.9g (sat 6.2g, mono 3g, poly 0.8g); **PROTEIN** 7.9g; **CARB** 15g; **FIBER** 1.8g; **CHOL** 114mg; **IRON** 2.3mg; **SODIUM** 355mg; **CALC** 81mg

BANANA-CHOCOLATE FRENCH TOAST

Hazelnut–chocolate spread and bananas between French toast will guarantee that everyone starts the day with a smile. Serve with cubed mixed fruit to round out the meal.

Hands-on time: 26 min. ★ **Total time: 26 min.**

¼ cup 1% low-fat milk
½ teaspoon granulated sugar
¾ teaspoon vanilla extract
⅛ teaspoon salt
2 large eggs, lightly beaten
6 (1½-ounce) slices whole-grain bread
4½ tablespoons hazelnut-chocolate spread
1 cup thinly sliced banana (about 8 ounces)
2 teaspoons canola oil
1½ teaspoons powdered sugar

1. Combine first 5 ingredients in a shallow dish.

2. Spread each of 3 bread slices with 1½ tablespoons hazelnut-chocolate spread; arrange ⅓ cup banana slices over each bread slice. Top sandwiches with remaining bread slices.

3. Heat a large nonstick skillet over medium-high heat. Add oil; swirl to coat. Working with 1 sandwich at a time, place in milk mixture, turning gently to coat both sides. Carefully place coated sandwiches in pan. Cook 2 minutes on each side or until lightly browned. Cut each sandwich into 4 triangles. Sprinkle with powdered sugar.

Serves 4 (serving size: 3 triangles)

CALORIES 390; FAT 13.8g (sat 3.6g, mono 6.8g, poly 3.2g); PROTEIN 11.7g; CARB 53.6g; FIBER 6g; CHOL 91mg; IRON 2.6mg; SODIUM 391mg; CALC 115mg

BREAKFAST POLENTA
with warm berry compote

Use the extra compote as a topping for pancakes, waffles, or ice cream.

Hands-on time: 23 min. ★ **Total time: 23 min.**

Compote:
- **1** tablespoon butter
- **3** tablespoons honey
- **1** tablespoon fresh lemon juice
- **Dash of ground cinnamon**
- **1** (12-ounce) bag assorted frozen berries

Polenta:
- **3** cups 1% low-fat milk
- **1/2** cup dry instant polenta
- **2** tablespoons sugar
- **1/2** teaspoon salt

1. To prepare compote, melt butter in a medium saucepan over medium heat. Add honey, juice, cinnamon, and berries; bring to a boil. Reduce heat; simmer 5 minutes or until thoroughly heated. Keep warm.

2. To prepare polenta, bring milk to a boil in a medium saucepan. Slowly add polenta, stirring constantly with a whisk. Stir in sugar and salt, and cook 5 minutes or until thick, stirring constantly. Serve with compote.

Serves 4 (serving size: 2/3 cup polenta and 1/3 cup compote)

CALORIES 285; FAT 4.9g (sat 3g, mono 1.4g, poly 0.2g); PROTEIN 8.5g; CARB 54.2g; FIBER 3.9g; CHOL 15mg; IRON 1.2mg; SODIUM 386mg; CALC 541mg

make it foolproof

Keep pancakes warm by placing them on a baking sheet in an oven at low temperature. Leave the pancakes uncovered to prevent them from becoming gummy.

BLUEBERRY BUTTERMILK PANCAKES

Start a happy weekend morning tradition with homemade pancakes for the family. Blueberries, either fresh or frozen, give ordinary flapjacks a big flavor boost.

Hands-on time: 27 min. ★ Total time: 27 min.

9   ounces all-purpose flour (about 2 cups)
1   tablespoon sugar
1   teaspoon baking powder
1   teaspoon salt
1/2   teaspoon baking soda
1 1/2   cups low-fat buttermilk
1/2   cup 1% low-fat milk
1   tablespoon canola oil
1   large egg, lightly beaten
Cooking spray
2   cups blueberries

1. Weigh or lightly spoon flour into dry measuring cups; level with a knife. Combine flour, sugar, baking powder, salt, and baking soda in a large bowl. Combine buttermilk, milk, oil, and egg in a bowl, and add to flour mixture, stirring until smooth.

2. Spoon 1/4 cup pancake batter onto a hot nonstick griddle or large nonstick skillet coated with cooking spray, and top with 2 heaping tablespoons blueberries. Turn pancake when top is covered with bubbles and edges look cooked. Repeat procedure with remaining batter and blueberries.

Serves 6 (serving size: 2 [5-inch] pancakes)

CALORIES 261; **FAT** 5.3g (sat 1.5g, mono 1.5g, poly 1.7g); **PROTEIN** 8.6g; **CARB** 45g; **FIBER** 2.4g; **CHOL** 38mg; **IRON** 2.2mg; **SODIUM** 536mg; **CALC** 159mg

CHEWY COCONUT GRANOLA BARS

Supereasy to make, these are perfect for breakfast, in the car, or as a snack.

Hands-on time: 15 min. ★ **Total time: 35 min.**

Cooking spray
2   teaspoons all-purpose flour
3   ounces all-purpose flour (about ⅔ cup)
1.6 ounces whole-wheat flour (about ⅓ cup)
1   teaspoon baking powder
½   teaspoon salt
1¼   cups packed brown sugar
¼   cup canola oil
2   tablespoons fat-free milk
2   large eggs
1½   cups whole-grain granola
¾   cup chopped dried mixed tropical fruit
½   cup flaked sweetened coconut

1. Preheat oven to 350°.

2. Coat a 13 x 9–inch metal baking pan with cooking spray; dust with 2 teaspoons all-purpose flour.

3. Weigh or lightly spoon 3 ounces all-purpose flour and 1.6 ounces whole-wheat flour into dry measuring cups; level with a knife. Combine flours, baking powder, and salt in a small bowl; stir with a whisk. Combine sugar, oil, milk, and eggs in a large bowl; beat with a mixer at high speed until smooth. Add flour mixture, beating at low speed until blended. Fold in granola and fruit. Spoon batter into prepared pan. Sprinkle with coconut.

4. Bake at 350° for 20 minutes or until golden. Cool completely in pan on a wire rack. Cut into bars.

Serves 16 (serving size: 1 bar)

CALORIES 154; FAT 5.8g (sat 1.5g, mono 2.5g, poly 1.1g); PROTEIN 2.7g; CARB 23.4g; FIBER 1.7g; CHOL 26mg; IRON 1mg; SODIUM 148mg; CALC 36mg

CHOCOLATE CHIP 'N' COFFEE MUFFINS

Every bite delivers a jolt of coffee flavor and chunks of chocolate.
Enjoy them each morning with your favorite cup of joe.

Hands-on time: 17 min. ★ **Total time: 35 min.**

²/₃ cup whole milk
5 tablespoons butter, melted
3 tablespoons instant coffee granules
1¹/₂ teaspoons vanilla extract
1 large egg, lightly beaten
9 ounces all-purpose flour (about 2 cups)
²/₃ cup sugar
¹/₂ cup semisweet chocolate chips
2 teaspoons baking powder
¹/₄ teaspoon salt
Cooking spray

1. Preheat oven to 400°.

2. Combine first 5 ingredients.

3. Weigh or lightly spoon flour into dry measuring cups; level with a knife. Combine flour and next 4 ingredients (through salt) in a large bowl; stir well with a whisk. Make a well in center of flour mixture. Add milk mixture to flour mixture; stir just until moist.

4. Spoon batter into 12 muffin cups coated with cooking spray. Bake at 400° for 18 minutes or until done. Remove muffins from pan immediately; cool on a wire rack.

Serves 12 (serving size: 1 muffin)

CALORIES 214; **FAT** 7.9g (sat 4.8g, mono 2.2g, poly 0.4g); **PROTEIN** 3.6g; **CARB** 32.9g; **FIBER** 1g; **CHOL** 29mg; **IRON** 1.3mg; **SODIUM** 163mg; **CALC** 66mg

EGGS BLINDFOLDED OVER GARLIC-CHEDDAR GRITS

Many grits lovers say the most flavorful variety is stone-ground yellow grits, which will also take longer to cook (but can be worth the wait). Take your pick before preparing this recipe: Stone-ground grits are more coarse than regular grits; instant grits have been precooked and dehydrated.

Hands-on time: 10 min. ★ Total time: 10 min.

Grits:

2 ½ cups hot cooked grits
3 tablespoons grated cheddar cheese
½ teaspoon garlic powder
½ teaspoon salt
½ teaspoon freshly ground black pepper

Eggs:

Cooking spray
4 large eggs, divided
½ cup ice cubes, divided
Freshly ground black pepper (optional)
Chopped chives (optional)

1. To prepare grits, combine grits, cheddar, garlic powder, salt, and ½ teaspoon pepper in a large bowl; keep warm.

2. To prepare eggs, heat a small skillet over medium heat. Coat pan with cooking spray. Break 2 eggs in pan; cook 1 minute or until whites are set. Add ¼ cup ice cubes to pan; cover and cook 2 minutes or until eggs are done. Remove from pan. Repeat procedure with remaining 2 eggs and ¼ cup ice. Serve eggs over grits. Garnish with black pepper and chives, if desired.

Serves 4 (serving size: 1 egg and about ⅔ cup grits)

CALORIES 184; FAT 7g (sat 2.7g, mono 2.5g, poly 0.9g); PROTEIN 9.8g; CARB 20.3g; FIBER 0.6g; CHOL 217mg; IRON 1.9mg; SODIUM 474mg; CALC 71mg

make it ahead
You can make the sauce up to three days ahead; prepare through step 1, cool, cover, and refrigerate. Bring back to a gentle simmer before proceeding.

EGGS POACHED IN CURRIED TOMATO SAUCE

Here's an exciting wake-up call: Eggs gently cooked in an Indian-inspired tomato sauce. Make this dish less spicy by removing the jalapeño's seeds.

Hands-on time: 42 min. ★ **Total time: 42 min.**

2	tablespoons peanut oil
1½	cups chopped onion
1	tablespoon minced garlic
1	tablespoon minced peeled fresh ginger
1	jalapeño pepper, minced
2	teaspoons curry powder
¼	teaspoon kosher salt
¼	teaspoon freshly ground black pepper

Dash of sugar

1	(28-ounce) can no-salt-added diced tomatoes, undrained
½	cup chopped fresh cilantro
½	cup light coconut milk
4	large eggs
4	whole-wheat English muffins, split and toasted
¼	cup chopped green onions

Cilantro leaves (optional)

1. Heat a large skillet over medium-high heat. Add oil; swirl to coat. Add onion and next 3 ingredients (through jalapeño); sauté 5 minutes or until vegetables are tender, stirring occasionally. Add curry powder and next 3 ingredients (through sugar); cook 2 minutes, stirring constantly. Drain tomatoes in a colander over a bowl; reserve liquid. Add tomatoes to pan; cook 5 minutes, stirring frequently. Add half of reserved tomato liquid; bring to a boil. Add chopped cilantro and coconut milk; return to a boil. Cover, reduce heat, and simmer 10 minutes. If sauce is too thick, add remaining reserved tomato liquid; maintain heat so that sauce bubbles gently.

2. Break each egg into a custard cup, and pour gently into pan over sauce. Cover and cook 5 minutes, just until whites are set and yolks have filmed over but are still runny. Arrange 1 muffin, cut sides up, on each of 4 plates. Carefully scoop 1 egg and about ½ cup sauce onto each serving. Sprinkle each serving with 1 tablespoon green onions; garnish with cilantro leaves, if desired.

Serves 4

CALORIES 357; **FAT** 14.4g (sat 4.4g, mono 5.2g, poly 3.6g); **PROTEIN** 14.1g; **CARB** 44.2g; **FIBER** 6g; **CHOL** 186mg; **IRON** 4.3mg; **SODIUM** 473mg; **CALC** 189mg

FINGERLING POTATO-LEEK HASH
with Swiss chard and eggs
To trim Swiss chard, pull or cut the stems away from the leaves.

Hands-on time: 43 min. ★ **Total time: 43 min.**

2 tablespoons extra-virgin olive oil

2 cups sliced leek (about 2 large)

12 ounces fingerling potatoes, cut in half lengthwise (about 4 cups)

2 garlic cloves, minced

1¼ teaspoons Spanish smoked paprika, divided

½ teaspoon salt, divided

½ teaspoon coarsely ground black pepper, divided

4 cups thinly sliced trimmed Swiss chard (about 1 bunch)

4 large eggs

1 ounce shredded Gruyère cheese (about ¼ cup)

1. Heat a large skillet over medium heat. Add oil to pan; swirl to coat. Add leek; cook 8 minutes, stirring frequently. Add potatoes and garlic; cook 15 minutes or until potatoes are tender, stirring occasionally. Stir in 1 teaspoon paprika, ¼ teaspoon salt, and ¼ teaspoon pepper. Add chard; cook 4 minutes, stirring constantly. Using a spoon, push potato mixture aside to make 4 egg-sized spaces. Crack 1 egg into each space; sprinkle ¼ teaspoon salt, ¼ teaspoon pepper, and ¼ teaspoon paprika over eggs. Cover and cook 3 minutes; sprinkle cheese over potato mixture. Cover and cook 2 minutes or until egg yolks are lightly set.

Serves 4 (serving size: about 1½ cups potato mixture and 1 egg)

CALORIES 261; **FAT** 13.5g (sat 3.5g, mono 7.6g, poly 1.8g); **PROTEIN** 11.6g; **CARB** 23.6g; **FIBER** 3.2g; **CHOL** 188mg; **IRON** 3.4mg; **SODIUM** 480mg; **CALC** 156mg

FRENCH TOAST
with maple-apple compote

Challah is a rich, traditional Jewish bread; substitute Hawaiian bread if challah isn't available. Maple and apples make this a nostalgic, warming meal.

Hands-on time: 39 min. ★ **Total time: 39 min.**

Compote:
Cooking spray
1   **tablespoon butter**
3   **cups sliced peeled Pink Lady apples (about 1½ pounds)**
¼   **cup maple syrup**
½   **teaspoon ground cinnamon**
French toast:
2   **tablespoons granulated sugar**
1   **teaspoon ground cinnamon**
1   **cup 2% reduced-fat milk**
2   **teaspoons vanilla extract**
⅛   **teaspoon salt**
4   **large eggs, lightly beaten**
12   **(1-ounce) slices challah**
4   **teaspoons butter**
Powdered sugar (optional)

1. Preheat oven to 250°. Place a wire rack on a baking sheet and place in oven.

2. To prepare compote, heat a large nonstick skillet over medium-high heat. Coat pan with cooking spray; melt 1 tablespoon butter in pan. Add apples to pan; sauté 8 minutes or until tender. Stir in maple syrup and ½ teaspoon cinnamon. Keep warm.

3. To prepare French toast, combine granulated sugar and 1 teaspoon cinnamon in a medium bowl, stirring with a whisk. Add milk, vanilla, salt, and eggs; whisk until well blended. Working with 1 bread slice at a time, place bread slice in milk mixture, turning gently to coat both sides.

4. Heat a large nonstick skillet over medium-high heat. Melt 1 teaspoon butter in pan. Add 3 coated bread slices; cook 2 minutes on each side or until lightly browned. Place on wire rack in oven to keep warm. Repeat procedure 3 times with cooking spray, remaining butter, and remaining bread slices. Serve French toast with compote. Sprinkle with powdered sugar, if desired.

Serves 6 (serving size: 2 pieces toast and about ⅓ cup compote)

CALORIES 370; **FAT** 12.1g (sat 5.3g, mono 4g, poly 1.3g); **PROTEIN** 11.3g; **CARB** 55.3g; **FIBER** 2.9g; **CHOL** 185mg; **IRON** 2.7mg; **SODIUM** 427mg; **CALC** 146mg

GRANOLA
with honey-scented yogurt and baked figs

Hands-on time: 18 min. ★ **Total time: 53 min.**

1   cup old-fashioned rolled oats
¹/₃   cup chopped pecans
1¹/₈   teaspoons vanilla extract, divided
1   large egg white
2   tablespoons brown sugar
³/₈   teaspoon ground cinnamon, divided
¹/₄   teaspoon salt, divided
¹/₈   teaspoon ground nutmeg
2   tablespoons maple syrup
Cooking spray
2   tablespoons plus 2 teaspoons honey, divided
9   firm, fresh dark-skinned figs, stemmed and quartered
3   cups plain fat-free Greek yogurt

1. Preheat oven to 300°. Combine oats and pecans in a small bowl. Combine ⅛ teaspoon vanilla and egg white in a medium bowl; beat egg mixture with a mixer at medium speed until foamy. Fold oat mixture into egg white mixture. Combine brown sugar, ¼ teaspoon cinnamon, ⅛ teaspoon salt, and nutmeg; fold sugar mixture into oat mixture. Fold in maple syrup.

2. Spread granola on a foil-lined baking sheet coated with cooking spray. Bake at 300° for 25 minutes, stirring once. Remove granola from oven; stir to loosen granola from foil. Cool on a wire rack.

3. Increase oven temperature to 350°. Combine 2 teaspoons honey and 1 teaspoon vanilla in a large bowl; add figs, stirring gently. Place figs, cut sides up, in a single layer on a foil-lined baking sheet. Sprinkle figs with ⅛ teaspoon cinnamon and ⅛ teaspoon salt.

4. Bake at 350° for 10 minutes or until fig juices begin to bubble. Remove from oven, and cool completely. Combine 2 tablespoons honey and yogurt in a small bowl. Spoon ½ cup yogurt mixture into each of 6 bowls; top each serving with about 2½ tablespoons granola and 6 fig quarters.

Serves 6

CALORIES 277; **FAT** 5.6g (sat 0.6g, mono 2.9g, poly 1.8g); **PROTEIN** 13.3g; **CARB** 45.7g; **FIBER** 4.2g; **CHOL** 0mg; **IRON** 1.2mg; **SODIUM** 152mg; **CALC** 117mg

make it foolproof

Phyllo dough is fragile, but you'll get great results with a few tips. First, thaw the phyllo in its package overnight in the refrigerator. As you work with it, keep it covered with plastic wrap to prevent it from drying out and breaking.

INDIVIDUAL APPLE STRUDELS

Crunchy, flaky, sweet—breakfast doesn't get more fun. You can make these several hours ahead; tent loosely with foil and leave at room temperature. Put in a 400° oven for a few minutes to warm and crisp just before serving.

Hands-on time: 34 min. ★ **Total time: 69 min.**

½ cup shelled dry-roasted pistachios
4 cups diced peeled apple (about 1½ pounds)
¼ cup turbinado sugar
1 tablespoon cornstarch
½ teaspoon ground cardamom
32 (14 x 9-inch) sheets frozen whole-wheat phyllo dough, thawed
3 tablespoons unsalted butter, melted
2 tablespoons powdered sugar

1. Preheat oven to 375°.

2. Place pistachios in a food processor; process until finely ground.

3. Combine apple, turbinado sugar, cornstarch, and cardamom in a large bowl; toss well.

4. Stack 2 phyllo sheets on a large cutting board or work surface (cover remaining dough to keep from drying). Lightly brush phyllo stack with butter; sprinkle with about 1 tablespoon ground pistachios. Top with 2 more phyllo sheets. Spoon about ½ cup apple mixture along 1 short edge of phyllo stack, leaving a 2-inch border on all sides. Fold over long edges of phyllo to cover about 1½ inches of apple mixture on each end. Starting at short edge with 2-inch border, roll up jelly-roll fashion. (Do not roll tightly, or the strudel may split.) Place strudel, seam side down, on a baking sheet lined with parchment paper. Repeat procedure with remaining phyllo sheets, butter, pistachios, and apple mixture to form 8 strudels total.

5. Pierce each strudel 2 times with a fork. Brush tops with remaining butter. Bake at 375° for 35 minutes or until crisp and golden brown. Sprinkle with 2 tablespoons powdered sugar. Serve strudels warm or at room temperature.

Serves 8 (serving size: 1 strudel)

CALORIES 278; FAT 10.8g (sat 3.9g, mono 4.5g, poly 1.7g); PROTEIN 5.3g; CARB 41.8g; FIBER 2.7g; CHOL 11.5mg; IRON 1.9mg; SODIUM 261mg; CALC 19mg

LIBANAIS BREAKFAST

Go on a culinary journey first thing in the morning, and enjoy this Middle Eastern–inspired breakfast with crisp pita toasts. Or, to make a breakfast buffet, serve with a simple cucumber salad and baba ghanoush.

Hands-on time: 20 min. ★ **Total time: 1 hr. 11 min.**

3   **(6-inch) pitas, each cut into 8 wedges**
¼   **cup extra-virgin olive oil, divided**
1   **cup water**
¼   **cup uncooked bulgur**
1   **cup chopped seeded plum tomato**
¾   **cup chopped fresh parsley**
3   **tablespoons finely chopped red onion**
2   **tablespoons chopped fresh mint**
3   **tablespoons fresh lemon juice**
¾   **teaspoon salt, divided**
½   **teaspoon freshly ground black pepper, divided**
⅛   **teaspoon ground red pepper**
6   **large eggs**

1. Preheat oven to 350°.

2. Arrange pita wedges in a single layer on a baking sheet. Lightly brush pita wedges with 2 tablespoons oil; bake at 350° for 20 minutes or until golden.

3. Combine 1 cup water and bulgur in a large bowl. Let stand 30 minutes or until bulgur is tender. Drain bulgur through a fine sieve; discard liquid. Place bulgur in a medium bowl. Add 2 table-spoons oil, tomato, parsley, onion, mint, juice, ½ teaspoon salt, ¼ teaspoon black pepper, and red pepper; toss well. Refrigerate 30 minutes.

4. Bring a medium saucepan of water to a boil. With a slotted spoon, carefully lower eggs into pan; cook 6 minutes. Drain and rinse eggs with cold running water until cool (about 1 minute). Peel eggs and cut in half. Place ⅓ cup tabbouleh and 4 pita wedges on each of 6 plates; top each serving with 2 egg halves. Sprinkle eggs with ¼ teaspoon salt and ¼ teaspoon black pepper.

Serves 6

CALORIES 262; FAT 14.2g (sat 2.8g, mono 8.5g, poly 1.7g); PROTEIN 11g; CARB 23.9g; FIBER 2.3g; CHOL 212mg; IRON 3mg; SODIUM 452mg; CALC 65mg

MAKE-AHEAD OOEY-GOOEY STICKY BUNS

Hands-on time: 28 min. ★ **Total time: 9 hr. 36 min.**

1 package dry yeast
(about 2 ¼ teaspoons)
1 teaspoon granulated
sugar
¼ cup warm water
(100° to 110°)
18 ounces all-purpose flour
(about 4 cups), divided
¼ cup granulated sugar
1 teaspoon ground nutmeg
¾ teaspoon salt
1 cup evaporated fat-free
milk, divided
¼ cup water
1 large egg, lightly beaten
Cooking spray
1¼ cups packed dark brown
sugar, divided
⅓ cup dark corn syrup
2 tablespoons butter
¾ cup chopped pecans
1 tablespoon ground
cinnamon

1. Dissolve yeast and 1 teaspoon granulated sugar in ¼ cup warm water in a small bowl; let stand 5 minutes. Weigh or lightly spoon flour into dry measuring cups; level with a knife. Place 16.9 ounces (about 3¾ cups) flour, ¼ cup granulated sugar, nutmeg, and salt in a food processor; pulse 2 times or until blended. Combine ⅔ cup milk, ¼ cup water, and egg. With processor on, slowly add milk mixture and yeast mixture through food chute; process until dough forms a ball. Process 1 minute more. Turn dough out onto a lightly floured surface; knead until smooth and elastic (about 8 minutes); add enough of remaining flour, 1 tablespoon at a time, to prevent dough from sticking to hands. Place dough in a large bowl coated with cooking spray, turning to coat top. Cover and let rise in a warm place (85°), 45 minutes or until doubled in size.

2. Combine ⅓ cup milk, 1 cup brown sugar, corn syrup, and butter in a small saucepan; bring to a boil, stirring constantly. Remove from heat. Divide pecans between 2 (9-inch) round cake pans coated with cooking spray. Top each with half of brown sugar mixture.

3. Punch dough down; let rest 5 minutes. Roll into a 24 x 10–inch rectangle on a lightly floured surface; coat entire surface of dough with cooking spray. Combine ¼ cup brown sugar and cinnamon in a small bowl; sprinkle over dough. Beginning with a long side, roll up jelly-roll fashion; pinch seam to seal (do not seal ends of roll). Cut roll into 24 (1-inch) slices. Arrange 12 slices, cut sides up, in each pan. Cover with plastic wrap coated with cooking spray, and let rise in refrigerator 8 to 24 hours or until doubled in size.

4. Preheat oven to 375°. Bake rolls at 375° for 23 minutes. Run a knife around outside edges of pans. Place a plate upside down on top of pan; invert onto plate.

Serves 24 (serving size: 1 bun)

CALORIES 187; **FAT** 3.9g (sat 1g, mono 1.8g, poly 0.9g); **PROTEIN** 3.6g; **CARB** 35.2g; **FIBER** 1.2g; **CHOL** 10mg; **IRON** 1.2mg; **SODIUM** 106mg; **CALC** 48mg

MAPLE-GLAZED SOUR CREAM DOUGHNUT HOLES

Hands-on time: 40 min. ★ Total time: 2 hr. 10 min.

6	**tablespoons warm water (100° to 110°)**
¼	**cup granulated sugar**
1⅛	**teaspoons dry yeast**
6.75	**ounces all-purpose flour (about 1½ cups), divided**
⅛	**teaspoon salt**
3	**tablespoons sour cream**
1	**large egg, lightly beaten**
Cooking spray	
6	**cups peanut oil**
1½	**cups powdered sugar**
2	**tablespoons maple syrup**
2	**tablespoons water**

1. Combine first 3 ingredients in a large bowl. Let stand 5 minutes or until bubbly. Weigh or lightly spoon 5.63 ounces (about 1¼ cups) flour into dry measuring cups; level with a knife. Combine 5.63 ounces flour and salt. Add sour cream and egg to yeast mixture; stir until smooth. Add flour mixture; stir until a moist dough forms.

2. Turn dough out onto a lightly floured surface. Knead until smooth (about 3 minutes); add enough of remaining 1.12 ounces (about ¼ cup) flour, 1 tablespoon at a time, to prevent dough from sticking to hands (dough will feel slightly sticky). Place dough in a clean bowl coated with cooking spray. Cover dough with plastic wrap. Let rise in a warm place (85°), 1 hour or until almost doubled in size. Punch dough down. Divide into 36 equal portions; roll each into a ball. Cover with plastic wrap coated with cooking spray; let stand 30 minutes.

3. Clip a candy/fry thermometer onto the side of a Dutch oven; add oil to pan. Heat oil to 375°. Combine powdered sugar, syrup, and 2 tablespoons water; stir until smooth. Place 9 dough balls in hot oil; fry 2 minutes or until golden and done, turning as necessary. Make sure oil temperature remains at 375°. Remove doughnut holes from pan; drain. Dip doughnut holes into syrup mixture; remove with a slotted spoon. Drain on a cooling rack over a baking sheet. Repeat procedure with remaining dough balls and syrup mixture.

Serves 12 (serving size: 3 doughnut holes)

CALORIES 178; **FAT** 5.9g (sat 1.4g, mono 2.5g, poly 1.6g); **PROTEIN** 2.4g; **CARB** 29.3g; **FIBER** 0.5g; **CHOL** 19mg; IRON 0.9mg; **SODIUM** 33mg; **CALC** 11mg

MIGAS CON SALSA VERDE

The ingredients in migas make it a dish that pleases on several flavor and texture notes. Enjoy this one-skillet Tex-Mex meal of eggs, tortillas, and cheese for breakfast, lunch, or dinner.

Hands-on time: 35 min. ★ **Total time: 55 min.**

1   **medium-sized red bell pepper**
6   **large eggs**
4   **large egg whites**
2   **tablespoons chopped fresh cilantro**
¼   **teaspoon salt**
4   **teaspoons olive oil**
4   **(6-inch) corn tortillas, cut into ½-inch strips**
1½   **cups chopped onion**
2   **garlic cloves, minced**
1   **jalapeño pepper, seeded and chopped**
6   **tablespoons salsa verde**
1   **ounce crumbled queso fresco (about ¼ cup)**

1. Preheat broiler.

2. Cut bell pepper in half lengthwise; discard seeds and membranes. Place pepper halves, skin sides up, on a foil-lined baking sheet; flatten with hand. Broil 10 minutes or until blackened. Place in a paper bag; fold to close tightly. Let stand 10 minutes. Peel and chop.

3. Combine eggs, egg whites, cilantro, and salt in a bowl, stirring with a whisk. Heat a large nonstick skillet over medium-high heat. Add olive oil to pan; swirl to coat. Add tortilla strips; sauté 2 minutes, stirring frequently. Reduce heat to medium. Add onion, garlic, and jalapeño; sauté 5 minutes or until tender, stirring occasionally. Add roasted bell pepper and egg mixture; cook 2½ minutes or until eggs are set, stirring occasionally. Divide egg mixture evenly among 4 plates; top each serving with 1½ tablespoons salsa and 1 tablespoon cheese.

Serves 4

CALORIES 273; **FAT** 14.5g (sat 3.8g, mono 6.6g, poly 2g); **PROTEIN** 17g; **CARB** 20.3g; **FIBER** 2.7g; **CHOL** 278mg; **IRON** 1.8mg; **SODIUM** 509mg; **CALC** 115mg

MONKEY BREAD

This is a breakfast treat that will revive childhood memories or make new ones: Bits of dough are rolled in cinnamon sugar and baked together. A creamy glaze coats the top, making them unforgettable.

Hands-on time: 45 min. ★ **Total time: 3 hr. 15 min.**

13.5 ounces all-purpose flour (about 3 cups)
4.75 ounces whole-wheat flour (about 1 cup)
1 teaspoon salt
1 package quick-rise yeast (about 2¼ teaspoons)
1 cup very warm fat-free milk (120° to 130°)
¼ cup very warm orange juice (120° to 130°)
¼ cup honey
2 tablespoons butter, melted
Cooking spray
½ cup granulated sugar
½ cup packed brown sugar
2 teaspoons ground cinnamon
4½ tablespoons fat-free milk, divided
2 tablespoons butter, melted
½ cup powdered sugar
1 tablespoon ⅓-less-fat cream cheese
1 teaspoon vanilla extract

1. Weigh or lightly spoon flours into dry measuring cups; level with a knife. Combine flours, salt, and yeast in the bowl of a stand mixer with dough hook attached; mix until combined. With mixer on, slowly add 1 cup warm milk, juice, honey, and 2 tablespoons butter; mix dough at medium speed 7 minutes or until smooth and elastic. Place dough in a large bowl coated with cooking spray, turning to coat top. Cover and let rise in a warm place (85°), free from drafts, 1 hour or until doubled in size. (Gently press two fingers into dough. If indentation remains, the dough has risen enough.)

2. Combine granulated sugar, brown sugar, and cinnamon in a shallow dish. Combine 3 tablespoons milk and 2 tablespoons butter in a shallow dish, stirring with a whisk.

3. Punch dough down; divide into 8 equal portions. Working with 1 portion at a time (cover remaining dough to prevent drying), roll into an 8-inch rope. Cut each dough rope into 8 equal pieces, shaping each piece into a 1-inch ball. Dip each ball in milk mixture, turning to coat, and roll in sugar mixture. Layer balls in a 12-cup Bundt pan coated with cooking spray. Repeat procedure with remaining 7 dough ropes. Sprinkle any remaining sugar mixture over dough. Cover and let rise in a warm place (85°), free from drafts, 1 hour or until almost doubled in size.

4. Preheat oven to 350°.

5. Uncover, and bake at 350° for 25 minutes or until golden. Cool 5 minutes on a wire rack. Place a plate upside down on top of bread; invert onto plate. Combine powdered sugar, remaining milk, cream cheese, and vanilla in a small bowl, stirring with a whisk. Microwave at HIGH 20 seconds or until warm. Drizzle over bread.

Serves 16 (serving size: 4 pieces and 1 teaspoon sauce)

CALORIES 234; **FAT** 3.4g (sat 2g, mono 0.8g, poly 0.3g); **PROTEIN** 4.5g; **CARB** 47.2g; **FIBER** 1.9g; **CHOL** 9mg; **IRON** 1.5mg; **SODIUM** 184mg; **CALC** 43mg

PAIN PERDU

Similar to French toast, Pain Perdu is a great way to use old bread for a meal—and it makes a beautiful breakfast for two. Serve it with any seasonal berries or other fruit.

Hands-on time: 25 min. ★ **Total time: 65 min.**

3/4   **cup 2% reduced-fat milk**
2   **tablespoons granulated sugar, divided**
1/2   **teaspoon ground cinnamon**
1 1/2   **teaspoons vanilla extract**
1/4   **teaspoon grated whole nutmeg**
3   **large eggs, lightly beaten**
8   **(1-ounce) slices diagonally cut day-old French bread (about 1 inch thick)**
2   **cups sliced strawberries**
2   **teaspoons grated orange rind**
4   **teaspoons butter, divided**
2   **tablespoons powdered sugar**

1. Combine milk, 1 tablespoon granulated sugar, cinnamon, vanilla, nutmeg, and eggs in a large bowl; stir with a whisk. Place bread slices in a 13 x 9–inch glass or ceramic baking dish; pour egg mixture over bread; turn to coat. Let stand at room temperature 20 minutes, turning occasionally, until egg is absorbed.

2. Combine strawberries, 1 tablespoon granulated sugar, and rind in a small bowl. Let stand 20 minutes.

3. Melt 2 teaspoons butter in a large nonstick skillet over medium heat. Add 4 bread slices to pan; cook 3½ minutes on each side or until golden. Repeat procedure with remaining butter and bread.

4. Place 2 bread slices on each of 4 plates. Sprinkle each serving with 1½ teaspoons powdered sugar; top each with ½ cup strawberry mixture.

Serves 4

CALORIES 349; **FAT** 9.7g (sat 4.5g, mono 2.9g, poly 1.5g); **PROTEIN** 13.8g; **CARB** 52g; **FIBER** 3.3g; **CHOL** 153mg; **IRON** 3.2mg; **SODIUM** 406mg; **CALC** 132mg

PEAR AND GRUYÈRE STRATA

Think of this as stuffed French toast in a casserole. Here, sweet cinnamon bread meets juicy pears and the savory bite of Gruyère cheese. You want a pear variety that will hold its shape and won't exude too much moisture as the strata bakes—we liked Anjou and Concorde.

Hands-on time: 20 min. ★ Total time: 9 hr. 25 min.

4　cups sliced peeled Anjou or Concorde pear
2　teaspoons butter, melted
6　tablespoons granulated sugar, divided
12　(1-ounce) slices cinnamon swirl bread, cut in half diagonally
Cooking spray
4　ounces shredded Gruyère cheese (about 1 cup)
1½　cups 1% low-fat milk
1　cup egg substitute
½　teaspoon ground cinnamon
1　tablespoon turbinado sugar
½　cup maple syrup

1. Combine pear, butter, and 1 tablespoon granulated sugar in a large bowl; toss gently.

2. Arrange half of bread in an 11 x 7–inch glass or ceramic baking dish coated with cooking spray. Spoon pear mixture over bread; top with cheese. Arrange remaining bread over cheese.

3. Combine 5 tablespoons granulated sugar, milk, egg substitute, and cinnamon, stirring with a whisk. Pour milk mixture over bread, pressing down to submerge. Cover and chill 8 hours or overnight.

4. Preheat oven to 350°.

5. Uncover dish. Sprinkle turbinado sugar over bread. Bake at 350° for 55 minutes or until a knife inserted in center comes out clean. Let stand 10 minutes. Cut into 8 equal pieces; drizzle with syrup.

Serves 8 (serving size: 1 strata piece and 1 tablespoon syrup)

CALORIES 355; **FAT** 10g (sat 4.3g, mono 3.7g, poly 0.6g); **PROTEIN** 13.1g; **CARB** 55.1g; **FIBER** 5.3g; **CHOL** 20mg; **IRON** 1.6mg; **SODIUM** 295mg; **CALC** 216mg

POACHED EGGS
with spinach and walnuts

Serve protein-packed eggs over a side of spinach sautéed with mushrooms, walnuts, and Gruyère cheese—this breakfast (or breakfast for dinner) is sure to give you plenty of energy. Enjoy with roasted winter squash on the side.

Hands-on time: 34 min. ★ **Total time: 34 min.**

1 tablespoon olive oil, divided
1 (10-ounce) bag baby spinach, chopped
3 garlic cloves, minced
3 vertically sliced shallots
1 tablespoon chopped fresh sage
3/4 teaspoon chopped fresh thyme, divided
1/2 teaspoon freshly ground black pepper, divided
1/4 teaspoon salt
1 (8-ounce) package cremini mushrooms, quartered
3/4 cup toasted walnuts, chopped and divided
2 tablespoons red wine vinegar
2 ounces shredded Gruyère cheese (about 1/2 cup)
8 cups water
2 tablespoons white vinegar
4 large eggs

1. Heat a large Dutch oven over medium-high heat. Add 1 teaspoon oil; swirl to coat. Add spinach; sauté 2 minutes. Remove spinach from pan; drain, cool slightly, and squeeze out excess moisture. Add remaining oil to pan; swirl to coat. Add garlic and shallots; sauté 3 minutes. Add sage, 1/2 teaspoon thyme, 1/4 teaspoon pepper, salt, and mushrooms; sauté 7 minutes. Stir in spinach, 1/2 cup walnuts, red wine vinegar, and cheese; cook 30 seconds.

2. Combine 8 cups water and white vinegar in a large saucepan, and bring to a simmer. Break each egg gently into pan. Cook 3 minutes. Remove eggs using a slotted spoon. Spoon 2/3 cup mushroom mixture onto each of 4 plates. Top each serving with 1 egg. Sprinkle with remaining thyme, pepper, and walnuts.

Serves 4

CALORIES 350; **FAT** 24.3g (sat 5.5g, mono 7.5g, poly 10.2g); **PROTEIN** 17.4g; **CARB** 18.4g; **FIBER** 5.1g; **CHOL** 196mg; **IRON** 4.4mg; **SODIUM** 383mg; **CALC** 257mg

CORN FRITTERS
with roasted tomatoes and lime aioli

Fritters are a breakfast tradition, particularly in the South. Put an upscale twist on them with a few flavor-boosting ingredients. Roasting the tomatoes in the oven intensifies their flavor; use roma or plum tomatoes.

Hands-on time: 24 min. ★ **Total time: 1 hr. 40 min.**

4   ripe tomatoes, halved (about 1 pound)
2   teaspoons olive oil, divided
½   teaspoon freshly ground black pepper, divided
2.25 ounces all-purpose flour (about ½ cup)
1   teaspoon baking powder
⅓   cup fat-free milk
1   large egg, beaten
1½   cups fresh corn kernels (3 ears)
⅓   cup finely chopped green onions
¼   teaspoon salt
3   tablespoons reduced-fat mayonnaise
2   tablespoons fresh lime juice
½   garlic clove, minced
1   teaspoon cold water
4   cups loosely packed arugula
4   (¼-ounce) slices prosciutto

1. Preheat oven to 375°.

2. Arrange tomato halves, cut sides up, on a baking sheet. Drizzle tomatoes with 1 teaspoon oil; sprinkle with ¼ teaspoon pepper. Bake at 375° for 1 hour and 30 minutes or until tomatoes are soft and have lost a lot of their moisture.

3. Weigh or lightly spoon flour into a dry measuring cup; level with a knife. Combine flour and baking powder in a medium bowl. Add milk and egg; stir until smooth. Stir in ¼ teaspoon pepper, corn, green onions, and salt.

4. Heat a large nonstick skillet over medium heat. Add ½ teaspoon oil; swirl to coat. Drop batter by level tablespoonfuls into pan to make 6 fritters; cook 2 minutes or until tops are covered with bubbles and edges are golden. Carefully turn fritters over; cook 2 minutes or until golden. Repeat procedure with remaining oil and batter.

5. Combine mayonnaise, juice, garlic, and 1 teaspoon cold water. Place 1 fritter on each of 4 plates. Top each with 1 tomato half and ½ cup arugula. Repeat layers with remaining fritters, tomato halves, and arugula, ending with fritters. Top each serving with 1 prosciutto slice; drizzle with 4 teaspoons aioli.

Serves 4

CALORIES 284; **FAT** 7.8g (sat 1.2g, mono 2.6g, poly 2.3g); **PROTEIN** 12.6g; **CARB** 48.4g; **FIBER** 7.4g; **CHOL** 49mg; **IRON** 2.9mg; **SODIUM** 526mg; **CALC** 185mg

make it ahead

For convenience, you can make the tomatoes and fritters in advance, and then reheat them to serve. Reheating the fritters in an oven or toaster oven will keep them from getting soggy.

make it ahead
Because you have to cook the beef a day in advance, you'll get a head start on this hearty breakfast (or breakfast-for-dinner). You'll have more beef than necessary—use it for another meal.

EGGS BARBACOA

Hands-on time: 46 min. ★ **Total time: 12 hr. 46 min. (including beef barbacoa)**

1 **(15-ounce) can pinto beans, rinsed and drained**
6 **tablespoons bottled lower-sodium salsa, divided**
2 **tablespoons water**
8 **(6-inch) corn tortillas**
Cooking spray
4 **large eggs**
¼ **teaspoon kosher salt**
¼ **teaspoon black pepper**
1 **cup hot Beef Barbacoa**
2 **ounces crumbled queso fresco (about ½ cup)**
¼ **cup sliced green onions**
¼ **cup chopped cilantro**
4 **lime wedges**

1. Place beans in a food processor; process until smooth. Combine beans, 2 tablespoons salsa, and 2 tablespoons water in a small saucepan over low heat until warm. Keep warm.

2. Heat a large nonstick skillet over medium-high heat. Lightly coat sides of tortillas with cooking spray. Place 1 tortilla in pan; cook 30 seconds on each side or until toasted. Repeat with remaining tortillas.

3. Add water to a large skillet, filling two-thirds full; bring to a boil. Reduce heat; simmer. Break 1 egg into each of 4 (6-ounce) custard cups coated with cooking spray. Place custard cups in simmering water in pan. Cover pan; cook 8 minutes. Remove custard cups from water. Sprinkle salt and pepper over eggs.

4. Place 2 tortillas on each of 4 plates; top each with 2 tablespoons bean mixture. Top beans with 2 tablespoons Beef Barbacoa. Place 1 poached egg on each plate to overlap tortillas. Top each with 1 table-spoon salsa. Sprinkle each with 2 tablespoons cheese, 1 tablespoon green onions, and 1 tablespoon fresh cilantro. Serve with lime wedges.

Serves 4

CALORIES 362; **FAT** 11.9g (sat 3.9g, mono 4.1g, poly 1.6g); **PROTEIN** 32.2g; **CARB** 33g; **FIBER** 5.7g; **CHOL** 273mg; **IRON** 4.3mg; **SODIUM** 604mg; **CALC** 132mg

beef barbacoa

1 **teaspoon black pepper**
1 **teaspoon dried oregano**
¾ **teaspoon kosher salt**
¾ **teaspoon ground cumin**
¾ **teaspoon ancho chile powder**
1 **(2¼-pound) boneless chuck steak, trimmed**
Cooking spray
2 **garlic cloves, thinly sliced**
1 **tablespoon fresh lime juice**

1. Preheat oven to 300°. Combine first 5 ingredients in a bowl; rub over beef. Heat a large Dutch oven over high heat. Coat pan with cooking spray. Add beef to pan; cook 3 minutes on each side or until browned. Add 1 cup water and garlic to pan, scraping pan. Cover and bake at 300° for 3 hours or until beef is very tender. Cool to room temperature. Cover and chill 8 hours or overnight.

2. Skim fat from surface of broth. Remove beef; shred with 2 forks. Return beef to pan; bring to a simmer over medium-high heat. Simmer 3 minutes or until liquid evaporates; stir in lime juice. Reduce heat to medium; cook 3 minutes or until crisp in spots.

Serves 10 (serving size: 2 ounces)

CALORIES 121; **FAT** 4.2g (sat 1.5g, mono 1.7g, poly 0.2g); **PROTEIN** 18.9g; **CARB** 0.8g; **FIBER** 0.2g; **CHOL** 57mg; **IRON** 2.3mg; **SODIUM** 179mg; **CALC** 11mg

MINI BACON AND EGG TARTS

Whose face wouldn't light up at the sight of these fun breakfast tarts? Green onions add color and flavor, but they're optional. Omit them, if you prefer.

Hands-on time: 24 min. ★ **Total time: 39 min.**

8   (1-ounce) slices white-
     wheat sandwich bread,
     crusts removed
Cooking spray
½   cup 2% reduced-fat milk
4   large eggs, lightly beaten
2   tablespoons chopped
     green onions (optional)
2   smoked bacon slices,
     cooked and crumbled
2   ounces shredded sharp
     cheddar cheese (about ½
     cup)

1. Preheat oven to 425°.

2. Lightly coat both sides of bread with cooking spray. Press bread slices into muffin cups. Bake at 425° for 10 minutes or until bread is lightly toasted. Cool slightly.

3. Reduce oven temperature to 350°.

4. Combine milk and eggs, stirring well with a whisk. Divide egg mixture among bread cups. Sprinkle onions, if desired, and bacon over tarts; top each tart with 1 tablespoon cheese. Bake at 350° for 15 minutes or until set.

Serves 4 (serving size: 2 tarts)

CALORIES 316; FAT 12.8g (sat 5.6g, mono 2.8g, poly 1.5g); PROTEIN 18.3g; CARB 31.2g; FIBER 3g; CHOL 202mg; IRON 1mg; SODIUM 515mg; CALC 163mg

make it ahead
You can cook the pork the night before. Allow it to cool, shred it, and store it in an airtight container in the refrigerator. Refrigerate the cooking liquid and garlic separately. When you finish the hash, allow more time for the pork to be thoroughly heated.

PORK AND SWEET POTATO HASH

This hash is equally good as a breakfast-for-dinner. Sweet potatoes and sliced mushrooms add an interesting twist to this familiar comfort food. Although the pork takes a while to cook, the simmering is hands-off time.

Hands-on time: 29 min. ★ **Total time: 1 hr. 54 min.**

1   (1-pound) boneless pork shoulder (Boston butt), trimmed
½   teaspoon kosher salt
½   teaspoon freshly ground black pepper
Cooking spray
3½ cups fat-free, lower-sodium chicken broth
6   garlic cloves, crushed
1   tablespoon olive oil
4   cups (½-inch) cubed peeled sweet potato (about 1 pound)
1   cup chopped onion
¼   teaspoon ground red pepper
1   (8-ounce) package cremini mushrooms, quartered
3   tablespoons sliced green onions

1. Heat a 12-inch cast-iron skillet over medium-high heat. Sprinkle pork with salt and black pepper. Coat pan with cooking spray. Add pork to pan, and sauté 8 minutes, turning to brown on all sides. Add broth and garlic to pan; bring to a boil. Cover, reduce heat to low, and simmer 45 minutes or until pork is fork-tender. Remove pork from pan, reserving cooking liquid and garlic. Cool pork slightly; shred with 2 forks.

2. Heat a large skillet over medium-high heat. Add olive oil to pan, and swirl to coat. Add potato and onion; sauté 6 minutes or until lightly browned, stirring occasionally. Add red pepper and mushrooms; cook 3 minutes. Add cooking liquid and garlic; bring to a boil. Reduce heat to medium, and cook, uncovered, 20 minutes or until liquid nearly evaporates, stirring occasionally. Stir in pork, and cook 1 minute or until thoroughly heated. Sprinkle with green onions.

Serves 4 (serving size: 1¼ cups)

CALORIES 338; FAT 15g (sat 4.6g, mono 7.6g, poly 1.5g); PROTEIN 24g; CARB 27g; FIBER 4.3g; CHOL 67mg; IRON 2.4mg; SODIUM 743mg; CALC 88mg

SAUSAGE AND EGG BURRITO

Hands-on time: 20 min. ★ **Total time: 20 min.**

⅓ cup thinly sliced radish
¼ cup thinly vertically sliced red onion
1 tablespoon fresh lemon juice
½ medium-sized ripe avocado, chopped
⅛ teaspoon kosher salt
¼ teaspoon freshly ground black pepper, divided
2 teaspoons butter
4 garlic cloves, coarsely chopped
2 ounces reduced-fat pork sausage
6 large eggs, lightly beaten
4 (8-inch) whole-wheat flour tortillas
1 (15-ounce) can organic pinto beans, rinsed, drained, and mashed
1 serrano chile, thinly sliced
¼ cup thinly sliced green onions

1. Combine first 4 ingredients in a bowl; sprinkle with ⅛ teaspoon salt and ⅛ teaspoon black pepper. Toss gently to coat.

2. Melt butter in a medium-sized nonstick skillet over medium heat. Add garlic and sausage to pan; cook 3 minutes or until sausage is browned, stirring to crumble. Stir in eggs; sprinkle with ⅛ teaspoon pepper. Cook to desired consistency, stirring to scramble. Remove from heat.

3. Heat tortillas according to package directions. Place 1 tortilla on each of 4 plates. Divide beans among tortillas, spreading to a thin layer, leaving a ¼-inch border. Divide egg mixture among tortillas; top with radish mixture and chile slices. Roll up burritos, jelly-roll fashion. Sprinkle 1 tablespoon green onions over each serving.

Serves 4 (serving size: 1 burrito)

CALORIES 410; **FAT** 19g (sat 5.1g, mono 8.5g, poly 3.1g); **PROTEIN** 20g; **CARB** 38g; **FIBER** 7.6g; **CHOL** 293mg; **IRON** 3.8mg; **SODIUM** 557mg; **CALC** 94mg

SAVORY BREAD PUDDINGS
with ham and cheddar

Hands-on time: 22 min. ★ Total time: 42 min.

8   **ounces multigrain bread with seeds, cut into ³/₄-inch cubes**
Cooking spray
³/₄   **cup fat-free milk**
3   **ounces shredded sharp cheddar cheese (about ³/₄ cup), divided**
¹/₄   **cup chopped green onions, divided**
¹/₄   **cup fat-free, lower-sodium chicken broth**
¹/₈   **teaspoon freshly ground black pepper**
3   **ounces lower-sodium ham, minced**
2   **large egg yolks, lightly beaten**
3   **large egg whites**
4   **teaspoons reduced-fat sour cream**

1. Preheat oven to 375°.

2. Place bread cubes on a jelly-roll pan; coat with cooking spray. Bake at 375° for 10 minutes or until lightly toasted, turning once. Remove from oven; cool.

3. Combine bread, milk, ½ cup cheese, 3 tablespoons onions, and next 4 ingredients (through egg yolks) in a large bowl. Place egg whites in a small bowl, and beat with a mixer at high speed until foamy (about 30 seconds). Gently fold egg whites into bread mixture.

4. Spoon about 1 cup bread mixture into each of 4 (7-ounce) ramekins coated with cooking spray. Divide ¼ cup cheese and 1 tablespoon onions among ramekins. Bake at 375° for 20 minutes or until lightly browned. Top each serving with 1 teaspoon sour cream.

Serves 4 (serving size: 1 bread pudding)

CALORIES 272; **FAT** 11.2g (sat 5g, mono 3.3g, poly 0.6g); **PROTEIN** 18.5g; **CARB** 28.4g; **FIBER** 8.6g; **CHOL** 140mg; **IRON** 2mg; **SODIUM** 536mg; **CALC** 400mg

NUTRITION NUMBERS AND KITCHEN MEASUREMENTS

Nutrition Analysis: What the Numbers Mean For You

To interpret the nutritional analysis in *Good Mood Food*, use the figures below as a daily reference guide. One size doesn't fit all, so take lifestyle, age, and circumstances into consideration. For example, pregnant or breast-feeding women need more protein, calories, and calcium. Go to choosemyplate.gov for your own individualized plan.

	Women ages 25 to 50	Women over 50	Men ages 25 to 50	Men over 50
Calories	2,000	2,000*	2,700	2,500
Protein	50 g	50 g	63 g	60 g
Fat	65 g*	65 g*	88 g*	83 g*
Saturated Fat	20 g*	20 g*	27 g*	25 g*
Carbohydrates	304 g	304 g	410 g	375 g
Fiber	25 g to 35 g	25 g to 35 g	25 g to 35 g	25 g to 35 g
Cholesterol	300 mg*	300 mg*	300 mg*	300 mg*
Iron	18 mg	8 mg	8 mg	8 mg
Sodium	2,300 mg*	1,500 mg*	2,300 mg*	1,500 mg*
Calcium	1,000 mg	1,200 mg	1,000 mg	1,000 mg

*Or less, for optimum health

Nutritional values used in our calculations either
come from the food processor, version 10.4 (ESHA research),
or are provided by food manufacturers.

Nutritional Analysis Abbreviations

SAT	saturated fat	**CARB**	carbohydrates	**g**	gram
MONO	monounsaturated fat	**CHOL**	cholesterol	**mg**	milligram
POLY	polyunsaturated fat	**CALC**	calcium		

Metric Equivalents

The information in the following charts is provided to help cooks outside the United States successfully use the recipes in this book. All equivalents are approximate.

Cooking/Oven Temperatures

	Fahrenheit	Celsius	Gas Mark
Freeze Water	32° F	0° C	
Room Temp.	68° F	20° C	
Boil Water	212° F	100° C	
Bake	325° F	160° C	3
	350° F	180° C	4
	375° F	190° C	5
	400° F	200° C	6
	425° F	220° C	7
	450° F	230° C	8
Broil			Grill

Liquid Ingredients by Volume

¼ tsp	=	1 ml				
½ tsp	=	2 ml				
1 tsp	=	5 ml				
3 tsp	=	1 Tbsp.	=	½ fl oz	=	15 ml
2 Tbsp.	=	⅛ cup	=	1 fl oz	=	30 ml
4 Tbsp.	=	¼ cup	=	2 fl oz	=	60 ml
5 ⅓ Tbsp.	=	⅓ cup	=	3 fl oz	=	80 ml
8 Tbsp.	=	½ cup	=	4 fl oz	=	120 ml
10 ⅔ Tbsp.	=	⅔ cup	=	5 fl oz	=	160 ml
12 Tbsp.	=	¾ cup	=	6 fl oz	=	180 ml
16 Tbsp.	=	1 cup	=	8 fl oz	=	240 ml
1 pt	=	2 cups	=	16 fl oz	=	480 ml
1 qt	=	4 cups	=	32 fl oz	=	960 ml
				33 fl oz	=	1000 ml = 1 l

Equivalents for Different Types of Ingredients

Standard Cup	Fine Powder (ex. flour)	Grain (ex. rice)	Granular (ex. sugar)	Liquid Solids (ex. butter)	Liquid (ex. milk)
1	140 g	150 g	190 g	200 g	240 ml
¾	105 g	113 g	143 g	150 g	180 ml
⅔	93 g	100 g	125 g	133 g	160 ml
½	70 g	75 g	95 g	100 g	120 ml
⅓	47 g	50 g	63 g	67 g	80 ml
¼	35 g	38 g	48 g	50 g	60 ml
⅛	18 g	19 g	24 g	25 g	30 ml

Length

(To convert inches to centimeters, multiply the number of inches by 2.5.)

1 in	=				2.5 cm		
6 in	=	½ ft		=	15 cm		
12 in	=	1 ft		=	30 cm		
36 in	=	3 ft	=	1 yd	=	90 cm	
40 in	=				100 cm	=	1 m

Dry Ingredients by Weight

(To convert ounces to grams, multiply the number of ounces by 30.)

1 oz	=	¹⁄₁₆ lb	=	30 g
4 oz	=	¼ lb	=	120 g
8 oz	=	½ lb	=	240 g
12 oz	=	¾ lb	=	360 g
16 oz	=	1 lb	=	480 g

INDEX

"A KITCHEN MEMORY" ESSAYS

ISBN-13: 978-0-8487-3914-0
ISBN-10: 0-8487-3914-0
Library of Congress Control Number: 2012949217
Printed in the United States of America
First printing 2013

Be sure to check with your health-care provider before making any
changes in your diet.

Oxmoor House

Editorial Director: Leah McLaughlin
Creative Director: Felicity Keane
Brand Manager: Michelle Turner Aycock
Senior Editor: Andrea C. Kirkland, MS, RD
Managing Editor: Rebecca Benton

Cooking Light® Good Mood Food

Editor: Shaun Chavis
Art Director: Claire Cormany
Project Editor: Megan Yeatts
Junior Designer: Maribeth Jones
Director, Test Kitchen: Elizabeth Tyler Austin
Assistant Directors, Test Kitchen: Julie Christopher, Julie Gunter
Recipe Developers and Testers: Wendy Ball, RD; Victoria E. Cox;
  Stefanie Maloney; Callie Nash; Leah Van Deren
Food Stylists: Margaret Monroe Dickey, Catherine Crowell Steele
Photography Director: Jim Bathie
Senior Photographer: Hélène Dujardin
Senior Photo Stylist: Kay E. Clarke
Photo Stylist: Mindi Shapiro Levine
Assistant Photo Stylist: Mary Louise Menendez
Senior Production Manager: Greg A. Amason
Production Manager: Tamara Nall Wilder

Contributors

Copy Editors: Jacqueline Giovanelli, Dolores Hydock
Proofreaders: Julie Bosche, Dolores Hydock
Indexer: Mary Ann Laurens
Interns: Megan Branagh, Frances Gunnells, Susan Kemp, Sara Lyon,
  Staley McIlwain, Jeffrey Preis, Maria Sanders, Julia Sayers
Photographers: John Autry, Sarah Bélanger, Beau Gustafson,
  Beth Dreiling Hontzas, Mary Britton Senseney,
  Becky Luigart-Stayner
Photo Stylists: Mary Clayton Carl, Katherine Eckert Coyne, Missie
  Neville Crawford, Leslie Simpson, Caitlin Van Horn
Food Stylists: Mary Drennen, Ana Price Kelly

Time Home Entertainment Inc.

Publisher: Jim Childs
Vice President, Strategy & Business Development:
  Steven Sandonato
Executive Director, Marketing Services: Carol Pittard
Executive Director, Retail & Special Sales: Tom Mifsud
Director, Bookazine Development & Marketing: Laura Adam
Executive Publishing Director: Joy Butts
Associate Publishing Director: Megan Pearlman
Finance Director: Glenn Buonocore
Associate General Counsel: Helen Wan

Cooking Light®

Editor: Scott Mowbray
Creative Director: Carla Frank
Executive Managing Editor: Phillip Rhodes
Executive Editor, Food: Ann Taylor Pittman
Special Publications Editor: Mary Simpson Creel, MS, RD
Senior Food Editors: Timothy Q. Cebula, Julianna Grimes
Senior Editor: Cindy Hatcher
Assistant Editor, Nutrition: Sidney Fry, MS, RD
Assistant Editors: Kimberly Holland, Phoebe Wu
Test Kitchen Director: Vanessa T. Pruett
Assistant Test Kitchen Director: Tiffany Vickers Davis
Recipe Testers and Developers: Robin Bashinsky,
  Adam Hickman, Deb Wise
Art Directors: Fernande Bondarenko, Shawna Kalish
Senior Deputy Art Director: Rachel Cardina Lasserre
Designers: Hagen Stegall, Dréa Zacharenko
Assistant Designer: Nicole Gerrity
Photo Director: Kristen Schaefer
Assistant Photo Editor: Amy Delaune
Senior Photographer: Randy Mayor
Senior Prop Stylist: Cindy Barr
Chief Food Stylist: Kellie Gerber Kelley
Food Styling Assistant: Blakeslee Wright
Production Director: Liz Rhoades
Production Editor: Hazel R. Eddins
Assistant Production Editor: Josh Rutledge
Copy Chief: Maria Parker Hopkins
Assistant Copy Chief: Susan Roberts
Research Editor: Michelle Gibson Daniels
Administrative Coordinator: Carol D. Johnson
CookingLight.com Editor: Allison Long Lowery
Nutrition Editor: Holley Johnson Grainger, MS, RD
Associate Editor/Producer: Mallory Daugherty Brasseale

To order additional publications, call
1-800-765-6400 or 1-800-491-0551.

For more books to enrich your life, visit
oxmoorhouse.com

To search, savor, and share thousands
of recipes, visit **myrecipes.com**